U.S. GOVERNMENT PRIVACY

Essential Policies and Practices for Privacy Professionals

Second Edition

Deborah Kendall, CIPP/US, CIPP/G, Executive Editor

An IAPP Publication

Cover design: Noelle Grattan, -ing designs, llc.
Developmental editor: Jocelyn Humelsine
Copy editor: Rebecca Mahoney
Compositor: Ed Stevens, Ed Stevens Design
Indexer: Wendy Catalano, Last Look Editorial Services

ISBN: 978-0-9885525-0-0
Library of Congress Control Number: 2012953076

About the IAPP

The International Association of Privacy Professionals (IAPP) is the largest and most comprehensive global information privacy community and resource, helping practitioners develop and advance their careers and organizations manage and protect their data.

The IAPP is a not-for-profit association founded in 2000 with a mission to define, support and improve the privacy profession globally through networking, education and certification. We are committed to providing a forum for privacy professionals to share best practices, track trends, advance privacy management issues, standardize the designations for privacy professionals, and provide education and guidance on opportunities in the field of information privacy.

The IAPP is responsible for developing and launching the first broad-based credentialing program in information privacy, the Certified Information Privacy Professional (CIPP). The CIPP remains the leading privacy certification for professionals who serve the data protection, information auditing, information security, legal compliance and/or risk management needs of their organizations. Today, many thousands of professionals worldwide hold a CIPP certification.

In addition, the IAPP offers a full suite of educational and professional development services and holds annual conferences that are recognized internationally as the leading forums for the discussion and debate of issues related to privacy policy and practice.

Contents

CHAPTER THREE

Other Laws and Regulations Focused on Government Agencies that Affect Their Privacy Practices

CHAPTER FOUR

Privacy and the Federal Government Intelligence Community

CHAPTER FIVE

Laws Affecting Both the Public and Private Sectors and Laws that Compel Disclosure of Information to the Government

CHAPTER SIX

Privacy Program Development and Organization

CHAPTER SEVEN

Records Management, Data Sharing and Disclosure

CHAPTER EIGHT

Privacy Auditing and Compliance Monitoring

Figures

Tables

Acknowledgments

The IAPP is pleased to present *U.S. Government Privacy, Second Edition* in support of our Certified Information Privacy Professional/U.S. Government (CIPP/G) program.

The development of this second edition was guided by advice from members of our Certification Advisory Board/U.S. Government. We would like to thank the board members:

Jonathan R. Cantor, CIPP/US, CIPP/G
Deputy Chief Privacy Officer, U.S. Department of Homeland Security

De Anna Greene, CIPP/US, CIPP/G, CIPP/IT
HIPAA Compliance Officer, Wyoming Department of Health

Michael Hawes, CIPP/G
Statistical Privacy Advisor, U.S. Department of Education

Julie S. McEwen, CIPP/US, CIPP/G, CIPP/IT
Principal Information Privacy & Security Engineer, The MITRE Corporation

Rebecca J. Richards, CIPP/US, CIPP/G
Senior Director, Privacy Compliance, U.S. Department of Homeland Security

Kathleen M. Styles, CIPP/G
Chief Privacy Officer, U.S. Department of Education

Elizabeth Varghese, CIPP/G
Cyber Security and Privacy Specialist, U.S. Department of Transportation

Charlene Wright Thomas, CIPP/G
Senior Advisor for Privacy Policy, U.S. Department of State

Additional guidance on shaping the Body of Knowledge, which serves to identify critical content for the program, was provided by Alexander C. Tang, CIPP/US, CIPP/G, Kirsten J. Moncada, CIPP/US, CIPP/G, Marc M. Groman, CIPP/US, and Maya A. Bernstein, CIPP/US, CIPP/G.

We are indebted to Harriet Pearson, CIPP/US who, while serving as a member of the IAPP Board of Directors, made the recommendation to develop the CIPP/G certification.

The initial program was underwritten by IBM and supported by members of our advisory board at the time: Emily Andrew, CIPP/US, CIPP/G, Jane Horvath, CIPP/G, CIPP/US, Deborah Kendall, CIPP/US, CIPP/G, John Lainhart, CIPP/US, CIPP/G, Joanne McNabb, CIPP/US, CIPP/G, CIPP/IT, Kenneth Mortensen, CIPP/US, CIPP/G, Stephania Putt, Zoe Strickland, CIPP/US, CIPP/G, CIPP/IT and Barbra Symonds.

The first edition of this book was edited by Julie S. McEwen, CIPP/US, CIPP/G, CIPP/IT and Stuart S. Shapiro, CIPP/US, CIPP/G of the MITRE Corporation. Additional MITRE contributors were Robert W. Johnson, CIPP/US, CIPP/G, Erika L. McCallister, CIPP/US, CIPP/G, Catherine M. Petrozzino, CIPP/US, CIPP/G, CIPP/IT, Sandra J. Sinay, CIPP/US, CIPP/G, Charissa L. Smith, CIPP/US, CIPP/G and David Weitzel, CIPP/US, CIPP/G. Their excellent work stands as the foundation of much of the content in this second edition.

Thank you to Deborah Kendall, CIPP/US, CIPP/G, Manager, Strategy and Processes, U.S. Postal Service (retired) who served as the executive editor of this second edition. Deborah served as a critical collaborator on this project, identifying contributors, guiding content development and shepherding the manuscript from draft to final copy.

The contributors to the second edition include influential privacy professionals working within and with the U.S. Government. These contributors are Claire Barrett, CIPP/US, CIPP/G, CIPP/IT, Jonathan R. Cantor, CIPP/US, CIPP/G, Michael Hawes, CIPP/G, Liz Lyons, CIPP/G, Patricia Mantoan, Julie S. McEwen, CIPP/US, CIPP/G, CIPP/IT, Kim Mott, CIPP/US, CIPP/G, Matthew J. Olsen, CIPP/US, CIPP/G, Rebecca J. Richards, CIPP/US, CIPP/G, Roanne R. Shaddox, CIPP/US, CIPP/G and Alexander C. Tang, CIPP/US, CIPP/G. We are enormously grateful that they shared their expertise within the pages of this book.

Brian Burke provided research and writing to ensure full coverage of the topics covered by this program. Marc M. Groman, CIPP/US, Julie S. McEwen, CIPP/US, CIPP/G, CIPP/IT and Elizabeth Varghese, CIPP/G provided comprehensive reviews of the draft manuscript. Their thoughtful and constructive comments served as a critical tool during the revision process. Thank you to Jocelyn Humelsine and Rebecca Mahoney for editing this book, and to Ed Stevens for layout. Their competence and attention to detail are evident in the production quality of this book.

It has been my pleasure to work with accomplished privacy professionals in and who work with the U.S. government. I'm delighted to present this book as a resource to the privacy community.

Richard Soule, CIPP/US, CIPP/E
Certification Director
International Association of Privacy Professionals

Introduction

You are holding the premier guide for privacy professionals working in all levels of U.S. government.

This second edition of *U.S. Government Privacy: Essential Policies and Practices for Privacy Professionals* not only lays out a comprehensive overview of U.S. public-sector law—such as the Freedom of Information Act of 1974, the Privacy Act of 1974 and the E-Government Act of 2002—but adjoining information privacy laws that affect both the public and private sectors. This newly minted edition also includes updates to the National Institute of Standards and Technology (NIST) and Office of Management and Budget (OMB) privacy guidance.

In particular, this text includes OMB "Guidance for Online Use of Web Measurement and Customization" (M-10-22); "Guidance for Agency Use of Third-Party Websites and Applications" (M-10-23), and the OMB Memorandum of April 7, 2010, on "Social Media, Web-Based Interactive Technologies and the Paperwork Reduction Act." This edition also accounts for NIST recommendation SP 800-122, "Guide to Protecting the Confidentiality of Personally Identifiable Information."

To further enrich this invaluable reference, we tirelessly worked with U.S. government-based privacy professionals at all stages of development. Led by the text's executive editor, former United States Postal Service Manager of Strategy and Process Deborah Kendall, CIPP/US, CIPP/G, contributors from a host of government agencies and the MITRE Corporation have compiled an indispensable resource.

As a result, *U.S. Government Privacy* includes new discussions on the Open Government Directive, the Confidential Information Protection and Statistical Efficiency Act, the newly added Controlled Unclassified Information category, the Family Educational Rights and Privacy Act, the Identity Theft Red Flags Rule and federal identity management and authentication.

I am thrilled with this updated edition. With profound insight from leading U.S. government privacy experts, I think you'll find this text an important part of your library. If you're studying for the CIPP/G, I know you will find this text to be an extremely helpful tool for successfully achieving certification, and I applaud your efforts to help elevate the privacy profession.

J. Trevor Hughes, CIPP
President and CEO
International Association of Privacy Professionals

CHAPTER ONE

Privacy Principles and Definitions

1. Privacy Basics

Many people consider the privacy role of the government in the United States as that of strictly regulating privacy practices in the commercial sector. This, however, is only part of the story. Government, in this day and age, collects, uses and retains massive amounts of personally identifiable information (PII) to provide services to the public. The use of this information is subject to substantial legislative and regulatory requirements. Some of these requirements are specific to the government, but others are more general and apply just as much to the government as to the private sector. This chapter touches on some of the broader requirements and refers the reader elsewhere for more detailed analysis of laws, regulations and practices.[1]

Why do various U.S. government laws and regulations exist in the first place? Simply put, privacy is a core value of democratic societies. It has long been recognized that privacy is an essential aspect of both freedom and human dignity. The importance of privacy to the political process is reflected in the value placed on anonymity when voting. Furthermore, the ability to develop personal opinions free from the scrutiny of others—least among them government itself—is the crucial precursor to casting a ballot. Similarly, human dignity demands autonomy derived in part from privacy. If individuals are to enjoy dignity in their activities and freedom from coercion, then personal judgments and decisions, as well as social interactions, require some sheltering from the gaze of others, including the government. Privacy as government practice speaks to something fundamental in the relationship between government and the governed.

The government provides benefits to and makes decisions regarding individuals every day, based on the information about them that the government collects, uses, and shares. Government actions often have a very significant impact upon individuals' lives.

The original text for this chapter was developed by Stuart S. Shapiro, CIPP/US, CIPP/G. New content for this revised edition was contributed by Kim Mott, CIPP/US, CIPP/G, and Claire Barrett, CIPP/US, CIPP/G, CIPP/IT, whose contributions are noted throughout the sections of the chapter.

For example, individuals can be denied benefits such as welfare payments, prevented from flying, or targeted for investigation all based on information about them that the government has. Thus, in some ways, the role of the chief privacy officer is even more critical in the federal government than in many parts of private industry.

2. Parsing Government Privacy in the United States

By necessity, privacy in government in the United States involves federal, state and even municipal government, though municipal-level privacy tends to be more about compliance with higher-level mandates. State efforts are a mixture of supplements to and compliance with federally mandated requirements—state versions of requirements that apply to the federal government and requirements that have no federal equivalent. It is impractical to comprehensively survey this mélange of state requirements in a work of manageable length. Therefore, this volume focuses on privacy at the federal level. We make a point, however, of highlighting some landmark state legislation and noting cases in which states have enacted laws that correspond to particular requirements at the federal level.

The focus of this text also is exclusively on the executive branch at both the federal and state levels. While the legislative and judicial branches are not without privacy issues, the executive branch, with its myriad agencies executing a broad array of missions and programs, is the principal environment in which the vast majority of government privacy professionals operate. It is the branch of government that has the greatest and most varied contact with the public, handles the most varied and voluminous PII, and is the primary target of privacy requirements that apply to the government.

2.1 Federal Agency Privacy Programs

Kim Mott, CIPP/US, CIPP/G

The Privacy Act of 1974 (as amended, 5 U.S.C. § 552a) serves as the legal foundation for executive branch federal privacy programs. The Privacy Act balances the federal government's need to collect personal information[2] from individuals while taking steps to protect that personal information. It establishes for individuals the right to privacy related to records that federal agencies collect, maintain and use.[3] The law requires agencies to take precautions when collecting, maintaining, distributing and disposing of PII. It contains both civil and criminal penalties for noncompliance.

The basic principle in federal privacy programs is to protect personal information in electronic or hard copy form. This includes prevention of unauthorized access, use, modification and disclosure of personal information and is accomplished through collaboration with different offices across an agency as well as through guidance provided by the Privacy Act, Office of Management and Budget (OMB) memoranda and National Institute of Standards and Technology (NIST) documentation. Privacy crosses all business lines and can impact an agency's public image and public trust and confidence. While federal agencies are not in business to make a profit, their bottom line is to provide services to the public and safeguard taxpayer dollars. An agency's business must be transparent and readily available to the public. Confidence and trust have to be established for an individual to feel safe and reassured that the information he or she provides is collected for a business purpose and is being protected.

One example of collaboration within an agency would be working with the Office of General Counsel to ensure appropriate legal authorities are cited in federal notices or their review of legal documents with vendors and ensuring that data is collected with proper legal authority and only shared as permitted by law. Another would be working with the Office of Acquisition to ensure that Federal Acquisition Regulation privacy clauses are included in contracts with vendors where personal information will be collected and stored; and working with information security to ensure adequate security measures are in place for personal information that is collected and stored to protect that information from unauthorized access. Collaboration also occurs among federal agencies. Interagency privacy committees provide an excellent opportunity for privacy professionals to meet and discuss current topics and concerns and to provide best practices that participants can take back to their respective agencies. The Chief Information Officers (CIO) Council Privacy Committee is a great way to interact with privacy professionals from various federal agencies.

Federal agencies have privacy programs of varying sizes. One thing all agencies are required to have is a designated senior agency official for privacy (SAOP), according to OMB Memorandum M-05-08. Executive departments and agencies were asked to identify a senior-level official who would be responsible for protection of information privacy. This guidance reaffirmed the federal government's commitment to protection of information privacy. Along with the SAOP, an individual who is designated with the title of privacy officer or other similar titles (e.g., director of privacy, privacy advocate) assists with this task. Generally, the privacy officer handles day-to-day privacy operations and the SAOP is the individual who signs agency documents such as the annual report required under Federal Information Security Management Act (FISMA) of 2002. The SAOP may be involved in privacy operations on a limited basis as well. For example, the SAOP may assist with reporting to oversight organizations regarding responses to privacy incidents.

The FISMA annual submission from federal agencies requires input from information security, privacy, and the inspector general offices and provides documentation on how an agency is managing its information security and privacy programs. The privacy office provides information on its websites for privacy impact assessments (PIAs) and system of records notices (SORNs), status of PIAs and SORNs and answers questions about training, privacy complaints received throughout the year, the types of reviews the office has completed, whether general awareness and job-specific training programs are offered to employees and contractors, and privacy information sent by the SAOP to employees.

FISMA report provides OMB and privacy professionals with a global view
rivacy program is doing. It allows the privacy officer the opportunity to see
complished and what areas need more attention in the coming year.
echnological environment has complicated the privacy officer's job. While
the goal is still the same, the information platforms and infrastructures are changing.
A few years ago personal information was collected, processed and stored by the
agency. Today, with the increased use of social media and mobile applications, third-
party vendors can handle the collection, use and storage of personal information. The
collection tool may have evolved, but the goal is still the same: to ensure that only the
personal information that is needed is collected, used, disseminated, and retained, and
that adequate security measures are in place to protect personal information.

3. Privacy Definitions

Kim Mott, CIPP/US, CIPP/G

Several different definitions of the term PII are referenced within the federal
government depending upon the context in which the term is used. The definition of
PII that is most commonly used in the federal government is from OMB M-07-16. It is
defined, in part, as follows:

> *Information which can be used to distinguish or trace an individual's identity, such
> as their name, social security number, biometric records, etc. alone, or when combined
> with other personal or identifying information which is linked or linkable to a specific
> individual, such as date and place of birth, mother's maiden name, etc.*[4]

The definition of PII in M-07-16 mentions that PII may be information that is
linked or linkable to individuals, which can make it difficult to determine whether or
not a piece of data is PII. OMB M-10-23, "Guidance for Agency Use of Third-Party
Websites and Applications", provides further guidance that agencies can use to help
them identify PII. It states that:

> *the definition of PII is not anchored to any single category of information or
> technology. Rather, it requires a case-by-case assessment of the specific risk that an
> individual can be identified. In performing this assessment, it is important for an
> agency to recognize that non-PII can become PII whenever additional information is
> made publicly available—in any medium and from any source—that, when combined
> with other available information, could be used to identify an individual.*[5]

The updated definition of PII reflects that not all PII is created equal and requires
an ongoing risk assessment to determine the appropriate level of protection for
each situation. One or two data elements normally present a low risk of harm to
an individual, while various data elements amassed from different sources can create
identifying information and thus create a higher risk of harm to the individual.

Organizations should consider whether certain data elements need to be collected at ~~data minimalization~~ all. By collecting only the minimum amount of data necessary, privacy risk is reduced. For example, a Social Security number (SSN) is one data element that has the ability to provide harm to the individual and requires more protection when used. In fact, OMB guidance states that an SSN alone can generate identity theft.[6] "Data elements that in isolation look relatively innocuous can amount to a privacy breach when combined."[7] This "mosaic effect" occurs "when combinations of data tidbits produce a picture that wasn't apparent from the individual pieces,"[8] and has the ability to bring non-PII data elements into PII. In particular, care has to be taken in order to prevent taking a data set that would be very difficult to link to an individual and making it easier to link. The Open Government Directive and subsequent Open Government Initiative bring this issue to the forefront. In an effort to be open and transparent, federal agencies still have to protect personal information provided to them. Both ideas can exist in harmony if agencies adhere to the notion that PII, regardless of where it is stored, has to be protected at a level commensurate with the level of risk to the data. This can be accomplished by performing a regular review of information that is posted on agency websites. There are software programs that can take aggregated information and bring it down to an identifiable level. To prevent this from occurring, it's best to work with agency experts, including your information security team.

4. Privacy and Trust

Respect for privacy is just as beneficial for the government as it is for the governed. While all kinds of nuanced reasons for this exist, the overriding rationale is simple: It is a matter of trust and confidence. Democratic government as an institution cannot endure if it does not enjoy the trust of the public, and this trust must extend to the ways in which the government handles data. The public entrusts huge amounts of often-sensitive PII to the government, particularly executive branch departments and agencies, and expects the government to treat that information with the care and respect it deserves. This care and respect involves not just what the government does with the PII it gathers and generates, but also what it does not do with that PII. The fact that some data collection is mandatory—that is, individuals and/or organizations are legally required to provide PII to the government—places an additional ethical obligation on the government to handle the information appropriately. The power to demand the provision of information comes with a corresponding imperative to properly use and protect that information.

What are the potential consequences when government privacy protections fail or are judged inadequate? First, individuals may suffer harm ranging from general anxiety to identity theft to discrimination to loss of services or benefits. Second, relevant government organizations may need to expend considerable time and money responding to the issue or event, including possible investigations by both overseeing and legislative bodies. Finally, to the extent that events diminish trust in government privacy practices, the resulting loss of credibility and public confidence could seriously impair the government's ability to carry out necessary activities and missions. Individuals may be more reluctant to provide PII to the government if not strictly required to do so, and legislatures may move to restrict the authority and ability of certain agencies or programs to collect and use PII.

Unfortunately, a steady stream of incidents involving PII has shaken trust in government privacy practices. One of the most widely reported of these privacy incidents and one of the most severe in terms of number of records affected was the theft of a laptop belonging to the U.S. Department of Veterans Affairs in May 2006.[9] The unencrypted PII on this device amounted to tens of millions of records, including SSNs and dates of birth. The incident raised a number of important questions about the procedures that were in place to handle data, such as whether there was a legitimate reason to have such sensitive data on the laptop in the first place and if management approval was required to put the data on the laptop. The laptop was eventually recovered and forensic analysis suggested that no one had accessed the information. This did little, though, to reduce the resources the department had to expend in response to the incident or the resulting public and congressional opprobrium. The 2007 edition of an annual survey that measures public trust in federal government privacy practices showed the devastating impact of this incident on public perceptions.

Other levels of government have been no more immune than the federal government to this kind of mishap. In March 2006, for example, a hacker exploited security flaws to gain access to PII stored in systems belonging to the Georgia Technology Authority.[10] Among the information in the over half-million exposed records were SSNs and the bank account details of state pensioners. And in January 2007, the *Kansas City Star* reported that Kansas City lost 26 Internal Revenue Service computer tapes that had been delivered to City Hall.[11] The taxpayer PII on the tapes included names, SSNs, bank account numbers and employer information.

The point, in all these cases, is not the culpability of particular government organizations; rather, that government is just as vulnerable to such incidents as the private sector, which regularly suffers privacy data breaches.[12]

At the same time, it's important to recognize that data breaches involving PII constitute just one kind of privacy incident, albeit the type most commonly in the news and most viscerally alarming to the public. Both the government and the private sector are just as susceptible to other kinds of privacy incidents as well. Privacy data breaches amount to a loss of control over PII, but other types of incidents involve such things as improper use of PII and harmful decisions based on erroneous PII. For example, several State Department contractors in 2008 viewed the passport files of the presidential candidates without authorization.[13] Organizations that focus purely on avoiding data breaches as a means of preserving or engendering trust remain vulnerable to other kinds of trust-damaging incidents. Implementing a comprehensive privacy program is the only way any government or private-sector organization can address privacy risk in all its various forms.

5. U.S. Federal and State Rights to Privacy   *implies a right to privacy*

Legal scholars generally agree that the U.S. Constitution does not explicitly articulate any general right to privacy. Explicit privacy rights at the federal level are solely the province of legal and regulatory requirements. In particular, the Privacy Act addresses the rights of individuals and obligations of the U.S. government concerning the use of individuals' PII as it exists within a "system of records," which covers both manual and automated record-keeping systems.

On the other hand, many experts believe that the Constitution implies a right to privacy, even if it is not explicitly called out. Their argument holds that certain aspects of the Constitution—for example, the Fourth Amendment protections against unreasonable search and seizure and the Fifth Amendment guarantee against self-incrimination—taken together imply a general right to privacy that goes beyond the textual specifics. Other scholars have made the related but distinct argument that, rather than implying a general right to privacy, the Constitution is premised on such a right. Otherwise, they contend, many provisions of the Constitution simply don't make any sense in terms of what motivated them or what they are intended to achieve.

6. Federal Privacy Programs

Kim Mott, CIPP/US, CIPP/G

To restore the public's faith in the federal government after the major breach that occurred when the laptop belonging to the Department of Veterans Affairs was stolen, the OMB provided additional recommendations for agencies. These recommendations included both privacy and security measures. Federal agencies were asked to continue adhering to the Privacy Act, review and reduce the volume of PII that was collected and reduce the use of SSNs. These actions would have the effect of reducing the risk to a federal agency because the risk exposure would be reduced when the amount of PII was reduced. Security programs were asked to assign impact levels to information and information systems, implement a minimum of security requirements and controls, provide federal information systems security authorization to operate, train employees and contractors in privacy and security requirements, use encryption to protect PII, and create rules of behavior so employees and contractors would understand their role in protecting sensitive information. Also, agencies were asked to report all incidents that involve PII to the United States Computer Emergency Readiness Team (US–CERT) within one hour of discovery or detection. US–CERT is run by the National Cyber Security Division of the Department of Homeland Security (DHS), and its mission is to "improve the nation's cybersecurity posture, coordinate cyber information sharing, and proactively manage cyber risks to the nation while protecting the constitutional rights of Americans. The US–CERT vision is to be a trusted global leader in cybersecurity—collaborative, agile, and responsive in a complex environment."[14]

ıother action item from M-07-16 was the requirement to draft an incident response policy that would document and address the steps taken if a breach occurred, how and when impacted people would be notified and how redress would take place. While breach notification has occurred in the past, this memorandum takes it a step further in requiring agencies to explicitly document specific follow-up action at the policy level. The memorandum provides six elements that should be addressed in the policy document when a breach occurs: whether breach notification is required; timeliness of the notification; source of the notification; contents of the notification; means of providing the notification; who receives notification; and public outreach in response to a breach.

Privacy offices began asking program offices to justify and, at the very least, be able to explain their collection of PII, and more importantly, SSNs. While the goal is to reduce the collection of PII and SSNs, it is also understood that some business processes continue to require SSNs. Information that is transferred between federal agencies continues to need an SSN as the unique identifier. An SSN is the only unique identifier that is recognized across federal agencies. Although agencies have reduced the use of SSNs by creating alternative unique identifiers within their agencies, this number doesn't translate outside the boundaries of the agency. Examples of when information is shared between federal agencies include training data, employee information when employees change agencies, or Equal Employment Opportunity reports submitted to the Office of Personnel Management annually.

7. Guiding Principles for Information Privacy

Revised by Claire Barrett, CIPP/US, CIPP/G, CIPP/IT

In the 1960s, the increasing power and capacity of computer systems led to proposals for, and prompted fears of, federal data banks that would centralize unprecedented volumes of PII.[15] Visions of greatly enhanced efficiency and coordination clashed with concerns over potential abuses and loss of privacy. The U.S. government responded in a variety of ways to this controversy, not least through congressional hearings. The response by the executive branch included establishment of the U.S. Department of Health, Education and Welfare (HEW) Secretary's Advisory Committee on Automated Personal Data Systems. In 1973, the committee released what is now recognized as a landmark report, *Records, Computers, and the Rights of Citizens*. In it, the committee recommended the development of statutory privacy protections and the adoption of the Code of Fair Information Practices for both computerized and manual records. As a result, the Code of Fair Information Practices was used as the basis of the federal Privacy Act, which is discussed at length in Chapter 2.

Over time, Fair Information Practices (FIPs) or Fair Information Practice Principles (FIPPs) have become the foundation of information privacy, both in the United States and around the world. Several different versions now exist, promulgated by various national and international bodies, but they maintain a high degree of common represent a general consensus on the proper handling of PII.

7.1 HEW Code of Fair Information Practices

The FIPs articulated in the 1973 HEW report are defined in the box below. Two of these are framed in very distinctive ways, particularly Principle 1, which addresses openness or transparency in terms unlike those found anywhere else. The prohibition against secret systems is a vital point, one meant to address fears of a "dossier society," in which government would define and treat individuals as abstract collections of PII, the existence and contents of which the public would not necessarily be aware. Principle 1 aimed to ensure public knowledge and government accountability and is a prerequisite to the other four practices. This principle holds particular importance for understanding one of the central aspects of the Privacy Act.

HEW Code of Fair Information Practices (1973)

1. *There must be no personal data record keeping systems whose very existence is secret*

2. *There must be a way for an individual to find out what information about him [or her] is in a record and how it is used*

3. *There must be a way for an individual to prevent information about him [or her] that was obtained for one purpose from being used or made available for other purposes without his [or her] consent*

4. *There must be a way for an individual to correct or amend a record of identifiable information about him [or her]*

5. *Any organization creating, maintaining, using, or disseminating records of identifiable personal data must assure the reliability of the data for their intended use and must take precautions to prevent misuse of the data*

Source: U.S. Department of Health, Education and Welfare, Secretary's Advisory Committee on Automated Personal Data Systems, *Records, Computers, and the Rights of Citizens,* Washington DC: Government Printing Office, 1973.

Principle 3 is interesting in its emphasis on the ability of the individual to prevent unauthorized uses of his or her PII, something more typically expressed in terms of choice or consent. However, Principles 2, 4, and 5 are not very different from their expressions in other sets of FIPs. One way or another, the 1973 code embodies most of the key concepts articulated in a more elaborate manner in the codes that it inspired.

7.2 The Organisation for Economic Co-operation and Development (OECD) Privacy Principles

Probably the most important of these later codes is Guidelines for the Protection of Privacy and Transborder Flows of Personal Data, put forth by the OECD in 1980.

The list below includes the individual principles that comprise the OECD set of privacy principles. Their relation to the 1973 FIPs is readily apparent. One notable elaboration, though, is the OECD accountability principle, which introduces the concept of the "data controller." The data controller is the entity behind any given collection and use of PII. Regardless of who actually performs these functions on the data controller's behalf, it is the data controller who bears responsibility for the PII and what is done with it. To some extent, the OECD Guidelines anticipated a world of outsourcing, though the Privacy Act does explicitly apply to government contractors as well as the federal government itself. The OECD Privacy Principles are referenced and used by some federal agencies in addition to the FIPs issued by HEW.

> *OECD Privacy Principles (1980)*
>
> *Collection Limitation Principle: There should be limits to the collection of personal data and any such data should be obtained by lawful and fair means and, where appropriate, with the knowledge or consent of the data subject.*
>
> *Data Quality Principle: Personal data should be relevant to the purposes for which they are to be used, and, to the extent necessary for those purposes, should be accurate, complete and kept up-to-date.*
>
> *Purpose Specification Principle: The purposes for which personal data are collected should be specified not later than at the time of data collection and the subsequent use limited to the fulfillment of those purposes or such others as are not incompatible with those purposes and as are specified on each occasion of change of purpose.*
>
> *Use Limitation Principle: Personal data should not be disclosed, made available or otherwise used for purposes other than those specified in accordance with [the Purpose Specification Principle] except:*
>
> > *a) with the consent of the data subject; or*
> >
> > *b) by the authority of law.*
>
> *Security Safeguards Principle: Personal data should be protected by reasonable security safeguards against such risks as loss or unauthorized access, destruction, use, modification or disclosure of data.*
>
> *Openness Principle: There should be a general policy of openness about developments, practices and policies with respect to personal data. Means should be readily available of*

establishing the existence and nature of personal data, and the main purposes of their *well as the identity and usual residence of the data controller.*

Individual Participation Principle: *An individual should have the right:*

a) to obtain from a data controller, or otherwise, confirmation of whether or not the data controller has data relating to him;

b) to have communicated to him, data relating to him

   – *within a reasonable time;*

   – *at a charge, if any, that is not excessive;*

   – *in a reasonable manner; and*

   – *in a form that is readily intelligible to him;*

c) to be given reasons if a request made under subparagraphs(a) and (b) is denied, and to be able to challenge such denial; and

d) to challenge data relating to him and, if the challenge is successful to have the data erased, rectified, completed or amended.

Accountability Principle: *A data controller should be accountable for complying with measures that give effect to the principles stated above.*

Source: Organisation for Economic Co-operation and Development, Guidelines Governing the Protection of Privacy and Transborder Data Flows of Personal Data, September 23, 1980.

7.3 APEC Privacy Principles

One generally recognized set of FIPs is published by the Asia-Pacific Economic Cooperation (APEC), a group of 23 regional economies that formed in 2005. The APEC Privacy Principles, which are endorsed by the U.S. government, are listed below. They are also based on the OECD Guidelines but seek to promote electronic commerce throughout the Asia-Pacific region by balancing information privacy with business needs. This balancing act is particularly evident in the Preventing Harm and the Access and Correction principles. The Preventing Harm principle emphasizes that remedies for privacy infringements should be aimed at preventing resulting harm and that those remedies should be proportionate to the likelihood and severity of the harm. The Access and Correction principle essentially establishes a cost-benefit criterion, discounting the need for access and correction capabilities when the cost of providing such capabilities would be disproportionate to the privacy risks. Of course, the APEC code is very much aimed at the private sector; the approach embodied in these two principles seems less appropriate for the government context, in which the rights of the public must take precedence over any burdening of the government.

APEC Privacy Principles (2005)

Preventing Harm: Recognizing the interests of the individual to legitimate expectations of privacy, personal information protection should be designed to prevent the misuse of such information. Further, acknowledging the risk that harm may result from such misuse of personal information, specific obligations should take account of such risk, and remedial measures should be proportionate to the likelihood and severity of the harm threatened by the collection, use and transfer of personal information.

Notice: Personal information controllers should provide clear and easily accessible statements about their practices and policies with respect to personal information that should include:

    a) the fact that personal information is being collected;

    b) the purposes for which personal information is collected;

    c) the types of persons or organizations to whom personal information might be disclosed;

    d) the identity and location of the personal information controller, including information on how to contact them about their practices and handling of personal information;

    e) the choices and means the personal information controller offers individuals for limiting the use and disclosure of, and for accessing and correcting, their personal information.

All reasonably practicable steps shall be taken to ensure that such notice is provided either before or at the time of collection of personal information. Otherwise, such notice should be provided as soon after as is practicable.

It may not be appropriate for personal information controllers to provide notice regarding the collection and use of publicly available information.

Collection Limitation: The collection of personal information should be limited to information that is relevant to the purposes of collection and any such information should be obtained by lawful and fair means, and where appropriate, with notice to, or consent of, the individual concerned.

Uses of Personal Information: Personal information collected should be used only to fulfill the purposes of collection and other compatible or related purposes except:

    a) with the consent of the individual whose personal information is collected;

    b) when necessary to provide a service or product requested by the individual; or,

    c) by the authority of law and other legal instruments, proclamations and pronouncements of legal effect.

Choice: Where appropriate, individuals should be provided with clear, prominent, easily under-standable, accessible and affordable mechanisms to exercise choice in relation to the collection, use and disclosure of their personal information. It may not be appropriate for personal information controllers to provide these mechanisms when collecting publicly available information.

Integrity of Personal Information: Personal information should be accurate, complete and kept up-to-date to the extent necessary for the purposes of use.

Security Safeguards: Personal information controllers should protect personal information that they hold with appropriate safeguards against risks, such as loss or unauthorized access to personal information, or unauthorized destruction, use, modification or disclosure of information or other misuses. Such safeguards should be proportional to the likelihood and severity of the harm threatened, the sensitivity of the information and the context in which it is held, and should be subject to periodic review and reassessment.

Access and Correction: Individuals should be able to:

a) obtain from the personal information controller confirmation of whether or not the personal information controller holds personal information about them;

b) have communicated to them, after having provided sufficient proof of their identity, personal information about them:

   – within a reasonable time;

   – at a charge, if any, that is not excessive;

   – in a reasonable manner;

   – in a form that is generally understandable; and,

c) challenge the accuracy of information relating to them and, if possible and as appropriate, have the information rectified, completed, amended or deleted.

Such access and opportunity for correction should be provided except where:

   – the burden or expense of doing so would be unreasonable or disproportionate to the risks to the individual's privacy in the case in question;

   – the information should not be disclosed due to legal or security reasons or to protect confidential commercial information; or

   – the information privacy of persons other than the individual would be violated.

If a request under (a) or (b) or a challenge under (c) is denied, the individual should be provided with reasons why and be able to challenge such denial.

Accountability: A personal information controller should be accountable for complying with measures that give effect to the Principles stated above. When personal information is to be transferred to another person or organization, whether domestically or internationally, the personal information controller should obtain the consent of the individual or exercise due diligence and take reasonable steps to ensure that the recipient person or organization will protect the information consistently with these Principles.

Source: Asia-Pacific Economic Cooperation, APEC Privacy Framework, Singapore: APEC Secretariat, 2005.

8. Impact of Technology on Privacy

As demonstrated through the discussion of the FIPs, the American framework for privacy risk management and protection is predicated on both legal obligations (Privacy Act, E-Government and sectorial laws such as The Health Insurance Portability and Accountability Act of 1996 as well as practical limitations on the ability to collect, collate and use information. While the legal framework is ever evolving, the reality is that technology evolves at a greater rate and to an extent in a less knowable manner. The past decade has seen a proliferation of various technologies designed to keep the public safe or to prevent or detect others causing harm, including advanced biometric collections (e.g., fingerprints, facial recognition, retina scans, handwriting analysis), radio frequency identification tagging and various surveillance technologies. Each of these technologies serves a purpose, albeit through intrusions (both with explicit consent and without) on individual privacy, which is often not well articulated and not expressed beyond a general statement of unease.

Exacerbating the tension is the need in some instances to use technologies that may intrude on the individual in order to protect information about the individual. Even more confounding is that within a single organization there may be mission requirements to implement security measures to protect digitally stored and transmitted information while simultaneously requiring the acquisition of highly sensitive personal information for the purposes of delivering services or providing for national security or law enforcement needs.

The FIPs, regardless of their articulation, provide a framework for examining privacy. However, the FIPs do have some limitations. For example, they do not address civil liberties in general which interface with privacy. They also say to evaluate whether the collection and use of PII meets the stated purposes for collecting and using the data, but do not state that the purpose for collecting and using data should be evaluated to see if that purpose is appropriate. It is important to take a broader view and look beyond the FIPs when identifying and mitigating privacy risks so that all aspects of privacy are evaluated.

9. Conclusion

Clearly, FIPs have evolved considerably since 1973. Yet while some interesting innovations have developed, the central themes have remained fairly consistent across the different versions. As embedded in the Privacy Act, the original HEW code has proven remarkably durable.

Both international and U.S. private-sector information privacy owe much to early U.S. government privacy. The United States was the scene of debates regarding privacy and information technology long before such concerns arose in other quarters. The results of that initial bout of reflection were the first set of FIPs and the federal Privacy Act.

More recently, the E-Government Act of 2002 mandated new requirements meant to address a world in which the sheer ubiquity of information and information technology, together with the development and application of new techniques ranging from biometrics to data mining, has prompted new concerns. Government privacy, with its complex of statutory responsibilities, organizational missions, socio-political contexts and technological infrastructure, is quickly becoming at least as challenging an environment for privacy professionals as for the private sector—if not more so.

Similarly, while trust is essential in both sectors, privacy in government—especially the post-9/11 government—carries connotations that dramatically distinguish it from privacy in the commercial sphere. The power to coerce and deny freedoms attaches to the government. Misused, abused or inadequately protected PII undermines the trust that the government relies on both operationally and politically.

At its most basic level, privacy in government demands trust and confidence that the government will comply with the privacy laws that apply to it. The next chapter surveys the requirements defined by the Privacy Act and the E-Government Act.

Endnotes

1   Peter P. Swire and Kenesa Ahmad, *U.S. Private-sector Privacy: Law and Practice for Information Privacy Professionals*. Portsmouth, NH; International Association of Privacy Professionals: 2012.

2   Throughout this book, the terms "personal information" and "personally identifiable information" (PII) are used interchangeably.

3   The Privacy Act, 5 U.S.C. § 552a.

4   Office of Management and Budget Memorandum M-07-16, "Safeguarding Against and Responding to the Breach of Personally Identifiable Information", May 22, 2007, www.whitehouse.gov/sites/default/files/omb/memoranda/fy2007/m07-16.pdf.

5   Office of Management and Budget Memorandum M-10-23, "Guidance for Agency Use of Third-Party Websites and Applications", June 25, 2010, www.whitehouse.gov/sites/default/files/omb/assets/memoranda_2010/m10-23.pdf.

6   Office of Management and Budget, "Recommendations for Identify Theft Related Data Breach Notification Guidance", September 20, 2006, http://m.whitehouse.gov/sites/default/files/omb/assets/omb/memoranda/fy2006/task_force_theft_memo.pdf.

7   Jaikumar Vijayan, "Sidebar: The Mosaic Effect," *Computerworld* (March 15, 2004).

8   *Id*.

9   David Stout and Tom Zeller, "Vast Data Cache About Veterans Is Stolen," *New York Times* (May 23, 2006).

10 Jaikumar Vijayan, "Hacker hits Georgia state database via hole in security software," *Computerworld* (March 30, 2006).

11 "26 IRS tapes missing from City Hall," *Kansas City Star* (January 19, 2007).

12 The advocacy group Privacy Rights Clearinghouse has maintained a running tally of publicly reported data breaches since January 2005. See www.privacyrights.org.

13 "State Department: Someone Snooped in Obama's Passport File," (March 21, 2008), www.cnn.com/2008/POLITICS/03/20/obama.passport/index.html.

14 US-CERT, United States Computer Emergency Readiness Team, www.us-cert.gov.

15 A full recounting of these events is provided in: Priscilla M. Regan, *Legislating Privacy: Technology, Social Values, and Public Policy*, (Chapel Hill: University of North Carolina Press, 1995).

CHAPTER TWO

The Privacy Act and
the E-Government Act

As the federal government collects increasing amounts of data in the Information Age, federal privacy professionals must learn and know the requirements of the Privacy Act of 1974 and the E-Government Act of 2002. These two statutes are the cornerstones for privacy protection within the nation when the U.S. government collects personally identifiable information (PII). Along with a good records management program, these laws and policies govern the collection and use of personal data from initial induction to final destruction.

1. The Privacy Act

Revised by Alexander C. Tang, CIPP/US, CIPP/G[1]

The Privacy Act (P.L. 93-579, 5 U.S.C. § 552a) has guided the privacy practices of U.S. federal agencies since its passage. This landmark legislation can be seen as an access statute, which calls for certain Fair Information Practices (FIPs) and requires, in most instances, public notice of the types of personal data (i.e., PII) to be collected, processed, stored and used by a federal agency "system of records." Through later amendment, the statute also requires disclosure of matching programs among agencies when the results of the match might affect the receipt of a government benefit. It ruled the policy landscape of federal privacy for nearly 30 years until the passage of the E-Government Act of 2002 and its requirements for privacy impact assessments (PIAs) for electronic information collection activities and website privacy policies.

While scholars continue to debate whether U.S. privacy law has a foundation in the U.S. Constitution, the preamble of the Privacy Act asserts that "the right to privacy is a personal and fundamental right protected by the Constitution of the United States," and establishes clear responsibilities for federal systems with respect to privacy.

The original text for this chapter was developed by Erika L. McCallister, CIPP/US, CIPP/G, Stuart S. Shapiro, CIPP/US, CIPP/G and David Weitzel, CIPP/US, CIPP/G. New content for this revised edition was contributed by Alexander C. Tang, CIPP/US, CIPP/G and Rebecca J. Richards, CIPP/US, CIPP/G, whose contributions are noted throughout the sections of the chapter.

Aspects of the Privacy Act

- *ulates collection, use and disclosure of personal information by federal agencies*
- *Covers both paper and electronic records*
- *Protects U.S. citizens and lawful permanent residents*
- *Applies to all federal agencies*
- *Applies only to a "record" contained within a system of records*
- *Requires publication of System of Records Notices (SORNs)*
- *Requires additional notice to individuals when collecting information from them*
- *Allows for "routine uses" of PII*
- *Requires that appropriate data quality and safeguards be maintained*
- *Includes systems operated by government contractors*
- *Includes special provisions that apply to computer-based, records matching programs*

The Privacy Act also establishes the statutory foundation for the application of modern FIPs to federal government operations by implementing the 1973 code discussed in Chapter 1. Among other things, the Privacy Act requires agencies to:

- Limit PII collection to that which is "relevant and necessary"
- Collect PII directly from the individual whenever possible
- Maintain the accuracy, currency and completeness of PII
- Limit disclosure of PII to those who need access for proper purposes
- Allow access to and correction of PII
- Secure systems containing PII

1.1 Definitions under the Privacy Act

The Privacy Act provides the following key definitions:

- **Agency:** "[I]ncludes any executive department, military department, Government corporation, Government controlled corporation, or other establishment in the executive branch of the Government (including the Executive Office of the President), or any independent regulatory agency."
- **Individual:** A "citizen of the United States or an alien lawfully admitted for permanent residence."
- **Record:** "Any item, collection, or grouping of information about an individual that is maintained by an agency. . . and that contains his name, or the identifying number, symbol, or other identifying particular assigned to the individual, such as a finger or voice print or a photograph."

- **System of Records:** "A group of any records under the control of any agency from which information is retrieved by the name of the individual or by some identifying number, symbol, or other identifying particular assigned to the individual."

- **Routine Use:** "[T]he use of [a] record for a purpose which is compatible with the purpose for which it was collected."

- **Matching Program:** "[A]ny computerized comparison of two or more automated systems of records or a system of records with non-Federal records for the purpose of . . . establishing or verifying the eligibility of, or continuing compliance . . . by, applicants for, recipients or beneficiaries of, participants in, or providers of services with respect to, cash or in-kind assistance or payments under Federal benefit programs, or recouping payments or delinquent debts under such . . . programs, or [any computerized comparison of] two or more automated Federal personnel or payroll systems of records or [any such system] with non-Federal records."

Several key aspects of the Privacy Act are:

- The law applies to U.S. citizens and legal permanent resident aliens only. However, some agencies have implemented policies that require them to protect the privacy of non-citizens in the same way that they protect the privacy of U.S. citizens or legal permanent resident aliens under the Privacy Act. For example, at the Department of Homeland Security (DHS), any PII that is collected, used, maintained, and/or disseminated in connection with a mixed system is treated as a system of records subject to the Privacy Act. A mixed system is a system that contains records both on U.S. citizens and legal permanent residents as well as non-citizens.[2]

- The law applies only to records in a system of records that are retrieved by a name or some other identifying number or symbol, such as a Social Security number. Some systems in the federal government collect information on individuals, but retrieve the information in other ways, such as a case number that cannot be linked directly to an individual. In such instances, the records are not a system of records under the definition provided by the Privacy Act. Federal government privacy professionals should work with their legal counsel to confirm which records are systems of records within their agency's systems.

- There have been calls for updating the Privacy Act. The Privacy Act was enacted many years ago, and, since the law was passed, information technology has changed significantly. It can be very challenging to apply the Privacy Act to the kinds of technology and systems environments that exist today. Federal government privacy professionals should take care to consider the original intent of the Privacy Act when working to uphold the law's provisions in their work.

1.2 Data Quality and Security

The Privacy Act requires agencies to ensure the quality of PII to provide fairness to the individual.[3] It is expected that the degree of data quality required will vary with the intended use of the PII. The relevant factors for PII quality are accuracy (sufficiently correct), timeliness (sufficiently up-to-date) and completeness (sufficient information).

The agency must make reasonable efforts to ensure that Privacy Act records meet these requirements (and that such records are relevant for agency purposes) before disseminating them to anyone other than another agency or under the Freedom of Information Act (FOIA).[4]

The act also mandates that agencies establish appropriate administrative, technical and physical safeguards to ensure security and confidentiality of the PII and to protect against anticipated threats or hazards to the security or integrity of such PII.[5] The act does not specify the safeguards to be adopted, which are prescribed by other laws, regulations and policies governing information security and records management within the federal government (e.g., Federal Information Security Management Act [FISMA] guidance issued by the Office of Management and Budget [OMB], National Institute of Standards and Technology [NIST], DHS and National Archives and Records Administration [NARA]).

1.3 SORN

The Privacy Act calls for certain activities when a federal agency creates or modifies a system of records (including elimination of records). It is important to recognize that a system of records may be paper based as well as electronic. When the agency collects and stores PII in records and the PII is actually retrieved by a personal identifier, the agency is required to establish the statutory need for the collection, disclose the collection, describe its contents and declare the routine uses for that agency or any other agency that will use the information. This disclosure, a SORN, must be made to OMB and Congress and must be published in the *Federal Register* in advance of the system becoming operational and when any new routine use (including any new data element that the agency will maintain, retrieve, and use) is adopted by an agency. The OMB has also directed agencies to make links to their current SORNs available from their websites. This requirement applies equally to pilot or test systems that are using actual "live" PII; the Privacy Act does not specify any exemptions for such systems.

SORNs are the principal way the Privacy Act implements the prohibition against secret systems in the 1973 Code of Fair Information Practices. SORNs amount to a public paper trail of all government "systems of records". Nongovernmental organizations (NGOs) play an important role in this process. Unlike the vast majority of the American public, privacy advocacy NGOs review the SORNs and other relevant notifications published in the *Federal Register*. When they find something they consider problematic, they readily voice their concerns.

The specific items in the SORN include:[6]

- Name and location of the system
- Categories of individuals whose PII is collected
- Each routine use
- Authority for maintenance of the system
- Policies for storage, retrieval, access control, retention and disposal of records
- Title and business address of the responsible agency official
- Agency procedures for an individual to inquire if a system contains records about the individual
- Agency procedures for an individual to gain access to records about the individual
- Categories of sources of records
- Disclosures to consumer reporting agencies and whether the system is exempt from access by the individual[7]

Critical Aspects of a SORN
- *Acts as legal notice to the public*
- *Must specify routine uses*
- *Must be revised and republished if a new routine use is created*
- *Prior to system operation, must be provided to OMB and Congress and published in the* Federal Register
- *Required for pilot or test systems using real PII*

1.4 Privacy Act Statement

In addition to SORNs, agencies must provide a separate statement (notice) to individuals when collecting Privacy Act information from them.[8] This statement must be included on the form used to collect the information from the individual or on a separate form that can be retained by the individual. Although not required by the Privacy Act, prior OMB clearance may be required in some cases under the Paperwork Reduction Act to review the agency's estimate of the paperwork burden imposed by the form. The Privacy Act statement must include the following items:

- The statute or other legal authority for soliciting the information
- The principal purpose(s) for which the information is intended to be used
- The routine uses to be made of the information (see the relevant SORNs)

- Whether the information is mandatory or voluntary, and the consequences not providing the information

Although this requirement applies to forms, the OMB recommends that such a statement also be given when collecting information orally from individuals. The OMB also notes that the act does not explicitly require such a statement when collecting information from a third-party source, but where feasible, the agency should inform the source about the purpose for which the information will be used and assure the third party that his or her identity will not be revealed to the subject individual (i.e., if such confidentiality is afforded by a Privacy Act exemption applicable to the relevant systems of records).[9]

1.5 Records Maintenance and Retention

Privacy Act records maintenance and retention requirements apply whether the records are maintained by the agency itself or by contractor personnel.[10] The retention requirements must be stated in the agency's SORN; the records are considered to be maintained by that agency, and subject to the agency's SORN, even when the records have been transferred temporarily for storage, processing or servicing to NARA.[11]

NARA retention schedules (discussed in more detail in Chapter 7) provide the basis for the records retention periods stated in the SORN. In an ideal world, the NARA and SORN retention periods would always be identical. As a practical matter, NARA's primary concern is preventing premature disposal of records, but sometimes the retention period specified in a SORN exceeds the period that is specified by the NARA schedule. Over-retention can have obvious privacy implications and poses long-term storage issues that are contrary to an efficient and effective records management program. In these cases, an explanation for the extended retention period should be provided in the SORN. Conversely, SORNs should not specify a retention period shorter than legally required under the applicable NARA retention schedule(s).

1.6 Agency Use of Data and Exceptions

Agency use of PII under the Privacy Act is bound by 12 exceptions. Without these exceptions, an agency would have to obtain the consent of individuals each time it intends to use or disclose their records. The breadth of the exceptions has rendered this process very infrequent.[12]

The 12 use exceptions to the Privacy Act are:[13]

- Performance of regular duties by an agency employee (need-to-know basis)
- FOIA disclosures
- Routine uses as specified in the applicable SORN
- Census Bureau or survey functions

- Statistical research if not individually identifiable
- Disclosure to the National Archives
- Law enforcement requests
- Compelling health or safety circumstances
- Congressional committee with appropriate jurisdiction
- Government Accountability Office (GAO) duties
- Court order
- Consumer reporting agencies

The most utilized of these Privacy Act data use exceptions are:
- Performance of agency duties
- Routine use
- Law enforcement
- Court order

1.6.1 Agency Utilization of Routine Use

Exemptions 1 (intra-agency use on a need-to-know basis) and 3 (published routine uses) form the backbone of day-to-day Privacy Act practice within federal agencies. Over time, however, routine uses have come to be written very broadly. Some commentators believe this has been merely for expediency, to avoid having to publish a revised SORN in the *Federal Register* if a use is modified. Others believe that the objective has been to limit the public's ability to know how PII is being processed, used and shared within agencies. Still others believe that agencies, as a practical matter, write broad routine uses to give themselves the widest flexibility in using and disclosing PII protected by the act. Whatever the reason, very broad routine uses can seriously undermine the purpose specification under FIPs. Privacy professionals in the federal government should carefully assess whether the routine uses, as written, provide sufficient information to the public about the protection of PII and should be prepared to challenge those within their organizations who wish to adopt broad routine use language that may to circumvent the intent of the Privacy Act.

1.7 Individual Access, Agency Procedures, Exempt Systems and Right to Court Review

With certain exceptions, an individual has significant access and disclosure rights under the Privacy Act. These rights include the right to access data about the individual kept by federal agencies and the right to file civil claims if the agency has breached the Privacy Act's requirements. Some records may not be kept under any circumstance unless specifically allowed by statute, such as any record regarding the exercise of an individual's First Amendment rights. In addition, the act allows agencies to exempt certain record systems from access by the individual and various other provisions of the act if such exemptions are published as an agency regulation in the *Federal Register* (e.g., Central Intelligence Agency and other classified systems, criminal law enforcement agency systems and personnel or contractor security investigation systems that would reveal a confidential source).[14]

1.7.1 Access and Correction

Certain rights to access, copy and request amendment of records are granted to the individual.[15] Once a request is made, the agency is required to acknowledge receipt of the request within 10 working days. It must promptly make corrections or inform the individual of the refusal to amend, the reason for the refusal, the procedures for review of the refusal and the name of the agency official to contact to dispute the refusal. The agency must allow a request for review of the refusal and process that request within 30 working days, unless the agency extends the review for good cause. If the agency has refused the individual's request, the individual is permitted to file a statement of disagreement with the agency. The agency is also required to inform people and agencies to whom the record is subsequently disclosed of any disputed portion of the record, together with a copy of the individual's statement and any optional statement by the agency of the reasons it refused to make the requested amendment. The agency must also inform persons or agencies to whom it previously disclosed the record of any correction or notation of dispute, except where the agency was not required to account for the prior disclosure (i.e., intra-agency disclosures and FOIA). In the event of an agency's refusal of the individual's request to amend, the individual is ultimately allowed judicial review.

1.7.2 Agency Procedures

The Privacy Act requires agencies to establish procedures implementing its provisions.[16]

These include procedures for access requests, establishing the identity of a person making a request and appeal of a denied access request.

1.7.3 Civil and Criminal Penalties

After exhausting the agency procedures outlined above, an individual can file suit in U.S. federal court in the following cases: a) the individual has had a request to amend a record refused by an agency; b) an agency refuses a request for access to records; or c) the agency fails to comply with the data quality safeguards identified above, or any other rights established under the act. Without deference to any agency determination or review, the court shall review the matter and may amend the individual's record, take whatever other action it deems appropriate and/or grant attorney fees, and in some cases, litigation costs against the agency.

In cases of refusal to amend a record or to comply with an access request, the court may require amendment of or access to the record, and may assess attorney fees and other "reasonably incurred" litigation costs. (The court may also privately examine the contents of the record to determine whether any exemption applies and access may be properly denied.) In lawsuits where the court determines that the agency intentionally or willfully failed to maintain records properly under the act, or to comply with any other provision of the act, the agency can be liable for actual damages sustained by the individual, but not less than $1000, plus attorney fees.[17] Such civil cases must be brought within two years of the date on which the cause of action arises or, if the agency materially and willfully misrepresented material information, within two years of discovery of the misrepresentation.

The act also provides for criminal penalties against agency officers or employees who have possession of, or access to, Privacy Act records for willfully disclosing them in violation of the act, and against such officers or employees for willful maintenance of an unpublished system of records. The act also deems it a crime for any person to obtain Privacy Act records knowingly and willfully from an agency under false pretenses.[18]

1.8 Computer-Matching Provisions

The Privacy Act was amended by the Computer Matching and Privacy Protection Act of 1988. The provisions under this amendment, as further amended in 1990, require federal agencies that use computerized means to match data between electronic federal Privacy Act record systems, or to match data from any such federal system with nonfederal records in connection with granting or recouping financial benefits (or for personnel or payroll purposes) to publicly disclose the matching in a written agreement between the agencies. The written agreement explains the scope and purpose of the matching and must include procedures and safeguards to protect individual privacy.

There are three important aspects of the computer-matching process:

- Generally does not apply to intra-agency matching
- Requires matching agreements overseen by agency data integrity boards (DIBs)
- Matching agreements must be made available to Congress and the public

1.8.1 Components of the Matching Program

The Privacy Act describes the major elements required for matching programs.[19] As noted above, there must be a written data-matching agreement between the agencies, specifying the purpose, justification and legal authority for the matching program, including a description of the records to be matched and procedures for notifying affected individuals that they may be subject to verification through matching programs.

The written agreement must also establish procedures for a) verifying the information produced by the matching program, b) retaining and destroying the information, c) providing administrative, technical and physical security of the matched records, d) prohibiting duplication and further disclosure unless required by law, e) allowing use by a recipient agency, including return and disclosure, and f) assessing the accuracy of records. The GAO is granted access to the records to verify compliance with the matching agreement.

Agencies may not operate a matching program until they provide a copy of the matching agreement to House and Senate oversight committees at least 30 days before the program begins. Matching agreements must also be made available to the public upon request. The agreement is only allowed to be in effect while the agency's DIB agrees, and not longer than 18 months, unless the agency DIB certifies the need to extend the agreement for an additional 12 months.

1.8.2 Rules Before Benefits Are Denied

Agencies must comply with certain requirements to ensure individual administrative due process before the matched data is used to suspend, reduce or deny a federal financial benefit or payment.[20] Agencies must independently verify the information, unless, following OMB guidelines, the DIB determines that the information used is accurate to a "high degree of confidence" and is limited to confirming the individual's identity and amount of benefits paid to him or her. An individual must receive a notice of the findings and be given an opportunity to contest the findings until the expiration of a time period established by the agency or by statute, or within 30 days if another time period has not been established. In the absence of a DIB determination, the agency's independent verification requires investigation and confirmation of the specific information used as a basis for the adverse action. This information includes, where applicable, the amount of an asset or income and the period that the individual had the asset or income. The data-matching provisions have an exception allowing an agency to take any appropriate action for public health or safety reasons without waiting for the notice period to expire.

No agency may disclose records to another agency for matching purposes if the source agency believes the matching agreement or the procedures for individuals to contest the match are not being followed by the recipient agency. Furthermore, no agency can renew a matching agreement unless the recipient agency certifies that it has complied with the agreement and the source agency has "no reason to believe" that the certification is inaccurate. Any new or significantly changed matching program must be reported in advance to appropriate House and Senate oversight committees and the OMB.

1.8.3 Creation and Use of the Data Integrity Board

The matching provisions of the Privacy Act require that each agency participating in a matching program create a DIB composed of senior officials and the agency's inspector general.[21] The DIB shall:

- Review, approve and maintain all matching agreements
- Review all existing matching programs annually to determine compliance with laws, regulations, guidelines and agreements, and assess the cost and benefits of the agreements

- Review the continued justification for each matching program annually
- Compile annual reports on matching programs for the agency head, OMB and public requests
- Serve as the matching program's information clearinghouse for accuracy, reliability and completeness of records used for data matching
- Provide interpretation and guide agency compliance
- Review agency matching programs' record-keeping and disposal policies
- Report, in its discretion, on other agency matching activities that are not under agreement

The DIB shall, with certain exceptions, require a cost-benefit analysis before approving any matching program. Disapproval of a matching agreement by the DIB may be appealed to OMB, which can override the disapproval. If both the DIB and the OMB disapprove a matching program proposed by the agency's inspector general, he or she may report the disapproval to the agency head and Congress.

1.9 The OMB's Role and Other Privacy Act Responsibilities

Under the Privacy Act, the OMB is charged with the responsibility to supervise agencies' implementation of the act's provisions. In order to perform this task, the act provides that the director of the OMB shall develop and prescribe guidelines and regulations, as well as provide assistance and oversight of their implementation by agencies.[22] (Although not explicitly prescribed within the act, additional legal guidance [overview] has been provided to federal agencies by the Department of Justice, Office of Privacy and Civil Liberties.) The Department of Justice asserts that its overview was not created to offer policy guidance—that is the OMB's responsibility—but that it is intended to legally analyze and refer to court decisions regarding the act's provisions.[23]

In the case of the OMB's policy guidance, the main directive is OMB Circular A-130 and its Appendix I, "Federal Agency Responsibilities for Maintaining Records About Individuals." The appendix identifies relevant responsibilities of the heads of agencies, including review of contracts, record-keeping practices, violations of the Privacy Act, personnel training, and SORNs. The appendix also identifies agency reporting requirements, and sets forth specific requirements for the Department of Commerce, Department of Defense, Office of Personnel Management, NARA, and the OMB itself. This OMB circular is discussed further in Chapter 6.

The OMB issued its original Privacy Act guidelines in the *Federal Register* in July of 1975, laying out responsibilities for Federal Agencies under the Act.[24] In order to update these guidelines, it issued supplemental guidance in December of the same year, and again in May of 1985.[25] In addition to this guidance, the OMB has issued provisions on the implications and relationships between the Privacy Act and other legislation, such as the Debt Collection Act of 1982[26] and the Personal Responsibility and Work Opportunity Reconciliation Act of 1996.[27] The OMB has continued to supplement its guidance over time with other issuances, including computer-matching guidance and other technical guidelines to carry out the requirements of the Privacy Act as well as the E-Government Act, which is discussed later in this chapter.[28]

1.10 Miscellaneous Provisions of the Act

In addition to the responsibilities discussed above, the act sets forth certain miscellaneous provisions designed to ensure that the privacy and civil liberties of individuals are protected. For example, subsection (n) of the act prohibits the unauthorized sale or renting of individual names and addresses. Section 7 of the act further prohibits any federal, state or local government agency from denying any individual any right, benefit or privilege provided by law based on an individual's refusal to disclose his or her SSN.

1.10.1 The Relationship Between the Privacy Act and FOIA

Although FOIA and the Privacy Act seem to have the opposite goals of ensuring access to records (FOIA) and preventing disclosure of records (Privacy Act), they are similar in their provisions for procedural rights to request records and receive a response.[29] The statutes work together to ensure access to agency records while protecting the privacy rights of individuals. The Privacy Act provides only U.S. citizens and lawful permanent residents right of access to their own records, whereas FOIA provides a general right of access to agency records for any requester (e.g., non-citizens, non-permanent residents, businesses) seeking access to such records. Privacy Act exemptions to access apply to entire systems of records, whereas FOIA exemptions apply to particular records and parts of particular records.

While FOIA allows agencies to withhold records that would constitute an unwarranted invasion of privacy from disclosure to persons or entities other than the individual, the Privacy Act often requires access to the same records by the person to whom the records pertain. Conversely, records that are part of systems exempted from certain provisions of the Privacy Act related to the subject individual are not necessarily exempt from disclosure to third parties under FOIA. To disclose a Privacy Act record under FOIA to a third party, however, the agency must receive a formal FOIA request and determine that the agency cannot withhold the record on grounds that it would constitute an unwarranted invasion of the subject individual's privacy. The Privacy Act does not permit discretionary disclosures (without a FOIA request) outside of the use exceptions discussed earlier. For first-party access requests from the subject individual, the agency must consider the exempt status of the requested record under both the Privacy Act and FOIA. Thus, the requested record must not only be part of an exempt system of records under the Privacy Act (see above) but must also be exempt from disclosure to the individual (on other non-privacy grounds) under the FOIA to bar an individual's access following that statute as well.

2. The E-Government Act

Revised by Rebecca J. Richards, CIPP/US, CIPP/G

The E-Government Act of 2002[30] was enacted in part to help bring the Privacy Act into the digital age. The requirements of the two laws are different but complementary. The E-Government Act promotes the use of electronic government services by the public and improves the use of information technology in the government. To establish and maintain public trust in electronic government services, the statute includes provisions for privacy and information security. Section 208 of the E-Government Act ensures "sufficient protections for the privacy of personal information" in government information systems.[31] Title III is referred to as The Federal Information Security Management Act of 2002 (FISMA), which requires executive branch agencies to maintain information security programs.

Section 208 of the E-Government Act has two major privacy provisions that help build privacy into the fabric of government agencies. First, it requires agencies to conduct a PIA before initiating a new collection of information in identifiable form and before developing or procuring information technology to collect, maintain or disseminate such PII.[32] Second, Section 208 requires agencies to maintain privacy policies on their websites and requires the privacy policies to be translated into a machine-readable format. The statute directs the OMB to issue detailed implementation guidance to the agencies.

Specifically, agencies are required to conduct a PIA before developing, procuring or significantly modifying information technology systems that collect, maintain or disseminate information in identifiable form from or about members of the public, or before initiating a new electronic collection of information in identifiable form for 10 or more people.

2.1 OMB Guidance on PIAs

OMB Memorandum M-03-22[33] provides agencies with specific implementation guidance for conducting PIAs and developing website privacy policies. OMB M-03-22 applies to all executive branch agencies and departments, contractors and cross-agency initiatives that use websites or other information technology for interacting with the public. It requires agencies to:

- Conduct PIAs and make them publicly available
- Post privacy policies on agency websites
- Translate privacy polices into a standardized machine-readable format
- Ensure privacy responsibilities are properly executed for information in identifiable form (IIF) processed by information technology
- Report annually to OMB on Section 208 compliance

OMB M-03-22 provides for several exceptions to the PIA requirement, principally those indicated below. The exception for national security systems is based on the definition in the Information Technology Management Reform Act of 1996, also known as the Clinger-Cohen Act (CCA). The CCA defines a national security system as any telecommunications or information system that involves intelligence, cryptologic activities related to national security, command and control of military forces, and equipment that is an integral part of a weapon system or that is critical to the direct fulfillment of military or intelligence missions. The definition explicitly excludes systems used for routine administrative and business functions, including payroll, finance, logistics and personnel management.

Principal PIA Exceptions

- *National security systems*
- *Systems that have previously undergone an evaluation similar to a PIA*
- *Internal government operations*
- *Websites, systems and information collections that do not involve the collection or maintenance of identifiable information about the public*
- *Minor changes to an information system or collection that do not create new privacy risk*

Source: "OMB Guidance for Implementing the Privacy Provisions of the E-Government Act of 2002," M-03-22, September 26, 2003.

The exception for information that relates to internal government operations effectively eliminates any need to perform a PIA on an information system or collection dealing exclusively with federal government personnel, including contractors. OMB M-03-22 notes that while such information is generally protected by the Privacy Act, agencies are encouraged to conduct PIAs for these systems as appropriate. More recently, OMB M-07-19, "FY 2007 Reporting Instructions for the Federal Information Security Management Act and Agency Privacy Management" reiterates this point in somewhat stronger terms, observing that:

> *Although neither Section 208 of the E-Government Act, nor OMB's implementing guidance mandate agencies conduct PIAs on electronic systems containing information about federal employees (including contractors), the OMB encourages agencies to scrutinize their internal business processes and the handling of identifiable information about employees to the same extent they scrutinize processes and information handling procedures involving information collected from or about members of the public.*[34]

OMB guidance sets forth the basic requirements that many federal agencies have built upon and issued additional guidance on when and how a PIA should be conducted. The E-Government Act is not the only statute that requires PIAs. PIAs are required of certain cabinet-level agencies for regulations and rules; for example, the

Homeland Security Act requires DHS to conduct PIAs on rules that may impact PII. In other instances Congress has passed a law specifically requiring a PIA for a particular program; for example, the 9/11 Commission Act requires a PIA to be conducted by the Office of the Director of National Intelligence, the Department of Justice and DHS on the Interagency Threat Assessment and Coordination Group (ITACG) program. While agencies may have specific guidance, the overall process and document for the creation of a PIA follows the same general flow.

2.2 What Is a PIA?

The PIA is both a process and a written outcome. An agency's privacy office partners with program managers, information technology managers, counsel and policymakers to assess all new or proposed department programs, systems, technologies or rulemakings (programs or systems) for privacy risks. It also recommends privacy protections and alternative methods for handling PII to mitigate privacy risks. A PIA is a decision-making tool used to identify and mitigate privacy risks at the beginning of and throughout the development life cycle of a program or system. It helps the public understand what PII the department is collecting, why it is being collected and how it will be used, shared, accessed and stored.

A PIA is an analysis of how PII is collected, used, disseminated and maintained. It examines how an agency has incorporated privacy concerns throughout its development, design and deployment of a technology, program or rulemaking. The purpose of a PIA is to demonstrate that program managers and system owners have consciously incorporated privacy protections through the development life cycle of a system or program. This involves making certain that privacy protections are built into the system from the initiation of development, not after the fact when implementing protections can be far more costly or could affect the viability of the project.

Each federal agency considers the nature and context of information it collects from the public and creates a process that flows from that. In Memorandum M-03-22, the OMB provides basic guidance on when and what questions need to be answered.[35]

2.3 When Is a PIA Required?

Generally, a PIA is required before a program or system that contains PII becomes operational.

- When developing or procuring any new program or system that will handle or collect PII
- For budget submissions to the OMB that affect PII
- With pilots or tests that affect PII
- When developing a program or system revisions that affect PII

- When issuing a new or updated rulemaking that involves the collection, use and maintenance of PII
- When issuing or updating a form that collects PII from 10 or more individuals in the public

Some agencies have a privacy threshold analysis or initial privacy assessment process in place that uses a short form to capture information. The information is reviewed by the agency's privacy official to determine whether a PIA (and, in some cases, a SORN) is required. This initial assessment identifies the basic information of the program, technology or collection with less emphasis on identification privacy risks and mitigation. It allows programs that are not privacy sensitive to demonstrate that a privacy official has reviewed its program and that a PIA is not required. OMB M-03-22 provides a list of examples of type of potential PIA triggers, which are summarized below.

Potential PIA Triggers

- *Conversion of records from paper-based to electronic form*
- *Conversion of information from anonymous to identifiable form*
- *System management changes involving significant new uses and/or application of new technologies*
- *Significant merging, matching, or other manipulation of multiple databases containing PII*
- *Application of user-authenticating technology to a system accessed by members of the public*
- *Incorporation into existing databases of PII obtained from commercial or public sources*
- *Significant new inter-agency exchanges or uses of PII*
- *Alteration of a business process resulting in significant new collection, use, and/or disclosure of PII*
- *Alteration of the character of PII due to the addition of qualitatively new types of PII*

Source: "OMB Guidance for Implementing the Privacy Provisions of The E-Government Act of 2002," M-03-22, September 26, 2003.

A PIA should be conducted when a program or system is developing or procuring any new technologies or systems that handle or collect PII. Similarly, if a system undergoes revisions, the PIA will need to be reviewed and determined whether an update is required. For example, if a program or system adds additional sharing of information with another agency or incorporates commercial data from an outside data aggregator, a PIA update would likely be required. If an organization decides to collect new information as part of a rulemaking, a PIA would be required. Even if a component has legal authority to collect certain information or build a certain program or system, a PIA is required before the program or system becomes operational.

The PIA requirement does not provide an exemption for pilot testing a program or system. If a PIA is ultimately required for a system, any pilot of that system must have the PIA completed prior to the pilot launch. This applies even if the pilot initially plans to use anonymous data but will use PII as it ends the pilot because the decisions affecting privacy are made leading up to the initiation of a pilot. Like operational systems, completion of a PIA prior to launch of a pilot ensures that privacy protections are considered during the development process instead of after a pilot has concluded when changes are potentially more costly and difficult to make.

2.4 Completing a PIA

OMB's PIA guidance is general, and federal agencies have each adopted their own PIA formats and processes in line with their distinct missions and policies and procedures. Before beginning a PIA, it is important to be familiar with the specific PIA process and template that is in use by the government organization that is responsible for the system or program on which the PIA is being completed. In general, there are three main steps that need to be followed in order to complete a PIA for a system or program:

- Gather information about the system or program
- Perform privacy risk analysis
- Identify outstanding issues requiring mitigation/resolution

The first step in completing a PIA is to collect all of the information about the system or program for which the PIA is being done and the system or program's environment. The information should be obtained by meeting with the program manager and system owners who are responsible for the system or program and also reviewing any existing documentation about the system or program. Information that should be gathered about the system or program and its environment includes:

- Privacy policies for the organization, program and/or system.
- Laws, regulations, and guidance with privacy implications that pertain specifically to the system or program.
- System description and system diagrams, including data flows within and between systems. The Concept of Operations (CONOPS) is often a good source to reference to find a system description.
- SORNs that are related to the system or program.

- System requirements (including security requirements).

- Interconnection agreements and/or any memoranda of understanding or memoranda of agreement that discuss the specifics of what PII is shared between organizations, how it is shared, retention periods for the data, and incident reporting requirements.

- Security accreditation documents, including the Security Plan, and results of security reviews or assessment/audit reports.

- Any prior PIAs related to the system or program.

- Database schemas or equivalent documents.

- Public information about the system, including outreach pieces on public websites.

The information that is gathered about the system or program is then analyzed by applying the FIPs to each of the required PIA content areas to assess the impact of the system or program on an individual's privacy. The required content of a PIA, as specified by M-03-22, is listed below.

PIA Content

- *What PII is to be collected*
- *Why the PII is being collected*
- *What are the intended uses of the PII*
- *With whom the PII will be shared*
- *What opportunities individuals have to decline to provide PII or to consent to particular uses of the PII*
- *How the PII will be secured*
- *Whether a system of records is being created under the Privacy Act*
- *Analysis of information life cycle and of choice made*

Source: "OMB Guidance for Implementing the Privacy Provisions of the E-Government Act of 2002," M-03-22, September 26, 2003

For example, information about what PII is collected by a system should be analyzed to see how well the system meets the requirement in the FIPs to collect only the PII that is needed for the purpose of the system. Privacy analysis should also look beyond the FIPs by considering civil liberties that interface with privacy, evaluating the purpose for collecting and using PII to see if it is appropriate, and assessing the broader social implications related to privacy. Privacy, like other system properties, such as performance and security, should be considered from the earliest conceptual stages of system development. The development of a PIA for an information technology system should mirror the system development life cycle; the PIA should become progressively less conceptual and more detailed as the system is developed. The information life cycle—collection, processing, use, disclosure, retention, and destruction—provides a framework for understanding how PII is handled and for identifying both relevant privacy risks at each state (including legal, regulatory, and policy compliance issues) and potential mitigations. Some agencies even structure the PIA document to explicitly reflect the stages of the information life cycle. The risk analysis can then feed back into the development or procurement process, appropriately influencing design decisions. Extensive and sophisticated risk analysis is not always necessary; M-03-22 explicitly recognizes that the depth and content of a PIA should be a function of the nature of the PII involved and the size and complexity of the information system or collection. While major systems handling large volumes of sensitive PII clearly demand relatively elaborate documentation and analysis, small collections of less-sensitive PII with highly circumscribed uses might be adequately assessed using something closer to a checklist.

Privacy risks are typically mitigated either through technical or policy changes, and these risk mitigation efforts should be discussed in the PIA. For example, the PIA document should summarize the reasoning behind key design choices that touch on privacy. What alternatives were considered and what are their pros and cons from a privacy standpoint? Which alternatives were selected and why? In particular, when a less privacy-sensitive alternative is selected, the rationale behind the selection should be clearly articulated.

In most instances, the end result of the process is a PIA that is published on the website of the agency. The PIA should identify the risks and the mitigation strategies, allowing the public to understand what the program or technology is, why it is being used and the privacy risks associated with it.

2.5 SORN Versus PIA

The Privacy Act requires agencies to publish SORNs in the *Federal Register* that describe the categories of records on individuals that they collect, use, maintain and disseminate. Generally, the requirements to conduct a PIA are broader than the requirements for SORNs. The PIA requirement is triggered by the collection or use of PII. SORNs are triggered by the collection or use of PII that is actually *retrieved* by a personal identifier. If the technology using the information is changed or updated, a PIA must be completed or updated to analyze the new impact of the technology, even if the collection or use of information remains the same and is already covered by an existing SORN or PIA. The SORN covering the system must also be reviewed to ensure its completeness and accuracy.

site Privacy Policies

of the E-Government Act requires agency website privacy policies to following information:

- What information is to be collected through use of the website
- Why the information is being collected
- The intended use by the agency of the information
- With whom the information will be shared
- What notices or opportunities for consent will be provided
- How the information will be secured
- The rights of individuals under the Privacy Act and other privacy laws

OMB M-03-22 provides implementation guidance for agency website privacy policies pursuant to Section 208 and modifies and replaces previous website privacy policy guidance.[36] OMB M-03-22 does not apply to agency intranet websites or national security systems.[37]

Consistent with OMB Memorandum 99-18, M-03-22 provides guidance on and requires agencies to post or provide links to their website privacy policies at their principal site, any known, major entry point to their site and any web page that collects substantial information in identifiable form.[38] In addition, the website privacy policy must be clearly labeled, easily accessed and written in plain language.

For the consent requirement, agencies must inform website visitors when requests for information are voluntary. Also, agencies must explain to visitors how they can provide consent for both voluntary and mandatory requests for information when the information will be used for purposes other than those mandated by statute or different from routine uses under the Privacy Act.

Agencies must inform users of the nature, purpose, use and sharing of collected information. If an agency is collecting information that will be included in a Privacy Act system of records, then the agency must notify website visitors of their rights under the Privacy Act. Moreover, visitors must be notified of applicable agency-specific privacy laws, such as the Health Insurance Portability and Accountability Act of 1996.[39] This information must be made available in the body of the website privacy policy, through a link to the applicable agency regulation or through a link to an official summary of statutory rights.

Agencies must explain in clear language that proper administrative, operational and technical controls are in place to protect the security and confidentiality of collected information. Also, agencies must state what information is automatically collected when the website is visited, such as IP address, type of operating system and time of visit.

Lastly, compliance with the Children's Online Privacy Protection Act (COPPA)[40] when collecting information from children under the age of 13 is a must (see Chapter 5 for more information), as is ensuring full adherence to the agency's stated privacy policies.

2.6.1 Privacy Policies in Machine-Readable Formats

OMB M-03-22 requires agencies to provide a machine-readable version of their website privacy policies that automatically lets a visitor know whether an agency's policy matches the visitor's privacy preferences. The Platform for Privacy Preferences (P3P) is the standard used to meet this requirement.[41]

Recognizing the increased use of the Internet and online tools by federal agencies to achieve greater transparency, citizen participation and collaboration, the OMB has issued M-10-22 and M-10-23 providing detailed guidance on the use of cookies and other web-tracking and customization technology, as well as third-party (e.g., social media) websites and applications.[42]

2.7 Web Tracking and Customization

Alexander C. Tang, CIPP/US, CIPP/G[43]

Agency websites and applications may use tracking or customization technologies to measure or analyze usage or to customize the user's experience by recording personal settings, preferences or other online user interactions with the site or application. Under OMB's guidance, the specific authorization requirements for the agency's use of such technology depend on whether it is limited to a single session (e.g., session cookie, "Tier 1") or is maintained across multiple sessions (e.g., persistent cookie, "Tier 2," unless it collects PII, which is "Tier 3"). Tier 3 technology, because it involves the collection and maintenance of PII and poses a greater potential privacy impact, requires that users be given the choice to opt in (rather than opt out) of such technology, and it must be reviewed by the agency's SAOP and approved in writing by its chief information officer (CIO). Before the CIO may grant such approval, the agency must solicit public comment on the proposed use through its Open Government web page for at least 30 days, unless, upon the CIO's written approval, the comment process "is reasonably likely to result in serious public harm." Agencies are not required to follow this specific approval and comment process for Tier 1 and 2 technologies, but users must still be allowed to opt out of those technologies as well, and the agency must adhere to its own internal policies for authorizing or securing the use of such technologies.

In all cases, regardless of tier, the agency must provide alternative access to comparable information or services for users who decline the technology and must disclose and explain the agency's use of the technology in the agency's privacy policy, including how users may access comparable information or services. Agencies must retain tracking and customization data for no longer than needed to achieve the intended objective, limit access to such data and comply with all applicable records management, privacy, security and other laws. Agencies must also annually review their compliance with OMB's requirements, immediately cease any use that violates the requirements and report violations to the OMB. Further, under no circumstances may an agency use any technology to track individual Internet usage outside the agency's website, share user data collected by the technology with other agencies without the user's consent, cross-reference the data with other user PII to determine a user's online activity, collect any PII from a user without explicit consent or for any other uses that the OMB may also prohibit.

2.8 Third-Party Sites and Applications

Alexander C. Tang, CIPP/US, CIPP/G[44]

Before using social media sites or other third-party sites and applications to engage the public, agencies must conduct a PIA for any site or application that will make PII available to the agency. For example, in the social media context, PII could include photos, comments or other content posted or made available by or about individuals who interact with the agency through the site. OMB's guidance outlines the specific issues that such a PIA must address, including the agency's purpose in using the third-party site or application; what PII is likely to be made available; how or whether the agency intends to use or share that PII; if and how long it will be maintained and how it will be secured; other privacy risks and mitigation steps; and whether the agency's use of the site or application will create or modify a Privacy Act system of records. Agencies may prepare one PIA for sites or applications that are "functionally comparable" but must create individual PIAs for sites or applications that raise distinct or unique privacy risks. Agencies must review the third party's privacy policy to determine what privacy risks may be involved, and whether the site or application is appropriate for agency use.

If an agency decides to use the site or application, the agency must follow requirements similar to those set out for agency websites. The agency should collect the minimum amount of available PII necessary to achieve a purpose required by statute, rule or executive order; disclose and explain the use of site or application in the agency's online privacy policy as detailed in OMB guidance; "brand" the agency's use of the site or application with an official seal or emblem to help the public distinguish it from nongovernment activities; and post a separate privacy notice on the site or application itself, to the extent feasible. This notice must: a) inform the public that the site is operated or controlled by a third party, not the government; b) explain that the agency's privacy policy does not apply; c) indicate whether and how the agency will maintain, share or use PII available through the site; d) warn users that third parties may have access to their PII; and e) provide links to the agency's official website and privacy policy. The privacy notice must be prominently displayed in all locations where a user might make PII available to the agency and must be clearly labeled and written in plain language. Any external links from the agency's website to the site or application must alert the user that he or she is being redirected to a nongovernment site or application with a different privacy policy. If the agency also embeds the third-party site or application in its own site, the embedded site or application must be disclosed and explained in the agency's privacy policy, as noted earlier. In determining whether to use third-party sites or applications, agencies are required to consult with their SAOPs, who have overall responsibility and accountability for ensuring the agency's implementation of privacy protections.[45]

2.9 Agency Responsibilities

OMB M-03-22 modifies OMB M-99-05, which ensures that information collected and used by agencies is handled in compliance with privacy laws by requiring each agency to appoint a senior official for privacy and to review agency practices to ensure compliance with the Privacy Act.[46] OMB M-03-22 adds the following responsibilities:

- Inform and educate employees and contractors about their responsibilities for protecting PII
- Identify individuals in the agency who have day-to-day responsibilities for implementing Section 208
- Designate the appropriate senior official to coordinate and act as a central contact for managing the website privacy policy implementation and maintenance
- Designate an official to serve as the reviewing official for PIAs

2.10 Reporting Requirements

OMB M-03-22 requires agencies to submit an annual compliance report to its office as part of their E-Government Act status report. The report must include the following information:

- **PIA status**
  - Listing of systems for which a PIA was conducted
  - Mechanism through which PIAs were made public
  - Whether each PIA was made public completely, partially or not at all
  - Whether each PIA was made available in conjunction with a SORN
  - The publication date
- **Persistent tracking technology status**
  - The need that compelled use of the technology
  - The safeguards implemented to protect the collected information
  - The agency official who approved the use
  - The privacy policy notification of the use
- **Machine-readable privacy policy status**
- **Contact information for officials responsible for information technology, web matters and website privacy policy**

2.11 Additional OMB Guidance

In 2006, the OMB issued two memoranda that related to privacy, OMB M-06-15 and OMB M-06-16.

OMB M-06-15 reminded agencies of their requirements under the Privacy Act to ensure that individuals with access to records covered by the Privacy Act have reviewed rules of conduct for using the records. It also requests that each agency conducts a review of policies, process and corrective action to ensure that the information maintained under the Privacy Act was properly secured. Shortly after this issuance, privacy reporting was incorporated into the FISMA reporting required to go to the OMB annually.

OMB M-06-16 laid out four specific requirements where PII was implicated. Generally, three of the requirements fall to the responsibility of the CIO: a) encrypt all data on mobile computers; b) allow remote access only with two-factor authentication; and c) use a timeout function for remote access and mobile devices. The fourth requirement for computer-readable extracts to be logged and destroyed after 90 days has largely remained the responsibility of the privacy officer. Different agencies handle this requirement through policy mechanisms to include distinguishing between ad hoc and routine Computer Readable Extracts and covering these through the system security plan.

3. Conclusion

The Privacy Act provides citizens and permanent resident aliens with notice, choice, access, redress and security of their personal data collected by the federal government. The E-Government Act provides transparency to all regarding the collection of personal data and safeguarding of that data based on sensitivity levels and the operations and collection of data via government websites.

Endnotes

1 The views expressed by the author do not necessarily represent those of the Federal Trade Commission or any Commissioner.

2 Department of Homeland Security, *DHS Privacy Policy Regarding Collection, Use, Retention, and Dissemination of Information on Non-U.S. Persons,* Privacy Policy Guidance Memorandum 2007-1, as amended, www.dhs.gov/xlibrary/assets/privacy/privacy_policyguide_2007-1.pdf.

3 5 U.S.C. § 522a(e)(5).

4 5 U.S.C. § 522a(e)(6).

5 5 U.S.C. § 522a(e)(10).

6 5 U.S.C. § 522a(e)(4).

7 Certain SORN elements in this list are prescribed in drafting guidelines issued by the Office of the Federal Register.

8   5 U.S.C. § 522a(e)(3).

9   See OMB 1975 implementing guidance, cited *infra*.

10 5 U.S.C. § 522a(e)(9).

11 5 U.S.C. § 522a(b)(6). Privacy Act records transferred to NARA before the act's effective date, as well as those permanently transferred to NARA for historical or other preservation reasons, are deemed to be maintained by NARA rather than the transferring agency. *Id.* NARA then becomes responsible for determining any access or disclosure to such records in accordance with the act.

12 Paul Schwartz and Joel Reidenberg, *Data Privacy Law*, 96 (Michie 1996).

13 5 U.S.C. § 552a(b)(1)–(12).

14 5 U.S.C. §§ 522a(j)(1)–(2); 5 U.S.C. § 522a(k).

15 5 U.S.C. § 522a(d).

16 5 U.S.C. § 522a(f).

17 Recent court cases have established that some actual damage must be demonstrated, e.g., *Doe v. Chao*, 540 U.S. 614 (2004), and *FAA v. Cooper*, 131 S. Ct. 3025 (2011) (excluding emotional harm).

18 5 U.S.C. § 522a(i)(1)–(3).

19 5 U.S.C. § 522a(o).

20 5 U.S.C. § 522a(p).

21 5 U.S.C. § 522a(u).

22 5 U.S.C. § 522a(v).

23 Department of Justice's Overview of the Privacy Act of 1974, 2010 Edition, www.justice.gov/opcl/1974privacyact-overview.htm.

24 40 Fed. Reg. 28948 (1975).

25 40 Fed. Reg. 56741-03 (1975); www.whitehouse.gov/sites/default/files/omb/assets/omb/inforeg/guidance1985.pdf.

26 48 Fed. Reg. 15556 (1983).

27 42 U.S.C. § 653; Pub. L. no. 104-193, § 316(f), www.whitehouse.gov/sites/default/files/omb/assets/omb/inforeg/katzen_prwora.pdf.

28 OMB's original Privacy Act implementing guidance, 40 Fed. Reg. 28948 (1975), and subsequent issuances are reproduced on the OMB website, www.whitehouse.gov.

29 U.S. House of Representatives, *A Citizen's Guide to the Freedom of Information Act and the Privacy Act of 1974 to Request Government Records*, 109th Cong. Rep. No. 109–226 (2005).

30 Public Law 107-347, 116 Stat. 2899 (2002).

31 *Id.*

32 The term *information in identifiable form* was introduced to cover cases in which PII might not be immediately recognized as such, such as when the Taxpayer Identification Number (TIN) of a business is actually an individual's Social Security number (SSN) as is typical for sole proprietorships. While this is the term referenced in the law, PII has become the de facto term.

33 OMB Memorandum 03-22, "OMB Guidance for Implementing Privacy Provisions of the E-Government Act of 2002," (Sept. 26, 2003) http://www.whitehouse.gov/omb/memoranda_m03-22.

34 OMB Memorandum M-07-19, "FY 2007 Reporting Instructions for the Federal Information Security Management Act and Agency Privacy Management," p. 19. (July 25 2007), www.whitehouse.gov/omb/memoranda/fy2007/m07-19.pdf.

35 OMB Memorandum M-03-22, "OMB Guidance for Implementing the Privacy Provisions of the E-Government Act of 2002," Sept. 26, 2003.

36 OMB Memorandum 00-13, "Privacy Policies and Data Collection on Federal Websites," (June 22, 2000) and OMB Memorandum 99-05, "Memorandum for Heads of Departments and Agencies," (Jan. 7, 1999).

37 National Security Systems is defined by 40 U.S.C.§ 11103.

38 OMB Memorandum 99-18, "Guidance and Model Language for Federal Website Privacy Policies," (June 1, 1999).

39 National Security Systems is defined by 40 U.S.C. §11103.

40 15 U.S.C. 6501 et seq.

41 W3C, "Platform for Privacy Preferences," available at: www.w3.org/TR/P3P/.

42 OMB Memorandum M-10-22, "Guidance for Online Use of Web Measurement and Customization Technologies," (June 25, 2010). The memorandum is primarily aimed at the tracking of public users, exempting internal agency activities (e.g., intranets or other nonpublic interactions), and tracking activities that are "part of authorized law enforcement, national security, or intelligence activities."; OMB Memorandum M-10-23, "Guidance for Agency Use of Third-Party Websites and Applications," (June 25, 2010).

43 The views expressed by the author do not necessarily represent those of the Federal Trade Commission or any individual Commissioner.

44 The views expressed by the author do not necessarily represent those of the Federal Trade Commission or any individual Commissioner.

45 See OMB Memorandum M-05-08, "Designation of Senior Agency Officials for Privacy," (Feb. 11, 2005).

46 OMB Memorandum 99-05, "Privacy and Personal Information in Federal Records," (May 14, 1998).

CHAPTER THREE

Other Laws and Regulations Focused on Government Agencies that Affect Their Privacy Practices

A key task for government privacy professionals is ensuring compliance with the letter and spirit of laws that apply specifically to government. The laws tend to be broad in scope, focusing on government generally (as opposed to a particular activity), and cover personally identifiable information (PII) in general (as opposed to particular subsets of PII). Therefore, they must be fundamentally embedded in government processes. While some of these laws revolve around access to information and others principally affect government operations, they all represent a floor—not a ceiling—for government privacy practices. While compliance with applicable laws is always essential, it's frequently insufficient to ensure a suitable level of privacy protection.

1. The Consolidated Appropriations Act of 2005

Revised by Deborah Kendall, CIPP/US, CIPP/G

Division H of the Consolidated Appropriations Act of 2005, also known as the Transportation, Treasury, Independent Agencies and General Government Appropriations Act, contains two significant provisions related to the federal privacy community:

1. A statutory mandate for chief privacy officers (CPOs)

2. The requirement that privacy audits be completed every two years

While there has been some debate about which agencies are subject to these provisions, the George W. Bush administration viewed the provisions as only applying to the agencies receiving appropriations under Division H at the time that the law was enacted.[1]

The original text for this chapter was developed by Erika L. McCallister, CIPP/US, CIPP/G, Stuart S. Shapiro, CIPP/US, CIPP/G and David Weitzel, CIPP/US, CIPP/G. New content for this revised edition was contributed by Deborah Kendall, CIPP/US, CIPP/G, Claire Barrett, CIPP/US, CIPP/G, CIPP/IT, Matthew J. Olsen, CIPP/US, CIPP/G, Alexander C. Tang, CIPP/US, CIPP/G, Patricia Mantoan, Jonathan R. Cantor, CIPP/US, CIPP/G, Michael Hawes, CIPP/G and Liz Lyons, CIPP/G whose contributions are noted throughout the sections of the chapter.

1.1 CPO

As required under Section 522(a) of the Consolidated Appropriations Act of 2005, a CPO must be created for each agency. The duties of the CPO include:

- Assuring the use of technologies to sustain privacy protections
- Assuring that technologies used to collect, use, store, and disclose information in identifiable form allow for continuous auditing of compliance with stated privacy policies and practices
- Assuring Fair Information Practices (FIPs) compliance for all Privacy Act systems of records
- Evaluating legislative and regulatory proposals involving federal "collection, use, and disclosure of personal information"
- Conducting privacy impact assessments of proposed rules on the privacy of information in identifiable form (IIF), including the type of PII and number of people affected
- Preparing an annual report to Congress on agency privacy activities including Privacy Act violations and internal controls

Section 522(a)(6) of the Consolidated Appropriations Act of 2005 requires the CPO to prepare a report to Congress on an annual basis about the activities of the department that affect privacy, including complaints of privacy violations, implementation of the Privacy Act, internal controls, and other relevant matters.

This act applies to a subset of agencies. However, other agencies, such as the Department of Homeland Security (DHS) have legislatively mandated CPOs, who are similarly tasked with generating annual privacy reports to Congress. The contents of these reports mirror the contents stated in the Consolidated Appropriations Act.

In addition, Section 522(c)294 of the act states that each covered agency shall prepare a written report of its use of information in an identifiable form, along with its privacy and data protection policies and procedures, and record it with the inspector general of the agency to serve as a benchmark for the agency.

Ideally, this report should be updated if the agency modifies either its use of IIF or its privacy and data protection policies and procedures.

On February 11, 2005, the Office of Management and Budget (OMB) issued Memorandum M-05-08 to all heads of executive departments and agencies, requesting that they identify and designate a senior agency official for privacy (SAOP) and provide the name, title and contact information to an OMB representative within 30 days. That official is responsible for overseeing, coordinating and facilitating the privacy compliance activities of the agency. In addition, the SAOP is responsible for policymaking in the agency's development, implementation and evaluation of privacy policy and regulation involving information privacy issues, including the collection, use, sharing and dissemination of personal information. The SAOP is also required to ensure that proper training is provided to agency employees and contractors regarding policies, procedures and regulations related to the handling of personal information.

Appropriations bills are occasionally used to enact controversial or problematic provisions that cannot be enacted in freestanding legislation. Due to Congress' concern about the Bush administration's tepid response to the protection of privacy in many cabinet-level agencies, provisions were passed requiring that agencies designate a chief privacy officer and prepare an annual report to Congress about the agency's privacy activities and Privacy Act violations. In addition, as many privacy advocates recommended, agencies are required to conduct privacy impact assessments (PIAs) on proposed rules impacting privacy, the types of PII collected and the number of people affected.

The designation of a CPO within agencies has improved accountability and openness within the federal government. The annual reports and other provisions provide increasing transparency on the collection and use of PII within the government.

2. The Federal Information Security Management Act

Revised by Deborah Kendall, CIPP/US, CIPP/G

The Federal Information Security Management Act of 2002 (FISMA) 44 U.S.C. 3541 *et seq.* was included as Title III of the E-Government Act of 2002. The law itself is rather straightforward. It:

- Authorizes the director of OMB to institute information security policies
- Empowers the National Institute of Standards and Technology (NIST) to establish the information security technical guidance, compliance testing and compliance reporting
- Empowers agency chief information officers (CIOs) and chief information security officers (CISOs) to implement the policies, technical guidance and testing/reporting regimes in their agencies

FISMA lays out a number of purposes for the act, including creating "a comprehensive framework for ensuring the effectiveness of information security controls" within the federal government; "government-wide management and oversight of … information security risks"; development of minimum security controls; oversight of agency information security; the use of "commercially developed information security products"; and agency decision making regarding the specific information security solutions chosen.[2] It also defines national security systems so that certain exceptions can be provided for them.

FISMA provides several definitions of key terms:[3]

- **Information security:** Protecting information and information systems from unauthorized access, use, disclosure, disruption, modification, or destruction in order to provide integrity, confidentiality, and availability

- **Integrity:** Guarding against improper information modification or destruction, and includes ensuring information nonrepudiation and authenticity
- **Confidentiality:** Preserving authorized restrictions on access and disclosure, including means for protecting personal privacy and proprietary information
- **Availability:** Ensuring timely and reliable access to and use of information

Comprehensive and interwoven privacy and security programs are essential for a department to fully mitigate risks related to the use, maintenance, and dissemination of sensitive data collected. Privacy and security programs are dependent on each other and have complementary goals. The comprehensive reporting requirements mandated by FISMA require a close relationship between the organization's CIO and CPO. Obviously, you can implement security measures without regard to privacy, but you cannot implement privacy protections without understanding the sensitivity of the data and the varying ways to mitigate the risks of unauthorized exposure. Identifying and inventorying all the PII collected by an organization assists the CIO and CISO in devising a comprehensive security plan to protect the data based on the degree of sensitivity, how widely accessible it is within the organization, and the possibility of exposure. FISMA requires these activities in addition to identifying agency websites, continuing privacy training, and ensuring that the CPO has a major role in all policies, directives and regulations involving the use and dissemination of PII within the agency.

Current FISMA reporting as outlined by the OMB includes:

- The number of federal systems that contain PII
- Website locations for the agency's PIAs and system of records notices (SORNs)
- Documentation outlining that the CPO participates in all agency information privacy compliance activities
- Agency privacy training activities
- PIA and web privacy policies processes
- Conduct of mandated reviews required by the Privacy Act of 1974, the E-Government Act and the Federal Data Mining Reporting Act of 2007
- The number of written privacy complaints received for each privacy issue by the agency
- Documentation-demonstrated review of the agency's compliance with information privacy laws, regulations and policies
- Agency use of web management and customization technologies
- Documentation that the CPO has provided formal written advice on privacy training; written agreements pertaining to information sharing, agency policies, orders, and directives governing the agency's handling of PII; and agency practices for conducting, preparing and releasing SORNs and PIAs.

2.1 The Role of the OMB

The OMB's core mission is to assist the president in implementing his vision across the executive branch.[4] Management is one of its critical processes, and includes the oversight of agency performance, federal procurement, financial management and information (including information technology (IT), paperwork reduction, privacy and security).[5]

FISMA gives broad policy-making powers to the director of the OMB.[6] These include:

- Developing and overseeing the implementation of information security policies, principles, standards and guidelines
- Requiring agencies to provide information security appropriate to the "risks and magnitude of harm" resulting from unauthorized access, use, disclosure, disruption, modification or destruction of agency or agency contractor information
- Coordinating the development of standards and guidelines by the NIST and agencies responsible for national security systems[7]
- Overseeing agency compliance and enforcing accountability
- Reviewing and approving agency information security programs on an annual basis
- Coordinating information security activities with general information resource management activities[8]
- Overseeing the federal information security response center
- Providing a yearly report to Congress that includes specific content

2.2 Agency Responsibilities

FISMA assigns extensive responsibilities to federal agencies.[9] Responsibility for FISMA compliance ultimately lies with the agency head, but day-to-day oversight can be delegated to the CIO and through the CIO to a senior agency information security officer. The agency officials must "provide information security protections commensurate with the risk and magnitude of the harm" from unauthorized acts. Compliance with OMB regulations and NIST guidelines is required. Information security activities must be integrated with agency planning processes and with annual agency budget submissions for information technology funding. Specific agency responsibilities include:

- Assessing the risk of unauthorized access
- Determining levels of information security
- Implementing policies to cost-effectively reduce risks to an acceptable level
- Conduct periodic testing and evaluation of information security
- Ensuring the agency has sufficient information security personnel
- Reporting annually on the effectiveness of the agency's information security program

2.3 CIO's Duties

Under the powers delegated by the agency head, the CIO is required to:

- Develop an agency-wide information security program
- Develop information security policies, procedures and control techniques
- Train and oversee a sufficient number of agency information security personnel
- Assist senior agency officials in carrying out their duties under FISMA

The CIO may further designate a qualified CISO to carry out the CIO's information security responsibilities and head an office with the mission and resources to assure agency compliance with FISMA.

2.4 Elements of the Information Security Program

FISMA requires specific elements in an OMB-approved agency information security program. These include:

- Conducting periodic assessments of information security risks
- Establishing risk-based, cost-effective policies and procedures that:
  - Reduce information security risks to acceptable levels
  - Ensure that information security is addressed throughout the information life cycle
  - Comply with FISMA-related OMB policy directives and NIST technical guidance
- Conducting security awareness training to inform trainees of risks and their responsibilities for compliance
- Conduct periodic testing of information security policies, procedures and practices, including attention to managerial, operational and technical controls
- Implementing a process for creating remedial action plans for deficient systems
- Establishing security incident procedures that include mitigation, notice to the federal information security center and, where appropriate, consultation with law enforcement authorities and the agency inspector general (IG)
- Developing continuity of operations plans and procedures

2.5 Annual Independent Evaluation

FISMA calls for an annual independent evaluation of the agency information security program.[10] The evaluation must test the effectiveness of the information security program for a representative subset of the agency's information systems. The assessment should review compliance with FISMA and related information security policies, procedures, standards and guidelines. A provision allows national security systems to be reported on separately.

The agency head or IG will select the independent auditor who evaluates the *yearly* agency's information system. If the agency does not have an IG or if the system is designated as a national security system, the evaluation may leverage other relevant audits, evaluations or reports by the agency. The audit also takes appropriate measures to limit the risk of inadvertent disclosure of data. Upon completion, the audit is provided to the OMB. Each year, the OMB summarizes the agency evaluations and reports to Congress. Separately, the comptroller general evaluates information security and reports to Congress on FISMA compliance.

2.6 Federal Information Security Incident Center

FISMA codifies the existence of a federal information security incident center.[11] The United States Computer Emergency Readiness Team (US-CERT):

- Provides timely technical assistance regarding security incidents.
- Compiles and analyzes security incident information.
- Informs agency information system operators about current and potential threats.
- Consults with the NIST and others regarding information security incidents. A special exception is made for agencies that operate national security systems.

2.7 CIO Council Federal Enterprise Architecture Security and Privacy Profile (FEA-SPP)

Claire Barrett, CIPP/US, CIPP/G, CIPP/IT

FISMA is the primary legislation driving federal agencies' information security activities. Designed around accountability, FISMA sets forth specific security activities and associated reporting requirements. Further implementation of FISMA occurs through OMB Circular A-130 (OMB A-130), numerous related regulations, and NIST standards and guidance. FISMA mandates a risk-management approach to securing federal information and information systems where individuals are given explicit responsibility to implement protection measures (controls) "commensurate with the risk and magnitude of the harm resulting from the unauthorized access, use, disclosure, disruption, modification, or destruction"[12] of agency information and information systems; and to integrate risk-management practices' strategic and operational planning processes.

The FEA-SPP[13] in its articulation of "Privacy Control Families"[14] serves two critical functions in the integration of privacy and security risk-management practices. First, it clearly articulates that while there is a symbiotic relationship between security and privacy, these practices are not identical; they are distinct practices, but intertwined.

Second, the FEA-SPP lays the groundwork for driving agency integration of privacy risk management into the fundamental design of technical systems and technologies. This helps agencies build consideration of privacy controls into the initial stages of their system development life cycle rather than treating as an afterthought. The Fair Information Practice Principles (FIPPs), as articulated in the FEA-SPP, also draw directly from the DHS FIPPs and are common across most privacy laws; they also provide a framework for organizing and addressing privacy requirements and capabilities.

Table 3.1: FEA-SPP Privacy Control Families

Privacy Control Family	Description
Transparency	Providing notice to the individual regarding the collection, use, dissemination, and maintenance of PII.
Individual Participation and Redress	Involving the individual in the process of using PII and seeking individual consent for the collection, use, dissemination, and maintenance of PII. Providing mechanisms for appropriate access, correction, and redress regarding the use of PII.
Purpose Specification	Specifically articulating the authority that permits the collection of PII and specifically articulating the purpose or purposes for which the PII is intended to be used.
Data Minimization & Retention	Only collecting PII that is directly relevant and necessary to accomplish the specified purpose(s). Only retaining PII for as long as is necessary to fulfill the specified purpose(s) and in accordance with the National Archives and Records Administration (NARA) approved record retention schedule.
Use Limitation	Using PII solely for the purpose(s) specified in the public notice. Sharing information should be for a purpose compatible with the purpose(s) for which the information was collected.
Data Quality and Integrity	Ensuring, to the greatest extent possible, that PII is accurate, relevant, timely, and complete for the purpose(s) for which it is to be used, as identified in the public notice.
Security	Protecting PII (in all media) through appropriate administrative, technical, and physical security safeguards against risks such as loss, unauthorized access or use, destruction, modification, or unintended or inappropriate disclosure.
Accountability and Auditing	Providing accountability for compliance with all applicable privacy protection requirements, including all identified authorities and established policies and procedures that govern the collection, use, dissemination, and maintenance of PII. Auditing for the actual use of PII to demonstrate compliance with established privacy controls.

2.8 NIST Special Publication 800-53, Revision 4, Security and Privacy Controls for Federal Information Systems and Organizations (SP 800-53)

Claire Barrett, CIPP/US, CIPP/G, CIPP/IT

In a complementary effort to the publication of the FEA-SPP, the NIST made a significant step in addressing the relationship between privacy and security risk management by publishing the draft revision to its SP 800-53[15] document with a substantive change in title: "Security and Privacy Controls." In addition, the NIST incorporated a new family of controls, again based on the FIPPs. The document recognizes that while effective privacy relies on a solid information security foundation, the scope of privacy goes beyond security and involves such issues as transparency, notice and choice, as well as issues of confidentiality, integrity and availability. The privacy controls, generally referred to as Appendix J, identify administrative, technical and physical mechanisms for addressing privacy risk at all levels of an organization.

While NIST Special Publication 800-53 is primarily about protecting information, organizations are meant to use the privacy controls appendix to address privacy risk emanating from activities that do not necessarily involve the collection and use of PII. The NIST discussion of the FIPPs differs from other similar documents in that it identifies specific actions to achieve the intent of each of the principles.

Table 3.2: Privacy Controls included in Appendix J of NIST 800-53

Cntl No.	Privacy Controls
TR	**Transparency**
TR-1	Privacy Notice
TR-2	System of Records Notices and Privacy Act Statements
TR-3	Dissemination of Privacy Program Information
IP	**Individual Participation and Redress**
IP-1	Consent
IP-2	Individual Access
IP-3	Redress
IP-4	Complaint Management
AP	**Authority and Purpose**
AP-1	Authority to Collect
AP-2	Purpose Specification
DM	**Data Minimization and Retention**
DM-1	Minimization of Personally Identifiable Information

DM-2	Data Retention and Disposal
DM-3	Minimization of PII Used in Testing, Training, and Research
UL	**Use Limitation**
UL-1	Internal Use
UL-2	Information Sharing with Third Parties
DI	**Data Quality and Integrity**
DI-1	Data Quality
DI-2	Data Integrity and Data Integrity Board
SE	**Security**
SE-1	Inventory of Personally Identifiable Information
SE-2	Privacy Incident Response
AR	**Accountability, Audit, and Risk Management**
AR-1	Governance and Privacy Program
AR-2	Privacy Impact and Risk Assessment
AR-3	Privacy Requirements for Contractors and Service Providers
AR-4	Privacy Monitoring and Auditing
AR-5	Privacy Awareness and Training
AR-6	Privacy Reporting
AR-7	Privacy-Enhanced System Design and Development
AR-8	Accounting of Disclosures

Source: NIST SP 800-53, Appendix J, http://csrc.nist.gov/publications/drafts/800-53-rev4/sp800-53-rev4-ipd.pdf

2.9 Other FISMA Provisions

The remaining portions of FISMA provide exceptions for national security systems, authorize appropriations and provide conforming amendments to other statutes. A vital provision of the law assigns significant responsibilities to NIST for promulgating standards and guidelines to implement information security programs. The breadth of this activity goes beyond the scope of an analysis of the FISMA statute; for further information, readers should consult the appropriate NIST website (http://csrc.nist.gov)

as well as related FIPS publications and 800-series documents, which support FISMA. Selected FIPS and NIST documents are also discussed in Chapter 6.

Table 3.3: Selected FIPS and NIST Publications and Special Publications for Information Security

Number	Title	Date Issued
FIPS 199	Standards for Security Categorization of Federal Information and Information Systems	February 2004
FIPS 200	Minimum Security Requirements for Federal Information and Information Systems	March 2006
SP 800-12	An Introduction to Computer Security: The NIST Handbook	October 1995
SP 800-14	Generally Accepted Principles and Practices for Securing Information Technology Systems	September 1996
SP 800-37 Rev. 1	Guide for Applying the Risk Management Framework to Federal Information Systems: A Security Life Cycle Approach	February 2010
SP 800-50	Building an Information Technology Security Awareness and Training Program	October 2003
SP 800-53 A Rev. 1	Guide for Assessing the Security Controls in Federal Information Systems and Organizations, Building Effective Security Assessment Plans	June 2010
SP 800-53 Rev. 4	Security and Privacy Controls for Federal Information Systems and Organizations	February 2012 (DRAFT)
SP 800-59	Guideline for Identifying an Information System as a National Security System	August 2003
SP 800-60 Rev. 1	Guide for Mapping Types of Information and Information Systems to Security Categories	August 2008
SP 800-61 Rev. 2	Computer Security Incident Handling Guide	August 2012
SP 800-64 Rev. 2	Security Considerations in the System Development Life Cycle	October 2008
SP 800-100	Information Security Handbook: A Guide for Managers	October 2006
SP 800-122	Guide to Protecting the Confidentiality of Personally Identifiable Information (PII)	April 2010

Sources: http://csrc.nist.gov/publications/PubsFIPS.html and http://csrc.nist.gov/publications/PubsSPs.html

3. The Freedom of Information Act (FOIA)

Revised by Deborah Kendall, CIPP/US, CIPP/G

In 1966, President Lyndon Johnson signed the Freedom of Information Act (FOIA) into law.[16] FOIA amends the Administrative Procedure Act by providing individuals the right to access federal government records and creating a process to allow them to exercise that right.[17] FOIA also provides administrative and judicial remedies for those denied access to records.

Prior to FOIA, the burden to obtain access to government records was placed on individuals who had to justify their need for government information and show they were "properly and directly concerned."[18] Individuals had no recourse when access to records was denied.[19] The U.S. Supreme Court explained the importance of FOIA when it held that FOIA promotes democracy by "ensuring an informed citizenry," which is "needed to check against corruption and to hold governors accountable."[20] FOIA has been amended several times, including in 1974 to strengthen its compliance provisions; in 1996 to provide for the electronic disclosure of records; and in 2007 with the enactment of the Open Government Act. These amendments address the administration of FOIA processing; attorney general and special counsel reporting requirements; creation of a new office (Office of Government Information Services) within NARA; and codification of the key roles played by the chief FOIA officers and FOIA public liaisons.

Using FOIA in conjunction with requests for information under the Privacy Act usually results in obtaining more information than just using FOIA alone. All agency records are subject to FOIA, while the Privacy Act applies only to records contained in a system of records maintained by the agency. However, individuals who are not covered by the Privacy Act (e.g., foreign nationals) must use FOIA to obtain government records.

Both FOIA and the Privacy Act provide independent rights of access to a first-party requester (i.e., the subject of the records). Third-party requests for Privacy Act records or under FOIA are treated differently. If the agency has a written consent of the subject of the records, the agency may process the request in the same manner as if it was from a first-party requester. However, without consent of the records subject, the release is not authorized. The agency must then determine if the records are releasable under FOIA. If a FOIA exemption applies—typically Exemption 6 or 7(c)—then the records cannot be released.

While FOIA requires disclosure of agency records, the Privacy Act does not permit withholding a record unless it is spelled out under a mandatory exemption adopted by an agency, such as testing or exam records. FOIA does permit withholding of records, if the record meets one of the nine discretionary exemptions.

FOIA is a federal statute that applies to executive branch agencies of the federal government, which include the cabinet departments, military departments, independent agencies and government corporations. FOIA does not cover the records of Congress, the federal courts, the executive office of the President, or other elected offices (such as the office of the vice president). FOIA does not apply state and local government records.[21] However, many states have laws similar to FOIA that do provide access to state and local government records.

3.1 Publicly Available Information

FOIA places an affirmative obligation on agencies to make certain information publicly available without a specific request. Each agency must publish in the *Federal Register* the following information:

- Descriptions of agency organization and office addresses
- Statements of the general course and method of agency operation
- Rules of procedure, descriptions of forms available and the places where forms may be obtained
- Substantive rules of general applicability adopted as authorized by law, statements of general policy and interpretations of general applicability
- Each amendment, revision or repeal of the foregoing

In addition, each agency must make information available relating to its opinions and policy interpretations. For records created on or after November 1, 1996, federal agencies are required to make these records available through hard copy and electronic copy, which has resulted in the creation of "electronic reading rooms" for each agency. The following information must be made available for public inspection and copying:

- Final opinions, including concurring and dissenting opinions, as well as orders, made in the adjudication of cases
- Statements of policy and interpretations that have been adopted by the agency and are not published in the *Federal Register*
- Administrative staff manuals and instructions that affect a member of the public
- Copies of all records that have been released to any person by specific request and are likely to be requested by others
- A general index of released records that are likely to be requested again

Each agency must also publish regulations describing the procedures and schedule of fees applicable to requests for records made pursuant to FOIA. The schedule of fees must conform to the guidelines set by the OMB. Each agency must publish regulations providing for expedited processing of requests and for multi-track processing of requests based on the anticipated time and/or effort required to respond.

Federal agencies must make their records promptly available upon receipt of a reasonable written request. FOIA requests can be made by anyone except other federal agencies, which includes individuals, partnerships, corporations, associations, state governments and even a foreign government. However, general eligibility to receive requested records was modified by the Intelligence Authorization Act for Fiscal Year 2003.[22] Agencies or parts of agencies that are part of the intelligence community, such as the National Security Agency or the Central Intelligence Agency, cannot disclose FOIA records to foreign governments or representatives of foreign governments.[23]

The term *record* was not explicitly defined in the original FOIA statute, and it was used interchangeably with the term *information*. In 1989, the Supreme Court established a two-part test to determine what information constitutes an "agency record" under FOIA.[24] First, the record must have been created or obtained by the agency. Second, the record must have been under the agency's control at the time of the request. Agency control is still a heavily litigated issue.[25] In 1996, the Electronic Freedom of Information Act amended FOIA and broadly defined "record" to include "any information that would be an agency record ... when maintained by an agency in any format, including in electronic format."[26]

Thus, FOIA requests can be made for printed documents, tape recordings, maps, photographs, computer disks and other similar items.[27] In 2007, the definition of "record" was expanded to include "information ... that is maintained for an agency under government contract, for the purposes of records management."[28]

3.2 FOIA Request Fees

The fees imposed on requesters must be reasonable, to cover the direct costs of duplicating, searching and reviewing requested information.[29] Fees are based on the characteristics of the requester.[30] There are three categories of requesters:

1. Commercial requesters who have a for-profit interest in the information can be charged for reasonable duplicating, searching and reviewing costs

2. Representatives of the news media, educational institutions and noncommercial scientific institutions can only be billed for reasonable duplication costs[31]

3. All others who do not fall into the other categories, such as individuals seeking information for personal use or public interest organizations, can be charged only for reasonable duplication and searching costs[32]

Anyone may request a fee waiver in the initial FOIA request. Fee waivers are granted "if the disclosure of the information is in the public interest because it is likely to contribute significantly to the public understanding of the operations or activities of the government and is not primarily in the commercial interest of the requester."[33]

3.3 FOIA Exemptions

FOIA provides nine discretionary exemptions to mandatory disclosure. An agency may disclose information even if it is covered by one or more of the exemptions.[34] However, an agency must release any nonexempt portions of records that are "reasonably segregable." Segregation can be accomplished through removal or redaction of the exempted portions of requested records.[35] If the nonexempt portions are "inextricably intertwined" with the exempt material, then the entire record is exempt.[36] Agencies must identify the location and amount of deleted information or withheld pages and provide the reason exemptions apply to the information.

The following nine exemptions are applicable to FOIA requests:

1. Records that relate to *national defense or foreign policy* and are properly classified. If classified documents are requested, the agency must review the classified status and determine if it still applies. The Department of Defense maintains many classified records, such as information on the building and operation of certain weapons defense systems.

2. Records related solely to the *internal personnel rules* and practices of an agency. This exemption applies to internal personnel procedures that are administrative with no public interest and to internal administrative manuals that could be used to circumvent law.

3. Records specifically exempted from disclosure by *statute*. The statute must require that the matters be withheld from the public in such a manner as to leave no discretion to the agency on the issue. An example is individual tax return information that is specifically protected from disclosure by statute.[37]

4. Records containing *trade secrets and commercial or financial information* obtained from a person and considered privileged or confidential. The records must have been created by a person outside of the government, which includes individuals, partnerships or corporations.

5. Records consisting of *interagency or intra-agency memorandums* or *letters* that otherwise would not be available by law to a party other than an agency in litigation with the agency. This exemption is used to prevent the release of draft decision policies, which encourages open debate. It also protects attorney work product and confidential communications between attorneys and clients.[38]

6. Records containing personnel files, medical files and other similar files that would constitute a clearly unwarranted invasion of *personal privacy*. It pertains only to individuals and not corporations or other nonperson entities. This

exemption requires agencies to balance an individual's privacy interest against the public's right to know. Federal civilian employees who are not involved in law enforcement generally have no expectation of privacy with regard to their names, titles, salaries, grades and duty stations. But federal employees do have a protectable privacy interest in purely personal details that do not shed light on agency functions such as their home addresses and telephone numbers.

7. Records or information compiled for *law enforcement* purposes. This exemption is limited to the following circumstances:

   a. The request could reasonably be expected to interfere with enforcement proceedings

   b. The request would deprive a person of a right to a fair trial or an impartial adjudication

   c. The request could reasonably be expected to constitute an unwarranted invasion of personal privacy; for example, this exemption has been regularly applied to withhold references to persons who are not targets of investigations but were merely mentioned in law enforcement records

   d. The request could reasonably be expected to disclose the identity of a confidential source

   e. The request would disclose techniques and procedures for law enforcement investigations or prosecutions

   f. The request could reasonably be expected to endanger the life or physical safety of any individual

8. Records contained in or related to examination, operating or condition reports prepared by, on behalf of or for the use of an agency responsible for the regulation or supervision of *financial institution*.

9. Records containing *geological and geophysical information* and data, including maps, concerning wells.

3.4 FOIA Exclusions

In some circumstances, an agency may treat an exempt record as an exclusion, where the agency is not required to confirm the existence of the record. There are three categories of records that may be treated as exclusions:

1. Law enforcement records pursuant to exemption 7(a) if:

   a. the investigation involves a violation of criminal law;

   b. there is reason to believe the subject of the investigation is unaware of the investigation; and

    c. disclosure could reasonably be expected to interfere with enforcement proceedings.

2. Informant records maintained by a criminal law enforcement agency

3. FBI records pertaining to intelligence, counterintelligence or terrorism

3.5 General Rule

FOIA requests must be made in writing, and must specifically describe the records sought as well as provide the name and address of the requester. Upon receipt of a request, each agency must respond to the requester within 20 business days, but may stop the clock on the 20-day period if it needs to obtain more information from the requester to fulfill the request or clarify fee issues.[39] This period ends when the requested information is received from the requester. For stoppage purposes, agencies are limited to one request for additional information.[40]

An agency's response should state that the request will be fulfilled, denied or requires additional time due to unusual circumstances. Unusual circumstances are narrowly defined and apply in specific situations, such as when the requested records are in a separate office; the request results in voluminous records; or another agency must be consulted because it has a substantial interest in the records. An agency must make reasonable efforts to search for the requested records in both manual and automated manners. A request may be denied when an exemption applies, a fee waiver has been denied or the requested records are not in the possession of the agency. In these cases, an agency must send an adverse letter that includes the reason for the denial, an explanation of the right to appeal and the time period permitted for making an appeal.

For all requests that will take more than 10 days to process, agencies must assign and provide the tracking numbers to the requesters and establish a telephone or Internet service that will provide requesters with the status of their requests, including the estimated completion date.[41]

Multiple requests that involve clearly-related material can be aggregated and considered as a single request, as long as the requesters are acting in concert. If multiple requesters are not acting in concert, then their permission must be obtained to aggregate their requests.

3.6 Expedited Processing

A requester may seek expedited processing for requests that demonstrate a compelling need or for other reasons as defined by the agency. A compelling need is defined statutorily as cases in which failure to obtain the requested records on an expedited basis could be reasonably expected to pose an imminent threat to the life or physical safety of an individual, or an individual usually engaged in disseminating information has an urgent need to inform the public concerning actual or alleged federal government activity.

Each agency must provide a response to requests for expedited process within 10 business days. Requesters do not have a right to judicial review of denials of requests for expedited processing.

3.7 Administrative Appeals

A requester has the right to an administrative appeal under many circumstances, such as the receipt of an adverse determination letter, an inadequate response, a fee waiver denial, a denial for expedited processing, collection of excessive fees, partial denial of requested records or any other type of denial. An inadequate response occurs when an agency sends an acknowledgment of receipt without any further information. Administrative appeals are important to agencies and requesters because they allow an agency to review its initial response to determine whether corrective steps are needed. Also, the Court of Appeals for the District of Columbia has held that exhaustion of the administrative appeal process is "generally required before filing suit in federal court."[42]

The requester must send a written appeal to the head of the agency or the appeals officer, and the agency must make a decision on the appeal within 20 business days. If an appeal is denied, the agency must notify the requester of his or her right to file a lawsuit in federal district court. If the agency completely fails to respond to the original request or the appeal within 20 days, the requester may immediately proceed to district court. At this point, the requester is considered to have exhausted all administrative remedies.

3.8 Litigation under FOIA

Having exhausted all administrative remedies, a requester may file a lawsuit in the federal district court where the requester resides or has his or her principal place of business; where the agency records are located; or in the District of Columbia. The court determines the matter *de novo*, meaning that the court starts over and disregards the findings from the administrative review.

The U.S. Department of Justice is responsible for responding to civil actions that involve alleged FOIA violations. The burden is placed on the government to justify withholding the information. The court may assess reasonable attorney fees and litigation costs against the government when the requester substantially prevails.[43] Moreover, if the court finds that agency personnel acted arbitrarily or capriciously in withholding the records, then special counsel may be assigned to investigate and make recommendations for corrective actions against the employees. The U.S. Attorney General is required to keep special counsel informed of any civil actions taken against agency personnel.

3.9 Reporting Requirements

FOIA also contains reporting requirements for federal agencies. All agencies subject to FOIA must submit an annual report on or before February 1 to the attorney general that provides the following:

- The number of denials of requests and the reasons for the denials

- The number of appeals made, the result of the appeals, the reason for the action on each appeal, a list of statutes used to deny requests and the number of times each statute was relied upon

- The number of pending requests before the agency as of September 30 of the preceding year, as well as the median and mean number of days the requests have been pending

- The number of requests received and processed by the agency

- The median and mean number of days taken by the agency to process different types of requests based on the dates the requests were received by the agency

- The number of requests that have been responded to within 20 days and the number in 20-day increments up to 200 days; the number of requests responded to within 201–300 days; the number of requests responded to within 301–400 days; and the number of requests responded to in over 400 days

- The average, median and total range of the number of days to provide granted information to requesters

- The average, median and total range of the number of days for an agency to respond to an administrative appeal

- Data on the 10 active requests with the earliest filing date

- The number of expedited review requests that are granted and denied, as well as the average and median number of days for adjudicating such requests

- The number of fee waivers that are granted and denied, as well as the average and median number of days for adjudicating requests

- The total amount of fees collected by the agency in processing requests

- The number of full-time staff devoted to processing requests and the total amount of time expended

The annual report and the raw data (upon request) must be made available to the public. The U.S. Attorney General must make an aggregate annual report available electronically and must provide the report to the U.S. House of Representatives by April 1 of each calendar year.

In addition, special counsel must report to Congress annually on civil actions taken against agency employees who have withheld records arbitrarily or capriciously.

3.10 The Chief FOIA Officer

Executive Order 13392[44] supplemented FOIA by reiterating the requirement for agencies to process requests in a courteous and expeditious manner. This order required each agency to establish a FOIA requester service that acts as the agency's central point of contact for FOIA requests. In addition, it required agencies to appoint a chief FOIA officer. The Open Government Act of 2007 codified this requirement and expanded on the responsibilities of the chief FOIA officer to include the following:

- Have agency-wide responsibility for efficient and appropriate compliance with FOIA
- Monitor FOIA implementation throughout the agency
- Recommend to the head of the agency any necessary adjustments in practices, personnel, policies or funding
- Review and report to the head of the agency and the U.S. Attorney General on the agency's FOIA performance
- Assign and provide to requesters an individualized tracking number for any request that takes longer than 10 days to process and provide a public access link via telephone or the Internet where requesters can obtain information on the status of their requests
- Facilitate public understanding of FOIA's statutory exemptions
- Designate one or more FOIA public liaisons who are "responsible for assisting in reducing delays, increasing transparency and understanding of the status of requests, and assisting in the resolution of disputes"[45]

3.11 The Office of Government Information Services

The Open Government Act of 2007 also created the Office of Government Information Services (OGIS) within the NARA. The mission of OGIS is to safeguard and preserve government records as well as advise federal agencies on records management practices.[46] The primary responsibilities of the OGIS are to review the FOIA policies and procedures of agencies, review FOIA compliance by agencies and recommend FOIA changes to Congress and the president.

The OGIS also offers mediation services to resolve disputes between agencies and requesters as an alternative to litigation. The mediation is nonbinding, and requesters may still litigate matters in district court.

4. Paperwork Reduction Act (PRA) of 1995

Revised by Matthew J. Olsen, CIPP/US, CIPP/G

The PRA[47] concerns information that is created, collected, disclosed, maintained, used, shared and disseminated by or for the federal government, regardless of whether it is PII. The primary goal is to calculate and reduce as much as possible the burden of providing information to the government while maintaining the quality of that information.

The requirements of the PRA cover "collections of information," which may exist in any format, and could include surveys, applications, questionnaires, reports or any scenario in which 10 or more persons are asked to provide the same information within a 12-month period.

Specific agency requirements under the PRA include:

- Calculation of the time required both by the agency and the respondent involved in collection of the information, reported as the number of hours multiplied by the anticipated number of respondents

- Providing a 60-day notice to the public of any covered collection of information by publishing this notice in the *Federal Register* and responding to any comments received

- Gaining approval of the OMB, lasting a maximum of three years, after which the agency must resubmit the collection for approval

4.1 Where Does Privacy Intersect with the PRA?

In meeting the goals of reducing the burden of information collection and ensuring the quality of information maintained by the federal government, the PRA, by default, helps ensure the minimization and proper use of PII that is collected and maintained.

Another intersection involves Section (e)(3) of the Privacy Act, which requires the agency to inform each individual whom it asks to supply information of four key issues. These must be included either on the form the agency uses to collect the information or on a separate form that can be retained by the individual. The issues are:

(A) the authority (whether granted by statute, or by executive order of the President) which authorizes the solicitation of the information and whether disclosure of such information is mandatory or voluntary;

(B) the principal purpose or purposes for which the information is intended to be used;

(C) the routine uses which may be made of the information as published pursuant to [Section] (4)(D) of [the Privacy Act]; and

(D) the effects on him, if any, of not providing all or any part of the requested information.

This notice, commonly referred to as a Privacy Act statement, would naturally appear on any form where the collection involved information maintained in a Privacy Act system of records.

Collections are transmitted to the OMB through the Regulatory Information Service Center and Office of Information and Regulatory Affairs Combined Information System (ROCIS). Besides the form or collection instrument itself, a ROCIS submission also includes privacy-related information, such as whether the submission also constitutes a PIA in accordance with OMB guidelines on instituting the provisions of Section 208 of the E-Government Act, and specifically asks whether the collection involved a Privacy Act system of records.[48]

Agency staff responsible for the transmission of collections to the OMB may not be the same staff responsible for privacy compliance. It is essential for all staff members to work in concert to ensure complete, accurate submission of collections to the OMB and to ensure the proper protection of PII through the development of Privacy Act statements, PIAs, and systems of records relating to those collections.

4.2 Interaction of the PRA and Emerging Technology

Federal agencies are increasingly using emerging technology to facilitate interactions with the public and promote transparency. This use of mobile or web-based interactive technologies, such as blogs, wikis and social networks, raises considerable questions in terms of compliance with the PRA.

To address these issues, the OMB on April 7, 2010, issued a memorandum, "Social Media, Web-Based Interactive Technologies and the Paperwork Reduction Act."[49] The memorandum clarifies that certain collections are not subject to the PRA, including online contests, public meetings facilitated by social media and general feedback requests, as long as the collection does not utilize a structured request and response format. For example, an agency contest asking contributors to create a video showing support for a program would not by itself trigger the PRA; however, if the agency were to request demographic information or answers to a set series of questions in association with the video submission, the PRA would be triggered.

> **Additional Resources on the PRA that Reference Privacy**
>
> *OMB Final Rule, FR Vol. 60, No. 167, August 29, 1995, "Controlling Paperwork Burdens on the Public; Regulatory Changes Reflecting Recodification of the Paperwork Reduction Act." www.whitehouse.gov/sites/default/files/omb/assets/OMB/inforeg/5_cfr_1320.pdf*
>
> *OMB "Guidance on Agency Survey and Statistical Information Collections," January 2006. www.whitehouse.gov/sites/default/files/omb/assets/omb/inforeg/pmc_survey_guidance_2006.pdf*
>
> *OMB "Standards and Guidelines for Statistical Surveys," September 2006. www.whitehouse. gov/sites/default/files/omb/assets/omb/inforeg/statpolicy/standards_stat_surveys.pdf*

5. The Data Quality Act

Revised by Alexander C. Tang, CIPP/US, CIPP/G[50]

In light of the increased use of the Internet by federal agencies as an easy, inexpensive and expedient way to disseminate information to the public, Congress passed the Data Quality Act of 2000 (DQA).[51] This act (also known as the Information Quality Act or Section 515, for the unnamed provision of the appropriations bill in which it was enacted) was designed to ensure the quality of information released by federal agencies. It appeared without hearings or legislative debate as a two-paragraph section somewhat obscured within a much larger appropriations bill.[52]

The DQA's impact on individual privacy is limited and indirect, as its principal focus is on the quality, and not the confidentiality, of information intended for publication. That said, DQA data quality procedures overlap with the data quality and integrity requirements of the Privacy Act, when an agency collects, generates or uses individual-level data in an agency system of records to prepare or support published studies or research covered by the DQA. The DQA does not govern whether such underlying data may or must be disclosed publicly in conjunction with the public study or research, which is instead determined under the Privacy Act or other confidentiality or public access laws (such as FOIA or other laws discussed further below) that may apply to the specific data in question.

The DQA modified the PRA[53] and directed federal agencies to issue information quality guidelines no later than one year after the OMB issued implementing guidance. The act applies to all executive branch agencies that are subject to the PRA, including executive departments, military departments, government corporations, independent regulatory agencies and other executive offices, such as the Executive Office of the President. The statute specifically excludes the Government Accountability Office, the Federal Election Commission, the governments of the District of Columbia and U.S. territories and "government-owned, contractor-operated" facilities.[54] It does not apply to state and local governments.

The DQA outlines four major requirements:

1. It directs the OMB to issue policy and procedural guidelines to federal agencies for "ensuring and maximizing the quality, objectivity, utility, and integrity" of disseminated information[55]
2. It requires agencies to issue their own sets of information quality guidelines
3. It mandates that each agency establish administrative mechanisms providing affected persons with the ability to have erroneous agency information corrected
4. It requires agencies to report annually to the OMB about the number and nature of complaints, and how the complaints were handled

The OMB published its final guidelines, "Guidelines for Ensuring and Maximizing the Quality, Objectivity, Utility, and Integrity of Information Disseminated by Federal Agencies" (hereinafter "OMB Guidelines") on September 28, 2001,[56] and republished them on February 22, 2002,[57] with definitions for the terms "quality," "utility," "integrity" and "objectivity":

"Quality" is defined to encompass the concepts of utility, objectivity and integrity. "Utility" refers to the usefulness of the information to its intended users. "Integrity" refers to the resistance of information to unauthorized access and revision, which could result in falsification. "Objectivity" refers to whether the information is accurate, clear, complete and unbiased.

Objectivity has been the most controversial requirement of the OMB Guidelines, because it places rigorous requirements on the dissemination of financial, scientific and statistical information. These types of information must undergo vetting by agencies to ensure that the sources of the information are identified, the results are reproducible, and the underlying data and methods are transparent. Data results that have been independently peer reviewed are subject to a rebuttable presumption of objectivity. In addition, the OMB Guidelines specified that the objectivity requirement does not override compelling interests, such as privacy, trade secrets and intellectual property rights. The guidelines thus recognize that agencies may not have the freedom to disclose supporting data if disclosure is not authorized by the Privacy Act or other legal restrictions that may apply in particular cases. Restricted data may include, for example, data that the agency obtained for its public research, subject to a limited-use agreement under the Health Insurance Portability and Accountability Act of 1996; certain individual-level census data; or other individually identifiable data collected for statistical purposes under Title V of the E-Government Act (i.e., the Confidential Information Protection and Statistical Efficiency Act of 2002 [CIPSEA]). Agency privacy staff members play a potentially critical role in advising program officials on how the agency may comply with the DQA's transparency mandate without inadvertently violating such privacy-related restrictions.

The OMB Guidelines elaborate on agency responsibilities established by the DQA and require that agencies adopt data quality as a performance goal, taking appropriate steps to incorporate information quality criteria into agency information dissemination practices. First, agencies must issue agency-specific data- quality guidelines that are appropriate for the categories of information it disseminates. Second, agencies must develop a process for reviewing the quality of information before it is disseminated. Third, agencies must establish the administrative mechanisms that allow affected persons to challenge the quality of information. Agencies must also establish an administrative appeal process when the affected persons disagree with the agency. Agencies must establish time periods for handling challenges and appeals. Fourth, agencies were required to write a draft report (by April 1, 2002), subject to OMB review, and final report (by October 1, 2002) providing their agency guidelines and explaining how it would ensure data quality and what administrative mechanisms were in place to handle challenges to the quality of information. Agencies were required to publish notices of the availability of the draft and final reports in the *Federal Register*, and to post these reports and administrative mechanisms on their websites. Fifth, agencies must designate a CIO or other responsible official to ensure compliance with the OMB Guidelines. Finally, agencies must report annually to the OMB regarding the number and types of complaints received and how the complaints were resolved.

Subsequently, the OMB issued a bulletin in 2004 regarding the types of peer review under the DQA for certain agency studies or publications that are deemed to be "influential scientific information" or "highly influential scientific assessments."[58] The bulletin notes that information about individuals who serve as peer reviewers may be part of a system of records subject to the Privacy Act, and agencies may need to publish a routine use to disclose that information under the DQA. In 2006, the OMB issued related guidance under the PRA on the design of surveys for collecting data from individuals and others.[59] In that guidance, the OMB acknowledges and discusses the need for agencies to inform respondents about their participation and confidentiality of their data, which may be used for studies or other agency publications subject to the DQA.

6. Federal Open Meetings Laws

6.1 Federal Advisory Committee Act

Revised by Patricia M. Mantoan

The Federal Advisory Committee Act (FACA), 5 U.S.C. App., is implicated when a federal agency establishes, manages or controls a group that includes one or more participants who are not federal employees for the purpose of obtaining the group's advice or recommendations on agency issues or policies. The FACA imposes several procedural requirements on federal agencies that convene advisory committees to enhance the transparency and accountability of the committee, such as issuing a committee charter, having open meetings, providing advance notice of meetings in the *Federal Register*, having a federal official attend the meetings, maintaining detailed meeting minutes and making advisory committee records available for public inspection and copying. The General Services Administration has issued regulations implementing the FACA for the executive branch at 41 C.F.R. part 102-3.

As explained by the U.S. Supreme Court, "FACA was enacted to cure specific ills, above all the wasteful expenditures of public funds for worthless committee meetings and biased proposals" (*Public Citizen v. United States Dep't of Justice*, 491 U.S. 440, 453 [1989]). "Its purpose was to ensure that new advisory committees be established only when essential and that their number be minimized; that they be terminated when they have outlived their usefulness; that their creation, operation, and duration be subject to uniform standards and procedures; that Congress and the public remain apprised of their existence, activities, and cost; and that their work be exclusively advisory in nature" (Public Citizen, 491 U.S. at 446).

In keeping with the FACA's transparency goals, federal agencies that manage the advisory committees, in general, routinely release to the public the names and affiliations of the committees' members, as well as other information about the committee's deliberations and its meetings. Privacy issues, however, might arise with other committee information. For example, federal agencies may maintain personal information pertaining to individual committee members in systems of records that are protected by the Privacy Act. Some member information—such as information reported on statutorily protected confidential financial disclosure forms (the Office of Government Ethics-450 form) for vetting members for possible conflicts of interest—or purely personal resume information, such as home addresses, home phone numbers and Social Security numbers—can be withheld by agencies if requested under the FOIA, 5 U.S.C. § 552. Specifically, the agencies may invoke appropriate FOIA exemptions to protect information, such as Exemption 3, which protects information that is required to be withheld under a statute, or Exemption 6, which protects against clearly unwarranted invasions of personal privacy.

In addition, agencies are permitted to close portions of advisory committee meetings when the committee is disclosing information that would cause a clearly unwarranted invasion of personal privacy and to redact committee records using FOIA exemptions, such as Exemption 6. Privacy issues from an advisory committee's meetings or records could arise, for example, if an advisory committee is evaluating the merits of an individual's grant application, and the committee's comments about the individual's application would cause a clearly unwarranted invasion of the individual's personal privacy if publicly disclosed.

In conclusion, federal agencies should carefully balance the transparency goals of the FACA with the privacy interests of individual committee members and other individuals affected by the committee's deliberations.

6.2 The Government in the Sunshine Act
Revised by Alexander C. Tang, CIPP/US, CIPP/G[60]

The Government in the Sunshine Act (GISA), 5 U.S.C. § 552b, requires federal agencies headed by collegial bodies of appointed individuals, such as the Federal Trade Commission or Federal Communications Commission, to hold open meetings that are announced in advance, unless the requirements for certain exemptions are met. As discussed below, an agency may, in certain cases, vote to close a meeting where an individual's privacy may be affected if the meeting were open to the public. Each agency is required to provide an annual report to Congress regarding changes in policies and procedures under GISA, the number of meetings held, exemptions applied and a description of litigation or formal complaints related to GISA compliance.

In general, for all meetings subject to the act, a public announcement must occur at least one week in advance and must state the time, place and subject matter of the meeting, whether the meeting is open or closed and the identity of a federal official designated to respond to information requests about the meeting. The items in the public announcement may be changed, but the announcement of changes should be made public at the earliest practicable time. No change is allowed unless it is publicly announced and submitted for publication in the *Federal Register*. For open meetings, a transcript, electronic recording or minutes must be promptly made available to the public at actual cost.

The exemptions to the open meeting requirement include matters held secret by executive order and meetings on personnel rules, trade secrets, accusations of crime, censure, information of a personal nature, certain law enforcement records (including those that would cause an unwarranted invasion of personal privacy or disclose the identity of a confidential source), information regarding supervision of financial institutions, premature disclosure of information that is likely to lead to financial speculation, premature disclosure that would frustrate implementation of a proposed agency action and certain legal filings or documents.

An agency may invoke one of the GISA exemptions by majority vote of the entire membership of the agency. An exemption applies to one particular meeting or to a series of meetings on the same particular matters.[61] Meetings may be closed if a person whose interests are directly affected by a portion of a meeting requests that the agency close that portion to the public. The agency is required to disclose the vote to close the meeting, by member, within one day in written form. Agencies may provide by regulation for the closing of meetings or portions of meetings at the beginning of such meeting, rather than before the meeting, if certain GISA exemptions apply. The agency, in lieu of providing the advance public notice normally required by the act, must publicly disclose the time, place and subject matter of the closed meeting at the earliest practicable time.[62]

In addition, the agency general counsel or chief legal officer is required to publicly certify that a meeting should be closed and state each relevant exemption that applies. The agency is required to maintain a complete transcript or electronic recording of each meeting or portion closed to the public.[63] Under certain GISA exemptions, if a meeting is closed, the agency may merely maintain meeting minutes that describe the matters discussed, summarize actions taken and the reasons for the actions, summarize views expressed, and record any roll call votes. Any documents used during the meeting must be identified.

For closed meetings, the transcript, minutes or electronic recording must be maintained for at least two years after the meeting or one year after the conclusion of any agency that was the reason for holding the meeting, whichever period is greater.

As noted above, the act recognizes that an agency may properly conduct a meeting in closed session when necessary to protect the personal privacy of specific individuals. When the agency's members vote to close a meeting on such grounds, the relevant

Sunshine Act exemptions also authorize the withholding of related meeting minutes, transcripts of any protected witness testimony, or other relevant meeting records in response to public access requests under the FOIA. As with FOIA exemptions, however, Sunshine Act exemptions would not be the authority to withhold such records or any other information from Congress, nor does it authorize an agency to close a meeting (on privacy or other grounds) if another law requires that the meeting be open to the public. Likewise, nothing in the Sunshine Act limits (or expands) an individual's access to agency records that the individual may be legally entitled to obtain about himself or herself under the Privacy Act.

7. Open Government Directive

Jonathan R. Cantor, CIPP/US, CIPP/G

The views presented in this section are those of the author and do not necessarily represent the views of the U.S. government or any of its departments or agencies.

When President Obama entered into office on January 21, 2009, he issued a memorandum calling for an "unprecedented level of openness in government,"[64] which launched the Open Government Initiative. On December 8, 2009, the Director of the OMB issued the Open Government Directive, which set forth detailed requirements focused on implementing the president's vision.[65] As its core, the initiative requires the federal government to incorporate the principles of transparency, participation and collaboration as part of its activities. As described by the memorandum, transparency helps agencies better share information and promotes accountability. Participation helps enhance effectiveness and improves decision making. And collaboration helps engage citizens in the work of the government. The president required the OMB to issue a directive to federal departments and agencies to take certain steps to implement the underlying principles of transparency, participation and collaboration discussed in the president's memorandum.

The directive requires departments and agencies to institutionalize the principles of open government by adopting certain behaviors and practices within specified time frames. The directive first requires departments and agencies to publish, to the extent possible, underlying data "in an open format and as granular as possible, consistent with statutory responsibilities and subject to valid privacy, confidentiality, security, or other restrictions"[66] consistent with administration policy in FOIA.[67] The stated goal is to have data available that can be downloaded, searched, indexed and retrieved by commonly used web applications without restrictions designed to limit reuse. In addition, a department or agency must detail "high-value information" currently available for download; plan a way to encourage the use of that data to heighten knowledge and transparency into processes and operations; and identify high-value data not yet available, as well as timelines and plans for how it would be made available.[68] Under the directive, "high-value information is information that can be used to increase agency accountability and responsiveness; improve public knowledge of the agency and its operations; further the core mission of the agency; create economic opportunity; or respond to need and demand as identified through public consultation."[69] It contained a specific requirement on departments and agencies to identify and publish on the Data.gov website three high-value data sets within a fixed time period of 45 days.[70] As part of this effort, departments and agencies have established an open government web page, and solicit feedback from and respond to the public on those pages.[71]

The directive also focused on improving the quality of information released and used by the government, and required departments and agencies to create a culture of open government and establish and publish an Open Government Plan to describe how each department and agency would implement the open government principles within the organization.[72] Agencies continually update their plans and have now published second versions. The public can easily see results of the effort through these Open Government Plans.

While the directive is revolutionary in its approach by breaking the need for members of the public to seek records and information through individual requests under FOIA and the Privacy Act, it also presents some challenges for privacy professionals. Some departments and agencies found that the high-value data they had includes information about people and either the services they provide to others, such as entitlement programs or education services, or the data they collect for compliance with laws and other policies, such as law enforcement programs, tax collection, employment or security.[73] While a sound privacy policy certainly encourages data controllers to provide the subject individual with easy access to records and information, it also warns about not improperly sharing with others. The focus on making so much data available in open formats in such granular detail creates a very real potential for the unintentional release of a data set that contains actual personal information or PII.

In this type of open format, such a PII release could easily move to a very large number of users who should not have access to this information, and, if the information were sensitive enough, cause a great deal of harm, inconvenience or embarrassment. Further complicating the risk is that the directive demanded very strict initial timelines, and thus departments and agencies needed to operate quickly, which made careful reviews very difficult. In addition to the risk of releasing PII erroneously in a data set, the data set releases that departments and agencies make under the directive also present the risk of being combined with other data sets made available by other organizations, including those from outside the federal government or even the United States, in a manner that could re-identify a person, even if the data were anonymous when planned for release. The combination of seemingly insignificant pieces of information about a person and assembling it back to identify a person is sometimes called the "mosaic effect."[74]

To guard against these risks, agencies take several approaches. In some departments and agencies, they are able to leverage expertise from already well-established disclosure review boards (DRB) with experience applying scientific methods to ensure data cannot be used in a manner to identify individuals. DRBs, however, are common only in those agencies that performed extensive research and statistical studies, and are not large enough to review open government activities of all large departments and agencies.[75] Yet some of their experience has been put to good use within those agencies and throughout the government. The OMB led a group of such government experts to design a screening methodology to help departments and agencies screen for potential PII in their data sets and help find ways to mask it. Through the Open Government Workgroup called for in the directive, the OMB also helps coordinate an interagency review effort to ensure that a planned release of a new data set will not lead to the re-identification of individuals or create other security risks.

Even with the tools available, however, when assisting releases that contain or are about individuals, the privacy professional must consistently balance the need to make data available with the risk to personal privacy.

8. Confidential Information Protection and Statistical Efficiency Act

Michael Hawes, CIPP/G[76]

Statistical activities within the federal government are decentralized across a large number of agencies. The OMB has designated thirteen "Principal Statistical Agencies" (e.g., the U.S. Census Bureau, the Bureau of Labor Statistics, and the National Center for Health Statistics) and identifies more than 80 additional federal agencies that perform statistical activities as a major portion of their work.[77] While many federal statistical agencies are able to collect information from the public under pledges of confidentiality authorized by their specific agency statutes (see Chapter 7), there was no strong federal government–wide confidentiality protection for statistical information until the late 1990s. Recognizing the need to provide clear and consistent protections for federal statistical collections, the OMB issued a memorandum, "Order Providing for the Confidentiality of Statistical Information," in June 1997.[78] This order provided basic federal legal protections for information collected by an OMB-designated "statistical agency or unit" for "exclusively statistical purposes." These protections were later expanded by CIPSEA, included as Title V of the E-Government Act of 2002, which introduced criminal penalties for the unauthorized disclosure of information collected under a statistical agency's pledge of confidentiality.[79]

9. Controlled Unclassified Information (CUI) Office Notice 2011-01: Initial Implementation Guidance for Executive Order 13556

Liz Lyons, CIPP/G

The views presented in this section are those of the author and do not necessarily represent the views of the U.S. government or the U.S. Department of Homeland Security and its components.

President Obama signed Executive Order (EO) 13556 on November 4, 2010, to ensure information is disseminated across the executive branch in a controlled and methodical way. Prior to this order, there was no attempt to establish a unifying method to categorize unclassified information and ensure common handling procedures when sharing information across federal agencies.

The Controlled Unclassified Information (CUI) program is "a system that standardizes and simplifies the way the executive branch handles unclassified information that requires safeguarding or dissemination controls, pursuant to and consistent with applicable law, regulations, and government-wide policies. The program emphasizes the openness and uniformity of government-wide practices. Its purpose is to address the current inefficient and confusing patchwork that leads to inconsistent marking and safeguarding as well as restrictive dissemination policies, which are often hidden from public view."[80]

The CUI EO prescribes a bottom-up approach, in which each department and agency is required to:

a. Identify all Sensitive But Unclassified (SBU) markings being employed in their particular department or agency;

b. Identify the authority for those markings, i.e. law, regulation, government-wide policy;

c. Review those markings to identify any areas for consolidation or the elimination of redundancy; and

d. Specifically define all categories, subcategories, and markings that the department or agency would like to continue to employ.[81]

CUI information does not include classified information; rather it is information that requires safeguarding or specific handling controls as prescribed by law or regulation.

At present there are over 100 different ways of labeling sensitive information. There is no definition or protocol used by the entire federal government to describe how a document should be marked, under what circumstances a document should be controlled and what procedures to follow to ensure its security. This results in confusion and inadequate protections for documents and other information shared within the federal government. It also results in too many documents being considered sensitive in an overly restrictive way. EO 13556 addresses these problems and provides a common definition and standardized process and procedures.[82]

NARA is designated as the executive agent to implement the EO, which includes issuing guidance and annual reports detailing how the federal government can fulfill the EO's requirements. The guidance instructs agency heads to establish and implement a program managing CUI data. Each agency's implementation plan must include training, maintenance and auditing to ensure compliance with the guidelines.

NARA also established a CUI registry for markings, categories and subcategories of CUI, based on information obtained from federal agencies about their current use of labels for sensitive information. The registry (http://www.archives.gov/cui/registry/category-list.html) went live on November 1, 2011, and includes a general category for privacy and 10 subcategories for specific aspects of privacy, such as health or financial information. The registry provides completely transparent instructions for labeling, safeguarding and disseminating CUI data.

Finally, NARA organized and clarified each agency's submissions regarding the circumstances and procedures for decontrolling data by category and subcategory. The registry specifies when law, regulation or generally accepted policy indicates that data no longer need to be considered CUI and should be re-designated and archived in an approved manner. Decontrol does not equal public release. CUI data is not allowed to be classified indefinitely unless required by a specific law, regulation or government-wide policy.

10. Federal Agency Data Mining Reporting Act of 2007

Liz Lyons, CIPP/G

The views presented in this chapter are those of the author and do not necessarily represent the views of the U.S. government or the U.S. Department of Homeland Security and its components.

> *Data mining means a program involving pattern-based queries, searches, or other analysis of 1 or more electronic databases, where:*
>
> *(A) A department or agency of the federal government, or a non-federal entity acting on behalf of the federal government, is conducting the queries, searches or other analyses to discover or locate a predicted pattern or anomaly indicative of terrorist or criminal activity on the part of any individual or individuals;*
>
> *(B) The queries, searches or other analyses are not subject-based and do not use personal identifiers of a specific individual, or inputs associated with a specific individual or group of individuals, to retrieve information from the database or databases; and*
>
> *(C) The purpose of the queries, searches, or other analyses is not solely –*
>> *i. The detection of fraud, waste, or abuse in a government agency or program; or*
>> *ii. The security of a government computer system.[83]*

"[Electronic] telephone directories, news reporting, information publicly available to any member of the public without payment of a fee, or databases of judicial and administrative opinions or other legal research sources" are not considered "databases" under the act.[84] Therefore, searches, queries, and analyses conducted solely in these resources are not "data mining" for purposes of the act's reporting requirement.

Two aspects of the act's definition of data mining are worth emphasizing. First, the definition is limited to pattern-based electronic searches, queries or analyses. Activities that use only PII or other terms specific to individuals (such as a license plate number) as search terms are excluded from the definition. Second, the definition is limited to searches, queries or analyses that are conducted for the purpose of identifying predictive patterns or anomalies that are indicative of terrorist or criminal activity by an individual or individuals. Research in electronic databases that produces only a summary of historical trends, therefore, is not data mining under the act.

If an agency is found data mining, it must submit a yearly report to Congress. The privacy office of that agency must be involved in producing the report. The report will be made public and describe all of the agency's data-mining activity, goals and an assessment of the effectiveness of the data mining activity.

Many federal agencies engage in data mining. For example, the Department of Homeland Security is authorized to engage in data mining and other analytical tools in furtherance of departmental goals and objectives.[85]

10.1 Example of Data Mining[86]

The DHS Immigrations and Customs Enforcement (ICE) maintains a system called Data Analysis and Research for Trade Transparency System (DARTTS). DARTTS generates leads for and otherwise supports investigations of trade-based money laundering, contraband smuggling, trade fraud and other import-export crimes. DARTTS analyzes trade and financial data to identify statistically anomalous transactions that may warrant investigation. These anomalies are then independently confirmed and further investigated by experienced Homeland Security investigators.

Between 2008 and 2010, for example, information from DARTTS was used to assist in an investigation into a California-based company that sold stuffed animals but was also involved in a money-laundering organization responsible for narcotics trafficking between the United States and Colombia. The ICE was able to disrupt, dismantle and ultimately stop the money-laundering organization by using data obtained from DARTTS as well as research and analysis provided by the trade unit. In 2010, the investigation culminated in the indictment and arrest of three officers in the company for conspiracy to defraud the United States and the seizure of evidence related to money laundering.

The ICE does not use DARTTS to make unevaluated automated decisions about individuals, and DARTTS data is never used directly as evidence to prosecute crimes.

DARTTS is solely an analytical tool that helps in the identification of anomalies. It is incumbent upon the investigator who finds an anomaly to further investigate the reason for the anomaly. If the anomaly can be legitimately explained, the investigator has no need to further investigate it for criminal violations and moves on to the next identifiable anomaly. Investigators are required to obtain and verify the original source data from the agency that collected the information to prevent inaccurate information from propagating. All information obtained from DARTTS is independently verified before it is acted upon or included in an investigative or analytical report. Investigators follow up on anomalous transactions to determine if they are in fact suspicious and warrant further investigation.

11. Conclusion

The requirements created by government information laws hold government agencies accountable for the privacy and security of PII entrusted to them. Government information laws create confidence in the handling of PII by requiring the protection of both information and information systems. These laws protect the rights of individuals by ensuring decisions are based on PII that has been collected and used in accordance with FIPs. Moreover, the laws protect the integrity of the democratic process by ensuring that individuals have access to government records and meetings while still protecting privacy, which enables the public to hold the government accountable for its actions.

Endnotes

1 The agencies covered explicitly are Transportation, Treasury, the General Services Administration, the Executive Office of the President, Architectural and Transportation Barriers Compliance Board, Election Assistance Commission, the Federal Elections Commission, the Federal Labor Relations Authority and the Federal Maritime Commission.

2 44 U.S.C. § 3541.

3 44 U.S.C. § 3542.

4 www.whitehouse.gov/omb/organization_mission/.

5 *Id.*

6 44 U.S.C. § 3543.

7 NIST activities have been extensive. See http://csrc.nist.gov.

8 The OMB has an extensive role in overseeing agency budgets, including agency information technology budgets.

9 44 U.S.C. § 3544.

10 44 U.S.C. § 3545.

11 44 U.S.C. § 3546.

12 The Federal Information Security Management Act, H. R. 2458-49, 44 U.S.C. § 3543.

13 www.cio.gov/Documents/FEA-Security-Privacy-Profile-v3-09-30-2010.pdf.

14 Federal Enterprise Architecture Security and Privacy Profile, Version 3.0, September 2010, www.cio.gov/documents/fea-security-privacy-profile-v3-09-30-2010.pdf.

15 http://csrc.nist.gov/publications/drafts/800-53-rev4/sp800-53-rev4-ipd.pdf.

16 Freedom of Information Act, 5 U.S.C. § 552.

17 Administrative Procedures Act, 5 U.S.C. § 1002 (1946).

18 111 Cong. Rec. S26820 (1965); H.R. Rep. No. 1497, 89th Cong., 2d Sess. (1966).

19 *Id*. at 5.

20 See *NLRB v. Robbins Tire & Rubber Co.*, 437 U.S. 214, 242 (1978).

21 U.S House of Representatives, A Citizen's Guide to the Freedom of Information Act and the Privacy Act of 1974 to Request Government Records, 109th Cong. Rep. No. 109-226 (2005).

22 Pub. L. No. 107-306, 116 Stat. 2383 (2002).

23 U.S. Department of Justice Office of Information and Privacy, FOIA Post: FOIA Amended by Intelligence Authorization Act (2002).

24 *U.S. Department of Justice v. Tax Analysts*, 492 U.S. 136, 144–45 (1989).

25 The most recent highly publicized FOIA case litigated on the issue of agency control was the request for access to the presidential visitor logs, which disputed whether the logs were in the control of the Office of the President or the Secret Service. See Mike Rosen-Molina, "Federal Judge Rules White House Visitor Logs Are Public Records," The Jurist (December 17, 2007), http://jurist.org/paperchase/2007/12/federal-judge-rules-white-house-visitor.php, opinion available at: https://ecf.dcd.uscourts.gov/cgi-bin/show_public_doc?2006cv1912-44.

26 Pub. L. No. 104-231, 110 Stat. 3048 (1996) (emphasis added).

27 U.S. House of Representatives, A Citizen's Guide to the Freedom of Information Act and the Privacy Act of 1974 to Request Government Records, 109th Cong. Rep. No. 109-226 (2005).

28 Open Government Act of 2007, Pub. L. No. 110-175 (2007) (emphasis added).

29 *Id*. The 2007 amendment to FOIA prohibits agencies from assessing search and duplication fees on requesters if agencies fail to comply with any statutory time limits, unless unusual circumstances apply.

30 5 U.S.C. § 552(a)(4)(A)(ii).

31 A "representative of the news media" was defined by the Open Government Act of 2007, Pub. L. No. 110-175 (2007), to mean "any person or entity that gathers information of potential interest to a segment of the public, uses its editorial skills to turn the raw materials into a distinct work, and distributes that work to an audience." The definition also provided for alternative media outlets, such as electronic newspapers. Additionally, it applies to freelance journalists who can demonstrate a solid basis for expecting publication, even if not employed by a news entity.

32 Noncommercial requesters, those who fall within categories two and three, are not generally charged for small requests because the first two hours of searching and the first 100 pages of duplication are free. U.S. Department of Justice, *Freedom of Information Act Guide* (2007).

33 5 U.S.C. § 552(a)(4)(A)(i).

34 Westby, Jody, *International Guide to Privacy*, Chicago, Illinois: ABA Publishing, 2004.

35 U.S. Department of Justice, *Freedom of Information Act Guide* (2007).

36 *Id.*

37 26 U.S.C. § 6103.

38 U.S. Department of Justice, *Freedom of Information Act Guide* (2007).

39 Beginning December 31, 2008, the 20-day period will commence on the date on which the request is first received by the *appropriate component* of the agency, but not later than 10 days after the request is first received by any component (amended by the Open Government Act of 2007).

40 Open Government Act of 2007, Pub. L. No. 110-175 (2007).

41 *Id.*

42 See *Oglesby v. The United States Department of the Army, et* al, 920 F.2d 57, 61 (D.C. Cir. 1990.) See also DOJ FOIA Regulations, 28 C.F.R. 16.6(c) (2008).

43 The Open Government Act of 2007, Pub. L. No. 110-175, defined "substantially prevailed" to mean that the complainant obtained relief through 1) judicial order, an enforceable written agreement or consent decree; 2) a voluntary, unilateral change in position by the agency, if the complainant's claim is not insubstantial.

44 Executive Order 13392: Improving Agency Disclosure of Information (Dec. 14, 2005).

45 The Open Government Act of 2007, Pub. L. No. 110-175 requires the agencies to fill the position of FOIA Public Liaison by December 31, 2007. The liaison aids requesters and assists in resolving disputes between requesters and the agency.

46 The National Archives, About the National Archives, www.archives.gov/about/info/mission.html.

47 44 U.S.C. § 3501 *et seq.*

48 OMB Memorandum M-03-22, "OMB Guidance for Implementing the Privacy Provisions of the E-Government Act of 2002," (September 26, 2003.), www.whitehouse.gov/omb/memoranda_m03-22.

49 www.whitehouse.gov/sites/default/files/omb/assets/inforeg/SocialMediaGuidance_04072010.pdf.

50 The views expressed by the author do not necessarily represent those of the Federal Trade Commission or any individual Commissioner.

51 See Treasury and General Appropriation Act for Fiscal Year 2001, Public Law 106-554 § 515, Appendix C, 114 Stat. 2763A-153 (2000).

52 Urs Gasser, *Information Quality and the Law, or, How to Catch a Difficult Horse,* The Berkman Center for Internet and Society, Harvard Law School, Research Publication No. 2003–08 (Nov. 2003).

53 44 U.S.C. § 3501 et seq.

54 44 U.S.C. § 3502.

55 Pub. L. No. 106-554, § 515, Appendix C, 114 Stat. 2763A-153 (2000).

56 See 66 FR 49718.

57 See OMB, "Guidelines for Ensuring and Maximizing the Quality, Objectivity, Utility, and Integrity of Information Disseminated by Federal Agencies," 67 FR 8452, February 22, 2002.

58 OMB Peer Review Bulletin, M-05-03 (Dec. 16, 2004), published at 70 Fed. Reg. 2664 (Jan. 14, 2005). www.whitehouse.gov/sites/default/files/omb/memoranda/fy2005/m05-03.pdf.

59 OMB Memorandum for the President's Management Council, "Guidance on Agency Survey and Statistical Collection" (Jan. 20, 2006), www.whitehouse.gov/sites/default/files/omb/inforeg/pmc_survey_guidance_2006.pdf.

60 The views expressed by the author do not necessarily represent those of the Federal Trade Commission or any individual Commissioner.

61 5 U.S.C. § 552b(d)(1).

62 5 U.S.C. § 552b(d)(4).

63 5 U.S.C. § 552b(f)(1).

64 January 21, 2009 Memorandum of President Barack Obama, "Transparency and Open Government", 74 Fed. Reg. 4685 (Jan. 26, 2009).

65 M-10-06, "OMB Memorandum for the Heads of Executive Departments and Agencies," "*Open Government Directive*," (December 8, 2009).

66 *Id.*, Attachment at 3.a.ii.

67 5 U.S.C. § 552. Obama Administration policy on the Freedom of Information Act (FOIA) was established by the President in his January 21, 2009 Memorandum on FOIA, 74 Fed. Reg. 4683 (Jan. 26, 2009), and Attorney General Eric Holder in his March 19, 2009 Memorandum on FOIA, www.justice.gov/ag/foia-memo-march2009.pdf.

68 M-10-06, "OMB Memorandum for the Heads of Executive Departments and Agencies," "*Open Government Directive*," (December 8, 2009).

69 *Id.*, at 3.a.i.

70 *Id.*, at 1.d.

71 Many departments and agencies use popular commercially available social media tools as part of this effort, which can present numerous privacy questions relating to the applications' use and sharing of personal information as well as technologies such as cookies used to track user behavior. The privacy issues with third-party applications and web customization tools are outside the scope of this section.

72 M-10-06, "OMB Memorandum for the Heads of Executive Departments and Agencies," "*Open Government Directive*," at 3.a., (Dec. 8, 2009).

73 5 U.S.C. § 552a.

74 See statement of Vikvek Kundrain "Removing the Shroud of Secrecy: Making Government More Transparent and Accountable," March 23, 2010, www.cio.gov/pages.cfm/page/Vivek-Kundra-Testimony-Resolving-the-Shroud-of-Secrecy.

75 While there are many such agencies, good examples are the Bureau of the Census in the Commerce Department, the National Center for Health Statistics of the Department of Health and Human Services and the Bureau of Labor Statistics of the Department of Labor.

76 This contribution is an official U.S. government product, and as such, is in the public domain.

77 Office of Management and Budget. "Statistical Programs of the United States Government, Fiscal Year 2012," www.whitehouse.gov/sites/default/files/omb/assets/information_and_regulatory_affairs/12statprog.pdf.

78 OMB "Order Providing for the Confidentiality of Statistical Information and Extending the Coverage of Energy Statistical Programs Under the Federal Statistical Confidentiality Order; Notice." *Federal Register* 62: 124 p.35044–35050 (June 27, 1997).

79 Public Law 107–347 § 513.

80 www.archives.gov/cui/documents/2011-what-is-cui-bifold-brochure.pdf.

81 www.archives.gov/cui/.

82 www.archives.gov/cui/documents/2011-what-is-cui-bifold-brochure.pdf.

83 42 U.S.C. § 2000ee-3(c)(1) and (2).

84 42 U.S.C. § 2000ee-3(b)(2).

85 *DHS Data Mining Report*, 2011, Foreword, www.cryptome.org/2012/03/dhs-data-spy-2011.pdf.

86 *DHS Data Mining Report*, 2011, pp. 17–20.

CHAPTER FOUR

Privacy and the Federal Government Intelligence Community

Liz Lyons, CIPP/G

The views presented in this chapter are those of the author and do not necessarily represent the views of the U.S. government or the U.S. Department of Homeland Security and its components.

Prior to the creation of the Department of Homeland Security (DHS), intelligence gathering in the United States focused on non-United States citizens and foreign lands. In comparison domestic intelligence agencies pursued intelligence–gathering under criminal investigations and relied on local law enforcement procedures and processes. As a result, the system to collect intelligence and share information is broad and complicated, with dozens of agencies and several laws under which most authorities operate.

Despite this confusion, the protection of privacy has been defended and respected throughout the creation of a domestic intelligence system.

1. The Federal Intelligence Community and the Information Sharing Environment (ISE)

To accomplish their missions, the U.S. intelligence and law enforcement communities must share information, which often includes personally identifiable information (PII). Privacy protection is important in the intelligence and law enforcement environments. Strong privacy protection can help build trusted partnerships, enhance information sharing and foster public confidence. This chapter discusses key documents that provide information and guidance for protecting privacy in the intelligence and law enforcement communities.

Executive Order 12333, United States Intelligence Activities, provides information about the goals, direction, duties and responsibilities with respect to the national intelligence effort and provides basic information on how intelligence activities should be conducted. The executive order states that agencies within the intelligence community are authorized to collect, retain or disseminate information concerning United States persons only in accordance with procedures established by the head of the agency concerned, and must be approved by the attorney general. The types of information that can be collected, retained and disseminated are listed in Executive Order 12333.

The executive order defines the term "United States person" as follows:[1]

> *United States person means a United States citizen, an alien known by the intelligence agency concerned to be a permanent resident alien, an unincorporated association substantially composed of United States citizens or permanent resident aliens, or a corporation incorporated in the United States, except for a corporation directed and controlled by a foreign government or governments.*

According to this order, a "United States person" could refer to an individual or a corporation. But this does not include government agencies, commissions, public universities and colleges. It is also unclear whether an association would be included in this definition. An example of an association would be a neighborhood association, a hobbyist group or a single-issue pressure group (such as an advocacy group, lobby group or special-interest group). The term "association" is also not defined in the order, and with no clear definition it is difficult to determine what constitutes an association and what is an organization; therefore, it is hard to determine if an association would be substantially composed of U.S. citizens or not.

In most cases, PII appears in information about individuals. However, information about a corporation could also include or be linked to information about individuals associated with the corporation; thus, agencies must pay careful attention to recognize this possibility and identify instances when PII is involved and where it is located.

1.1 Privacy and the Federal Government Intelligence Community: ISE Privacy Guidelines

The ISE is a conceptual framework for facilitating the sharing of terrorism-related information among federal, state, local and tribal agencies, the private sector, and foreign partners. The ISE was mandated by the Intelligence Reform and Terrorism Prevention Act of 2004 (IRTPA): "The President shall ... create an ISE ... [that operates] in a manner consistent with national security and with applicable legal standards relating to privacy and civil liberties."

ISE guidance includes steps to ensure the information privacy and other legal rights of Americans are protected in the development and use of the information-sharing environment.[2] The IRTPA mandated that the guidelines be issued within 270 days of the act's passage.

If a federal agency wants to participate in the ISE, then the IRTPA requires it to implement protections "at least as comprehensive as the ISE privacy guidelines." These guidelines set a baseline, but there is no ceiling; participating agencies may exceed the requirements of the ISE privacy guidelines to create a higher level of privacy protection. The ISE creates the conditions by which federal, state, local and tribal agencies can share information while protecting the privacy and civil liberties of American citizens.

The ISE privacy guidelines provide high-level direction on protecting privacy. The guidelines apply to information (called "protected information") about U.S. citizens and lawful permanent residents. Protected information is subject to information privacy or other legal protections under the Constitution and federal laws of the United States. The guidelines address:

- Identification of protected information
- The use of notice mechanisms
- Data quality
- Data security
- Accountability, enforcement and audit
- Redress
- Execution, training and technology
- Awareness
- Working with nonfederal entities
- ISE governance (which involves the identification of an ISE privacy official within each agency)

The existence of the guidelines does not remove the need for agencies to issue memoranda of understanding to establish specific privacy-sensitive procedures for data sharing.

A Privacy and Civil Liberties Implementation Guide for the Information Sharing Environment provides a suggested process for federal departments and agencies to implement the ISE privacy guidelines.

A Privacy and Civil Liberties Implementation Manual for the ISE also offers a collection of useful resource documents. The Key Issues Guidance is of particular interest for privacy; it includes a discussion of what ISE members should address in their redress and notice mechanisms.

1.1.1 Privacy Principles for the ISE

The ISE privacy guidelines establish a set of core privacy and civil liberties principles for intelligence agencies to follow. These principles are as follows:

- Identify and review protected information that may be shared via the ISE
- Enable ISE participants to determine the nature of protected information that may be shared and any applicable legal restrictions

- Share protected information in the ISE only to the extent it is terrorism, weapons of mass destruction, or homeland security information
- Assess, document, and comply with all applicable laws and policies
- Establish data accuracy, quality, and retention procedures
- Deploy adequate security measures to safeguard protected information
- Implement adequate accountability, enforcement, and audit mechanisms to verify compliance
- Establish a redress process consistent with legal authorities and mission requirements
- Implement ISE Privacy Guidelines requirements via appropriate change to business processes and systems, training, and technology
- Make the public aware of the agency's policies as appropriate
- Ensure that, in order to share information in the ISE, nonfederal entities— including state, local, tribal, territorial, and foreign governments— develop and implement appropriate policies and procedures that provide protections that are at least as comprehensive as those contained in the ISE Privacy Guidelines
- Designate a senior official accountable for implementation (ISE Privacy Official)[3]

1.1.2 Implementation of the Privacy Guidelines

All federal agencies complied with the first step for implementing the ISE privacy guidelines when they appointed a senior privacy official at each department.

Agencies then developed their own privacy protection policy to implement the ISE privacy guidelines. The policies matched the guidelines regarding retention of data, access, notice and audit mechanisms. As a result of each agency implementing a specific privacy policy, data is shared through the ISE in a uniform manner. Memoranda of understanding are written to detail how information is shared and how long it is retained.

2. Office of the Director of National Intelligence (ODNI)

Overseeing the intelligence community is the Office of the Director of National Intelligence (ODNI). The IRTPA established the director of National Intelligence (DNI) as the head of the intelligence community and the principal advisor to the president and the National Security Council. The ODNI ensures intelligence is provided to the executive branch and shared in the best possible way within the intelligence community. There are 17 diverse intelligence groups throughout the federal government, and the ODNI is tasked with improving and integrating the intelligence structure and organization. The ODNI consists of the National Counterterrorism

Center, the National Counterproliferation Center, the National Counterintelligence Executive and the Intelligence Advanced Research Projects Activity.

Within the ODNI, the IRTPA created a civil liberties protection officer, who is also responsible for privacy and reviews and incorporates privacy and civil liberties into the policies and procedures of the ODNI. The officer also reviews complaints regarding possible abuses of civil liberties and privacy from the administration of any programs from the ODNI. Finally, the officer ensures compliance with the Fair Information Practice Principles and conducts privacy impact assessments when needed.

3. Implementing Recommendations of the 9/11 Commission Act of 2007

Congress announced the necessity to create the Privacy and Civil Liberties Oversight Board because "[o]ur history has shown us that insecurity threatens liberty. Yet, if our liberties are curtailed, we lose the values that we are struggling to defend."[4]

The board consists of a full-time chairman and four additional members. The members are appointed by the president and confirmed by the Senate. The members serve for a term of six years, and no more than three members can be attached to the same political party.

The functions of the board include providing advice and counsel on policy development and implementation of legislation related to the war against terrorism. The board also reviews actions that the executive branch takes and ensures there is a balance with privacy and civil liberties. The board consults agencies during the development and use of privacy policies related to the ISE. Specifically, the board is charged with reviewing terrorism information-sharing practices of executive branch departments and agencies to determine their impact on privacy and civil liberties. The board members represent subject matter experts in privacy and civil liberties.

3.1 Department Privacy Officer

Congress implemented many of the recommendations of the 9/11 Commission through the DHS. As mentioned in Chapter 1, DHS has the first statutorily mandated privacy office in the federal government. The chief privacy officer (CPO) reports directly to the secretary of Homeland Security, and the office works to preserve and enhance privacy protections for all individuals and promote transparency of DHS operations. In addition, the office "works to minimize the impact of DHS programs on an individual's privacy, particularly an individual's personal information, while achieving the department's mission to protect the homeland."[5] The DHS Privacy Office does not just protect the privacy of U.S. citizens; the office also "handles non–U.S. person PII held in mixed systems in accordance with the fair information practices, as set forth in the Privacy Act. Non-U.S. persons have the right of access to their PII and the right to amend their records."[6]

The CPO is able to investigate programs within DHS as deemed necessary and require subpoenas, subject to the approval of the secretary, of any evidence the CPO feels is required for an investigation. In addition, the CPO can coordinate with the inspector general in investigations of possible violations or abuse concerning a program within DHS. If the inspector general chooses not to investigate, the privacy office can continue the investigation and produce a separate report.

3.2 Privacy and Civil Liberties Officers

The law states that various agencies such as Defense, State, Treasury and any others the Privacy and Civil Liberties Oversight Board identifies must have not fewer than one senior officer to serve as a privacy and/or civil liberty officer. Most often, the same person fulfills these two functions.

In this role, the officer advises the secretary of the agency on privacy and civil liberties issues in regards to regulations, policies and procedures concerning the war on terror. The officer also has the ability to investigate and review policies and procedures within the agency to ensure that privacy, civil rights and civil liberties are properly considered. The officer ensures that the agency has the ability to receive complaints from individuals who believe the agency at fault in possibly violating their privacy, civil rights or civil liberties. Finally, if an agency wants to "retain or enhance a particular governmental power,"[7] the agency must show they have properly considered the impact on privacy, civil rights and civil liberties, and that there are appropriate procedures and guidelines in place.

The law requires that these privacy and civil rights officers—again, often one person holds both positions—report to the head of their agencies and are provided with the full resources needed to complete their mission.

Civil rights and civil liberties officers work to prevent abuses of civil rights and liberties and profiling on the basis of race or religion by employees of the federal government. Their offices review policies and procedures of various government agencies to ensure these protections are incorporated into the programs. In addition, there is a compliance role with requirements from the Constitution, statutes and regulations relating to individuals affected by programs run by the federal government.

Civil rights and civil liberties officers also coordinate with privacy offices to ensure that both issues are integrated and relevant in all agency programs and procedures. Like the privacy officers, the civil rights and civil liberties officers submit reports to Congress detailing what actions have been taken to ensure the protection of civil rights and liberties in the agencies' programs and procedures.

Finally, the officers can investigate complaints of possible abuses of civil rights or civil liberties.[8]

4. Conclusion

The intelligence community and information-sharing environment work hard to ensure privacy is protected throughout the entire process of gathering and disseminating information. In coordination with a privacy and civil rights and civil liberties officer, the U.S. government is moving forward with privacy protection in all spheres of the government.

Endnotes

1   Executive Order 12333 — United States intelligence activities, as amended by E.O. 13284 on Jan. 23, 2003 and E.O. 13355 on Aug. 27, 2004, Part 3, Section 3..4(i). www.archives.gov/federal-register/codification/executive-order/12333.html. The provisions of Executive Order 12333 of Dec. 4, 1981, appear at 46 FR 59941, 3 CFR, 1981 Comp., p. 200.

2   All ISE privacy documents described in this section are available at http://ise.gov/ise-privacy-guidelines-implementation-manual.

3   http://ise.gov/sites/default/files/PrivacyImpGuide_0.pdf.

4   Subtitle F Privacy and Civil Liberties, §1061, (B)(3).

5   DHS Data Mining Report, 2011, pg. 10.

6   DHS Privacy Policy Guidance Memorandum, 2007-1, January 19, 2007, p. 2, www.dhs.gov/xlibrary/assets/privacy/privacy_policyguide_2007-1.pdf.

7   42 U.S.C. § 2000ee-1(a)(4), www.gpo.gov/fdsys/pkg/USCODE-2011-title42/html/USCODE-2011-title42-chap21E-sec2000ee-1.htm.

8   Section 705(a) of the Homeland Security Act of 2002 (6 U.S.C.§ 345(a)) (amended).

CHAPTER FIVE

Laws Affecting Both the Public and Private Sectors and Laws that Compel Disclosure of Information to the Government

1. Laws with Privacy Implications for Private Industry and Government Agencies

Revised by Julie S. McEwen, CIPP/US, CIPP/G, CIPP/IT

A number of privacy-related laws exist in the United States that are primarily directed at the private sector, but also may have implications for the federal sector in some cases. This chapter addresses several of these statutes. It also provides a brief overview of what government privacy professionals need to know relative to privacy in the private sector and highlights your need to safeguard and protect the data if your agency is a recipient of the data.

1.1 The Health Insurance Portability and Accountability Act (HIPAA)

Government privacy professionals whose work in any way touches the areas of healthcare and health insurance must have an understanding of HIPAA.[1] HIPAA creates the legal and regulatory context for the handling of healthcare and health insurance information. It also applies to government organizations in some contexts.

1.1.1 Covered Entities and Business Associates

HIPAA defines covered entities as:

- Healthcare clearinghouses
- Health plans
- Healthcare providers who electronically transmit health information in connection with certain transactions for which the secretary of the Department of Health and Human Services (HHS) has adopted standards under HIPAA

The original text for this chapter was developed by Robert W. Johnson, CIPP/US, CIPP/G and Sandra J. Sinay, CIPP/US, CIPP/G. New content for this revised edition was contributed by Julie S. McEwen, CIPP/US, CIPP/G, CIPP/IT and Deborah Kendall, CIPP/US, CIPP/G whose contributions are noted throughout the sections of the chapter.

HIPAA applies to both private and public organizations (e.g., healthcare providers would include both public and private hospitals, among others), and health plans encompass Medicare and Medicaid. HHS describes restrictions on government access to health information as follows:[2]

> Under the HIPAA Privacy Rule, government-operated health plans and health care providers must meet substantially the same requirements as private ones for protecting the privacy of individual identifiable health information. For instance, government-run health plans, such as Medicare and Medicaid plans, must take virtually the same steps to protect the claims and health information that they receive from beneficiaries as private insurance plans or health maintenance organizations (HMO). In addition, all federal agencies must also meet the requirements of the Privacy Act of 1974, which restricts what information about individual citizens—including any personal health information—can be shared with other agencies and with the public.

In addition to the defined covered entities, HIPAA recognizes that other entities also may maintain or transmit protected health information (PHI) on behalf of or in the provision of service to a covered entity; these are referred to as business associates. Business associates must comply with the same requirements as the covered entity. These requirements must be defined in written business associate contracts.

HIPAA is enforced by HHS and state attorneys general. HIPAA violations can result in both civil and criminal penalties, with intentional disclosure subject to fines of up to $250,000 and imprisonment for up to 10 years. Covered entities, whether private or public, are required to cooperate with efforts by the HHS Office for Civil Rights, which is responsible for investigating complaints.

1.1.2 Security Rule and Privacy Rule

HIPAA originally was conceived to improve the efficiency of the healthcare system by standardizing the use of electronic medical transactions. Because of security and privacy concerns associated with individuals' medical information, the law required HHS to put regulations in place to ensure that security and privacy concerns are addressed (thus, the Security and Privacy Rules). The HIPAA Privacy Rule addresses the use of individuals' medical information, or PHI, by entities subject to HIPAA.[3] The rule seeks to ensure that PHI is appropriately protected while making it available as needed for healthcare purposes or to protect public health. The Privacy Rule sets national minimum standards, but the standards do not preempt more stringent state requirements. Therefore, even if a covered entity is compliant with HIPAA, the entity must ensure it is also in compliance with applicable state laws.

The Security Rule defines standards for the protection of electronic PHI. Generally, covered entities are required to employ safeguards to protect the confidentiality, integrity and availability of PHI. The safeguards are meant to be generally technology neutral and should be implemented in a way that balances the security threat with the operational need for access to PHI. The safeguards should also reflect "the size, complexity and capabilities of the covered entity."[4]

1.1.3 Protected Health Information

The HIPAA Privacy Rule defines PHI as individually identifiable health information that is transmitted or maintained in any form or media by a covered entity. Individually identifiable health information relates to:

- An individual's past, present or future physical or mental health or condition
- The provision of healthcare to an individual
- The past, present or future payment for the provision of healthcare to an individual

This information must either identify an individual, or reasonably be believed to identify that person. PHI does not include health information that an entity maintains in its capacity as an employer or health information in education records covered by the Family Educational Rights and Privacy Act.[5] PHI also does not include health information that has been de-identified; that is, information from which it is no longer possible to determine an individual's identity. A covered entity may use an independent, qualified statistician to document the methods used to de-identify data and make a determination as to whether the risk of re-identifying the data is small. Under HIPAA, a covered entity may also assign a type of record identifier, such as a code, to health information so any information that is de-identified can be re-identified by only the covered entity. The code cannot be derived from the original identifiers in the information. HIPAA also contains provisions that permit the use of limited data sets from which direct identifiers, such as name and address, have been removed. Use or disclosure of limited data sets requires that a data use agreement is in place with the entity with which the information is being shared.

1.1.4 Use and Disclosure

One of the primary purposes of the Privacy Rule is to limit the instances in which an individual's PHI may be used or disclosed by a covered entity. Generally, covered entities may only use or disclose PHI in connection with treatment for a condition, payment for services rendered or to support healthcare operations. The rule specifically details when PHI must be used or disclosed, when it may be used or disclosed with or without attaining the individual's authorization, and when an individual must be given the opportunity to agree with or object to the use or disclosure.

Covered entities are required to disclose PHI in two specific instances:

1. To individuals or their representatives when they request access to their own PHI, or an accounting of disclosures of, their own PHI
2. To HHS during a compliance investigation, review or enforcement action

Covered entities also may use and disclose PHI without an individual's authorization in the following instances:

- For treatment, payment and healthcare operations, except for psychotherapy notes and marketing purposes, as specifically defined
- Specified public interest uses and disclosures, including those uses required by law; for public health activities; in cases of abuse or neglect; for law enforcement purposes; for serious threats to health and safety; and for legal proceedings
- Use and disclosure incidental to approved uses and disclosures
- For research, public health and healthcare operations when the data has been limited by removing specified identifiers, including identifiers such as name, address, Social Security number (SSN) and account number

Covered entities may use and disclose PHI when the individual is incapacitated and the use or disclosure may be in the individual's best interests, and then later give the individual an opportunity to agree or object. Typical instances include identifying information in a health facility directory and the disclosure of limited PHI to family or friends who are directly involved in the individual's care or payment for care (such as a relative picking up a prescription from a pharmacist).

Covered entities must obtain an individual's written authorization when the use or disclosure is not for purposes of treatment, payment or healthcare operations. This authorization must be specific and easily understandable. In addition, specific authorization is required when using or disclosing psychotherapy notes and when the use or disclosure is for marketing purposes.

1.1.5 Access and Notice

Another primary purpose of HIPAA is to ensure that individuals have the right to access, copy, and if necessary, correct their PHI. They also have the right to an accounting of all disclosures made of their PHI. Covered entities must ensure they have sufficient procedures in place so access and accountings are completed in a timely manner.

In most cases, covered entities are required to provide notices of their privacy practices. The Privacy Rule requires certain specific elements and procedures for issuing the notices. Primarily, a notice must describe how the covered entity will use, disclose and protect an individual's PHI. It must also describe the individual's rights to access, accountings, correction and redress.

1.2 The Health Information Technology for Economic and Clinical Health Act (HITECH Act)

Enacted as part of the American Recovery and Reinvestment Act of 2009, the HITECH Act, among other objectives, further addresses privacy and security issues involving PHI as defined by HIPAA. The HITECH privacy provisions include the introduction of categories of violations based on culpability that, in turn, are tied to tiered ranges of civil monetary penalties, which the HIPAA enforcement regulations have been amended to reflect. The act also applies the HIPAA security regulations directly to the business associates of HIPAA-covered entities and clarifies restrictions on the disclosure and sale of health information as well as requirements on the accounting of certain PHI disclosures. Like the HIPAA Privacy Rule, the HITECH privacy provisions establish a requirements floor and do not automatically preempt state requirements.

The most noteworthy elements of the HITECH privacy provisions focus on breach notification. A breach involves unauthorized acquisition, access, use or disclosure of information that compromises the security or privacy of the information. The implementing rule elaborates on this latter aspect, interpreting it as a "significant risk of financial, reputational, or other harm to the individual."[6] This aligns both with state breach notification laws and with breach notification guidance within the federal government, and implies the need to perform a risk assessment to establish whether a breach has actually occurred.[7]

In establishing breach notification requirements for PHI, the act defines unsecured PHI as that which is not secured through the use of a technology or methodology specified by the secretary of HHS. This guidance, issued in April 2009, specifies encryption and destruction as acceptable ways of rendering PHI "unusable, unreadable or indecipherable" to unauthorized individuals.[8] Information to which one of these measures has not been properly applied is considered "unsecured." Only a breach involving unsecured PHI triggers the notification requirements.

Upon discovery of a breach of unsecured PHI, the covered entity must notify affected individuals within 60 calendar days. If the breach involves the information of more than 500 individuals in a particular state, county, city or town, the entity also must notify media outlets in that geographic area. However, a notification delay for law enforcement purposes is permitted. Regardless of the size of the breach, the HHS secretary must be notified—immediately in the case of breaches involving the information of 500 or more individuals; and annually in the case of smaller breaches. Business associates of covered entities must inform the covered entities upon discovery of a breach of unsecured PHI.

The notice provided to affected individuals must contain the following components:

- A brief description of what happened
- A description of the types of unsecured PHI that were involved
- The steps individuals should take to protect themselves from potential harm resulting from the breach
- A brief description of what the covered entity is doing in response to the breach
- Contact procedures enabling individuals to ask questions and/or obtain additional information about the breach

Breach notification requirements also apply to vendors (entities other than covered entities under HIPAA) providing "personal health records" (PHRs), which are maintained by individuals rather than healthcare providers, as is the case with electronic health records (EHRs). Upon discovery of a breach of unsecured PHR identifiable health information—individually identifiable health information as defined in the Social Security Act—the vendor must notify all affected individuals who are U.S. citizens or residents and as well as the Federal Trade Commission (FTC). Third-party service providers to such vendors are obligated to notify the vendor upon discovery of a breach.

1.3 The Children's Online Privacy Protection Act

Almost every federal government entity has at least one website directed at children. In many cases, these websites are required to comply with the Children's Online Privacy Protection Act of 1998 (COPPA).[9] Government privacy professional need to understand the specific concerns associated with a government entity interacting online with children.

COPPA was enacted in 1998; the FTC issued its final rule in 1999,[10] and COPPA became effective on April 21, 2000. COPPA places requirements on certain websites that collect personal information from children under the age of 13. Specifically, those sites must:

- Include appropriate notice
- Seek verifiable consent from a parent for any collection of personal information
- Provide for the right of a parent to review personal information provided by the child
- Establish and maintain reasonable procedures to protect the confidentiality, security and integrity of personal information collected from the child

In addition, websites may not condition participation in certain site activities on providing personal information.

While COPPA is specifically directed at commercial websites and online service providers, by federal policy it has been extended to federal websites by Office of Management and Budget (OMB) Memoranda M-00-13 and M-03-22.

The FTC enforces COPPA based on submitted complaints and potential violations discovered from monitoring. COPPA allows for civil penalties of up to $11,000 per violation. Websites have had to pay over $1 million in settlements with the FTC for COPPA violations. The actual amount of the payment may vary based on how egregious the violation was, the number of children involved, the type of information collected, the uses of the information and similar factors. COPPA grants enforcement authority to specified federal agencies and states.

1.3.1 Compliance Requirements

In most cases it is clear who must comply with COPPA. Compliance is mandated for any operator of a commercial or federal government website or online service directed at children under the age of 13, or any operator of a general-audience website or online service with actual knowledge that they are collecting personal information from children under the age of 13.

Occasionally, the question arises of who the operator of a website or online service provider actually is. The FTC will consider several factors in determining who is an operator, such as: who owns and controls the collected information; who is financially responsible for the information collection and maintenance; any preexisting contractual relationships regarding the information; and the role of the website in the collection activity.

Another question that may arise is whether a website is "directed to children." In making this determination, the FTC will look at the intended and actual audience of the website, as well as the website content, including subject matter, visual or audio components, the age of any models, the language of the site, and the types of promotions used.

COPPA specifically excludes nonprofits that would otherwise be exempt from coverage of Section 5 of the Federal Trade Commission Act, although nonprofits that operate for the profit of their commercial members *are* subject to Section 5 and consequently would be required to comply with COPPA. In any case, the FTC recommends that nonprofits comply with COPPA.

1.3.2 Personal Information

The definition of personal information in the law and rule of COPPA is fairly expansive. It includes the expected individually identifiable information, such as name, physical address, e-mail address, phone number, SSN, photograph, and persistent identifiers, such as customer serial numbers in cookies or other information that would permit physical or online contacting of a child. However, it also includes non-individually identifiable information concerning the child or parent when such information is combined with other individually identifying information.

1.3.3 Notice

COPPA requires two types of notice: (1) a notice of the privacy policy associated with the collection of personal information from children under the age of 13; and (2) a direct notice to parents. The website must post a prominent link to its privacy policy on its homepage and on each page of the website where information may be collected. The FTC has made it clear that a small link at the bottom of a page is not sufficient. The link must be highlighted in some way, such as in a larger font size or contrasting font color and background. In addition, the privacy policy itself must:

- Provide the name and contact information of the site operator(s)
- Describe what personal information is being collected and whether it is being collected actively or passively (this may include whether the site is collecting IP addresses or using cookies)
- Describe how the information will be used
- Describe whether the information will be disclosed to third parties
- Inform parents of their right to consent to the collection and use of personal information without consenting to disclosure to a third party

- Inform that the site is prohibited from conditioning a child's use of the site on collecting more personal information than necessary
- Describe the procedures that parents must follow to review and have the collected personal information deleted, as well as how to revoke consent for further collection and use of the information

The website also must make a reasonable effort to directly notify parents of the website's practices regarding collection, use and disclosure of the child's personal information. This notice must contain the same information as the notice on the website. It also must notify the parent that the site wishes to collect information from the child. If the collection, use or disclosure requires parental consent, the notice also must include that information and instruct the parent as to how to provide consent. If the collection, use or disclosure does not require parental consent because of a defined exception (described below), the information in the notice varies based on the exception.

Perhaps the most significant requirement of COPPA is that the website must, in most cases, obtain verifiable parental consent *before* a website collects, uses or discloses personal information from a child under the age of 13.[11] The rigor that a website must use to ensure that the website operator has received parental consent depends on the use of the information. The FTC uses a sliding-scale mechanism to determine what type of confirmation is required.[12] The FTC balances the cost of attaining consent with the risk of harm based on the intended uses. If the information is to be used only internally—for example, communicating updates to the website—the website operator may use e-mail, provided that the e-mail response from the parent includes additional contact information, such as a phone or fax number to allow for subsequent confirmation; or, if a time delayed e-mail is sent to the parent, to confirm consent. If the information will be shared with third parties, the site must use a method that provides higher confidence that the consent occurred. Acceptable methods include:

- Signed form from the parent (mailed or faxed)
- Verified credit card number
- Call from a parent to a toll-free number staffed by trained personnel
- Digitally signed e-mail
- E-mail with a preexisting personal identification number obtained from one of the preceding verification methods

COPPA also defines certain collections that do not require prior parental consent, although reasonable efforts may be required to notify parents after the information is collected. These include when information is collected for:

- Purposes of obtaining parental consent
- Responding directly to a child for one time only and then the information is deleted

- Responding directly to a child more than once
- Purposes of the child's safety
- Solely for legal or law enforcement purposes

1.3.4 Confidentiality, Security, and Integrity Procedures: Safe Harbor

COPPA requires that the website operator must establish and maintain reasonable procedures to protect the confidentiality, security and integrity of any collected information.

Websites are considered to be in compliance with COPPA if they comply with FTC-approved self-regulatory guidelines. These guidelines are developed by organizations that then submit them to the FTC for approval. The FTC will consider public comment on whether the guidelines provide sufficient protections, whether the guidelines have effective mechanisms for assessing compliance and whether the guidelines offer compliance incentives. The list of approved safe-harbor guidelines is on the FTC website.

In order to address changing technology, the FTC proposed revisions to COPPA in September 2011. A summary of the major changes proposed is provided below.[13]

- The definition of "personal information" will be revised to include geolocation information and certain types of persistent identifiers used for functions other than the website's internal operations, such as tracking cookies used for behavioral advertising.
- The definition of "collection" will be revised so that operators may allow children to participate in interactive communities without parental consent, as long as the operators take reasonable measures to delete children's personal information before it is made public.
- Parents will be presented with key information regarding privacy practices in a "just-in-time" notice instead of relying only on the information provided in a privacy policy.
- New methods to obtain verifiable parental consent will be added to the existing list, including electronic scans of signed parental consent forms, video conferencing, and use of government-issued identification checked against a database, provided that the parent's ID is deleted promptly after verification is complete.
- The method of parental consent known as "e-mail plus," will be eliminated. This allows operators to obtain consent through an e-mail to the parent, coupled with another step, such as sending a delayed e-mail confirmation to the parent after receiving consent.
- Operators that participate in an FTC-approved safe harbor program will be able to use a consent method permitted by that program.
- Operators will be required to ensure that any service providers or third parties to whom they disclose a child's personal information have reasonable

procedures in place to protect it. Operators will be required to retain the information for only as long as reasonably necessary. They will also be required to take reasonable measures to protect against unauthorized access to or use in connection with the disposal of information.

Safe harbor programs will be required to audit their members at least annually and report the audit results periodically to the FTC.

1.4 The Financial Services Modernization Act

While it may not be readily apparent, the Financial Service Modernization Act of 1999, also referred to as the Gramm-Leach-Bliley Act (GLBA), has significant implications for many government privacy professionals.[14] GLBA directly applies to government entities that provide financial services such as student loans and mortgages.

In the course of conducting federal business, some government agencies work with financial institutions to provide members of the public with the ability to pay for products provided by the government, such as passports and licenses. In addition, much of the development of individual-notice policy and practice is in the area of financial services because of the GLBA. A basic understanding of GLBA concepts will benefit all privacy professionals, whether they have a hand in the financial services provision or not.

GLBA primarily was intended to remove restrictions to allow certain types of financial institutions to merge. Laws such as the Glass-Steagall Act, which GLBA repealed, had restricted such mergers. Removing the merger restrictions created concerns that financial institutions would have uncontrolled access to an excessive amount of personal information. Consequently, GLBA placed three requirements on the financial institutions' handling of personal information. The financial institutions must:

- Provide notice on how personal information is handled and shared
- Give consumers the option to opt out of particular sharing
- Provide adequate safeguards for personal information

The FTC has worked with other financial institution regulators to define the specifics of these requirements, which are spelled out in both the Privacy Rule and the Safeguards Rule. The Privacy Rule implements "notice requirements and restrictions on a financial institution's ability to disclose nonpublic personal information (NPI) about consumers to nonaffiliated third parties." The Safeguards Rule sets the standards to "ensure the security and confidentiality of customer records and information; protect against any anticipated threats or hazards to the security or integrity of such records; and protect against unauthorized access to or use of such records or information that could result in substantial harm or inconvenience to any customer." GLBA sets the minimum national standard, but it does not preempt state law, and states may impose tougher standards on covered entities.

1.4.1 Nonpublic Personal Information (NPI)

GLBA places privacy requirements on NPI, which is defined as personally identifiable financial information, as well as lists, descriptions or other groupings of consumers derived using personally identifiable financial information that is not publicly available. This will include information that the consumer provides to obtain a financial product or service, information resulting from a financial product or service transaction, and information otherwise obtained in connection with providing a financial product or service.

1.4.2 Covered Entities

Any financial institution that provides financial products or services to consumers must comply with GLBA. The GLBA Privacy Rule further defines a financial institution as an entity that is significantly engaged in financial activities, as described in Section 4(k) of The Bank Holding Company Act of 1956.[15] Whether an entity is "significantly engaged" will be based on a review of all of the facts and circumstances. Generally, this means that an entity is a financial institution if it is significantly engaged in activities such as lending, exchanging, investing for others, insuring, providing financial advice or marketing securities.

GLBA makes a distinction between consumers and customers, which affects the privacy protections extended to the individual. Under GLBA, a "consumer" is defined as an individual who obtains or has obtained a financial product or service from a financial institution to be used primarily for personal, family, or household purposes. For example, consumers might be loan applicants or individuals using a check-cashing company.

Financial institutions are required to provide consumers with:

- An initial privacy notice if the financial institution shares information beyond the defined exceptions
- Notice of the right, and sufficient opportunity, to opt out prior to sharing NPI with a third party
- Notice of any changes to privacy practices

A "customer," according to GLBA, is defined as a consumer who has an ongoing customer relationship with a financial institution—for example, through a credit card or a loan. Financial institutions are required to provide customers with:

- An initial privacy notice no later than when the customer relationship is established
- Notice of the right, and sufficient opportunity, to opt out prior to a third-party sharing of NPI
- An annual privacy notice during the length of the customer relationship
- Notice of any changes to privacy practices

1.4.3 Privacy Notices

GLBA has requirements for both initial and annual notices. In all cases, a privacy notice must be a clear, conspicuous and accurate statement of the privacy practices, including:

- What information is collected
- What information the financial institution shares
- With whom the information is shared
- How the information is protected
- An explanation of the consumer's right to opt out
- Any disclosures the financial institution is required to make under the Fair Credit Reporting Act

The FTC issued a Model Privacy Notice form in November 2009 that is to be used by financial institutions as the model format for their notices to consumers.[16] The notice may be provided by mail or in-person delivery. The type of delivery must be reasonable, based on the consumer relationship.

In many cases, a consumer will have a reasonable opportunity to opt out prior to a third party sharing of information. The GLBA privacy notice must provide this information and describe reasonable means available to a consumer to opt out of a particular sharing. Typical means for opting out include a toll-free telephone number, a detachable stub on a mailed form or an electronic form (if the consumer has agreed to receive notices electronically).

1.4.4 The GLBA Safeguards Rule

GLBA, through the Safeguards Rule, requires that financial institutions have a security program that includes administrative, technical and physical safeguards to protect the security, confidentiality and integrity of NPI. These security programs should reflect the size, complexity and nature of the financial institution.

The GLBA Safeguards Rule specifically requires that every financial institution must:

- Designate an employee to coordinate the security program
- Identify and assess the risks to consumer information throughout the institution
- Design, implement, monitor, and test the security program
- Evaluate and adjust the program as circumstances change

GLBA prohibits "pretexting" or gaining access to consumers' financial information by using false pretenses, such as impersonation or fraud.[17] It also prohibits soliciting others to engage in pretexting.

GLBA is enforced by the following authorities: The FTC; the Office of the Comptroller of the Currency; the Federal Reserve System; the Federal Deposit Insurance Corporation; the Office of Thrift Supervision; the National Credit Union

Administration; the Securities and Exchange Commission; and state insurance authorities. In addition, the Consumer Financial Protection Bureau, which was created by the Dodd-Frank Wall Street Reform and Consumer Protection Act of 2010, enforces consumer financial laws, including GLBA.[18]

1.5 Family Educational Rights and Privacy Act

The Family Educational Rights and Privacy Act (FERPA)[19] establishes requirements regarding the privacy protection of student educational records. It applies to all academic institutions that receive funds under applicable U.S. Department of Education programs. FERPA gives parents certain rights with respect to their children's education records. These rights transfer to the student when he or she reaches the age of 18 or attends a school beyond the high school level. Students to whom the rights have transferred are referred to as "eligible students."[20]

Government agencies should be aware of FERPA requirements. In the course of conducting government business, there may be instances where educational records are shared with government entities. FERPA provides parents and eligible students with the right to:

- Review their education records
- Seek amendment of their education records which they believe are inaccurate or misleading
- Limit disclosure of personally identifiable information (PII)
- Notify the Department of Education about the failure of an academic institution to comply with FERPA regulations

In order to release a student's education record to a third party, academic institutions must first have written permission from the parent or eligible student. FERPA allows schools to disclose records without consent to the following parties or under the following conditions:[21]

- School officials who have legitimate educational interest
- Other schools to which a student is transferring
- Specified officials for audit or evaluation
- Appropriate parties in connection with financial aid to a student
- Organizations conducting certain studies for or on behalf of the school
- Accrediting organizations
- Appropriate officials or third parties to comply with a judicial order or lawfully issued subpoena
- Appropriate officials in cases of health and safety emergencies
- State and local authorities, within a juvenile justice system, pursuant to specific state law

"Directory" information is defined as student information, such as a student's name, address, telephone number, date and place of birth, honors and awards, and dates of attendance. Schools may disclose directory information without consent. However, they must tell parents and eligible students about directory information. They also must provide parents and eligible students with a reasonable amount of time to request that the school not disclose directory information about them. Schools also must notify parents and eligible students annually of their rights under FERPA.[22]

1.6 Identity Theft Red Flags and Address Discrepancies under the Fair and Accurate Credit Transactions Act of 2003 ("The Red Flags Rule")

The Red Flags Rule requires covered businesses and organizations to implement a written Identity Theft Prevention Program that is used to detect identity theft in their operations. By identifying identity theft indicators, known as red flags, businesses and organizations can take precautions to prevent occurrences of identity theft. The Red Flags Rule requires financial institutions and creditors that hold consumer accounts and allow multiple payments or transactions, or any other types of accounts for which there is a risk of identity theft, to develop and implement an Identity Theft Prevention Program for new and existing accounts. Financial institutions are defined as all banks, savings associations and credit unions, regardless of whether they hold a transaction account belonging to a consumer, and anyone else who directly or indirectly holds a transaction account belonging to a consumer.

The definition of "creditor" was changed when the law was amended in 2010. The changed law covers creditors who, in connection with a credit transaction, obtain or use consumer reports or furnish information to consumer reporting agencies. Under the revised law, creditors are also organizations that advance funds to or on behalf of someone else, with the exception of any funds for expenses that are incidental to a service provided by the creditor to an individual.[23]

The Red Flags Rule applies to government agencies or nonprofit organizations if they perform functions that meet the definitions of financial institution or creditor. For example, local government organizations may operate utilities that regularly bill customers after they have received utility services, which means they are covered under the Red Flags Rule.[24] Covered entities are required to develop a program that includes reasonable policies and procedures that enable their organizations to prevent identity theft as well as to detect and mitigate identity theft. Specifically, the program should enable covered entities to:

- Identify relevant patterns of activity that may indicate identity theft
- Incorporate business practices to detect indicators of identity theft

- Develop and document appropriate responses to indications of possible identity theft so that identity theft can be prevented and mitigated
- Update their programs from time to time so they reflect changes in risks from identity theft

The Red Flags Rule also includes guidelines to help financial institutions and creditors develop and implement a program, including a supplement that offers examples of red flags.[25]

2. Laws that Compel Disclosure of Information to the Government

Revised by Deborah Kendall, CIPP/US, CIPP/G

Generally speaking, most laws carefully consider and afford stringent protections around the use, sharing and disclosure of sensitive personal information. However, some statutes—and provisions contained within certain statutes—mandate the recording and reporting of personal information in specified circumstances to both private and governmental entities. These statutes are frequently referred to as "anti-privacy" laws, in that they compel disclosure of personal information.

Since the terrorist attacks on September 11, 2011, new anti-privacy provisions have been enacted and existing laws amended to expand the government's authority to mandate the recording and disclosure of personal information in order to better to detect, identify and deter criminal activity, particularly as it relates to acts of domestic and international terrorism.

2.1 The Bank Secrecy Act

The Financial Recordkeeping and Reporting of Currency and Foreign Transactions Act of 1970, more commonly known as the Bank Secrecy Act of 1970 (BSA), requires U.S. financial institutions and money service businesses (MSBs), which are entities that sell money orders or provide cash transfer services, to record, retain and report certain financial transactions to the federal government. This requirement is meant to assist the government in the investigation of money laundering, tax evasion, terrorist financing and various other domestic and international criminal activities.

The BSA requires specified financial institutions to keep records of cash purchases of negotiable instruments, file specific reports for cash transactions exceeding $10,000 USD (daily aggregate amount), and report suspicious activity that may be indicative of criminal activity. Failure to comply with reporting requirements will result in significant penalties.

All records and reports mandated by the BSA are exempt from disclosure under the Freedom of Information Act (discussed in Chapter 3). The most common BSA records and reports (and the information disclosed in each) include:

- **Monetary Instrument Log (MIL):** A financial institution must retain a record for cash purchases of monetary instruments (such as money orders, cashier's checks, and travelers checks) ranging from $3,000 to $10,000.

- **Currency Transaction Reports (CTRs):** A financial institution must file a CTR with the Financial Crimes Enforcement Network (FinCEN), via FinCEN Form 10, for each daily single and/or aggregated cash transaction(s) in excess of $10,000, including deposits, withdrawals and transfers. Information contained within the CTR includes the name, address, date of birth, bank account number, and SSN or taxpayer identification number of each individual who is a party to the transaction.

- **Suspicious Activity Report (SAR):** SARs generate leads that law enforcement agencies use to initiate criminal investigations. As such, these are one of the government's main weapons in the battle against money laundering and other financial crimes. MSBs must file a SAR for any suspicious cash transaction where the customer seems to be attempting to avoid BSA reporting requirements (such as a CTR or MIL), where it is suspected that the funds are from an illegal source or where the funds appear to serve no known business purpose. The MSB may not reveal to the individual or business that a SAR, filed via FinCEN Form 109, has been initiated. Very detailed personal information must be reported within the SAR, including a checklist of items that must be considered and then reflected within a narrative description of the transaction itself. The U.S. Postal Service (USPS) is a federal entity that routinely submits SARs for its money order business in post offices when the transaction meets the statutory threshold. The USPS maintains a system of records notice for this collection and sharing and provides additional security for this data while at rest and when transferred to FinCEN.

- **Report of International Transportation of Currency or Monetary Instruments (CMIR):** It is legal to transport any amount of currency or other monetary instruments into or out of the United States. If the aggregate amount at issue, however, exceeds $10,000 USD (or its foreign equivalent), a CMIR must be filed by each person and/or entity that physically transports, mails or ships the currency/monetary instrument(s), or causes the same to occur. The CMIR is filed with U.S. Customs and Border Protection via FinCEN Form 105.

- **Report of Foreign Bank and Financial Accounts (FBAR):** Any person subject to the jurisdiction of the United States who has an interest in or signature authority over any financial account(s) and/or securities in a foreign country must file an FBAR if their aggregate value at any point in the calendar year exceeds $10,000. The FBAR is filed with the U.S. Department of the

Treasury via Form TDF 90-22.1. Information that must be disclosed includes the individual's name, address, date of birth, SSN, account number, the name(s) and SSN(s) of any joint owners, the value of the account and the name of the financial institution where the account is held.

Since its enactment, the BSA has been amended and expanded in both scope and industries covered by several subsequent anti-money laundering laws, including the USA Patriot Act. Because BSA operations are related to criminal and/or terrorist investigations, the individual is never notified that a financial institution or the USPS (among other MSBs) is collecting personal data and sharing it with FinCEN in order to combat money laundering. FinCEN provides access to every U.S. attorneys' office and 59 law enforcement agencies, including the Federal Bureau of Investigation (FBI), Secret Service, and Customs and Border Protection. Privacy officials in those agencies should be aware that this data is being disseminated and ensure that proper information security controls are in place for this information while under the agency's control, and request that data that is no longer needed is purged appropriately.

2.2 The Foreign Intelligence Surveillance Act

The Foreign Intelligence Surveillance Act of 1978 (FISA)[26] regulates the way that U.S. intelligence agencies conduct foreign intelligence surveillance activities, including wiretaps and the interception of communications. The act sets forth the judicial approval process that is required when the government targets U.S. persons located within the United States.[27] FISA allows warrantless surveillance to be conducted without a court order for up to one year, provided that the surveillance is for foreign intelligence information, targets foreign powers, and will not capture the contents of any communication to which a U.S. person is a party. Generally speaking, FISA *does not* apply to activities directed at persons overseas.

When drafting FISA, Congress carefully crafted a definition for the term "electronic surveillance" to identify the activities that fall within FISA's scope and to distinguish between surveillance directed at persons overseas and surveillance of those in the United States.[28] This definition was framed, however, in terms of wire and radio communications, which were the technologies available in 1978. Such a definition did not encompass (nor could it have foreseen) the revolutionary advances in telecommunications technology, including cellular phones and e-mail. With this advancing technology, the careful balance established by Congress to distinguish between surveillance governed by FISA and surveillance directed at targets outside the United States became decidedly less clear.

Like many older statutes, and due in part to the advances in technology, FISA has been amended on numerous occasions since its enactment almost 30 years ago.[29] One significant amendment is the Protect America Act of 2007.[30]

2.3 The Protect America Act (PAA)

Prior to the amendment in the PAA, the U.S. government often needed to obtain a court order before collecting vital intelligence against a terrorist or other foreign intelligence target located in a foreign country. This was needed because the definition of electronic surveillance and the new technologies used were not adequately addressed by FISA. Further, obtaining a court order to collect foreign intelligence on targets located in foreign countries resulted in unnecessary delays and gaps in intelligence collection efforts, and was contrary to Congress's intent when passing FISA.

The PAA restored FISA to its original focus of protecting the rights of persons in the United States, while not acting as an obstacle to gathering foreign intelligence on targets located in foreign countries. The act also modernized FISA in four important ways:

1. It clarifies FISA's definition of electronic surveillance, making it clear that no court order is required for the intelligence community to gather foreign intelligence on targets located or reasonably believed to be in foreign countries. Electronic surveillance targeting a person in the United States continues to require a court order.

2. It provides a role for the FISA court in reviewing the procedures the intelligence community uses to ensure that collection remains directed at persons located overseas. The U.S. attorney general is required to submit to the FISA court the procedures by which the federal government determines that the authorized acquisitions of foreign intelligence do not constitute electronic surveillance and thus do no trigger FISA's court approval requirements.

3. It provides a mechanism for the FISA court to direct third parties to assist the intelligence community in its collection efforts. The act permits the director of National Intelligence and the attorney general to direct communications service providers to supply the information, facilities and assistance necessary to conduct authorized foreign intelligence activities. In the event such a person fails to comply with a directive, the attorney general may invoke the aid of the FISA court to compel compliance with the directive. By the same token, the act allows third parties to challenge a directive in the FISA court.

4. It protects third parties from private lawsuits arising from assistance they provide the government in authorized foreign intelligence activities targeting individuals located outside the United States.

Note that the final two items include additional requirements levied on third parties, including telecommunications providers, mandating their cooperation with intelligence surveillance and collection efforts.

2.4 Foreign Intelligence Surveillance Act of 1978 Amendments Act of 2008

On July 10, 2008, the president signed into law the Foreign Intelligence Surveillance Act of 1978 Amendments Act of 2008 (also known as the FISA Amendments Act of 2008). Specifically, the revised act prohibits individual states from investigating, sanctioning, or requiring disclosure by complicit telecoms or other persons. It permits the government not to keep records of searches and destroy existing records (even though an existing record schedule requires a 10-year retention period).

The act also:

- Grants immunity to telecoms from lawsuits for past or future cooperation with the government.

- Increases the time for warrantless surveillance from 48 hours to seven days if the FISA court is notified; receives an application; and the circumstances relate to a U.S. person located outside of the United States with probable cause that they are agent of a foreign power. After seven days, if the FISA court has not acted or denies the application, the information cannot be used as evidence.

Some of these provisions are pending judicial review via lawsuits to block implementation.

2.5 The Right to Financial Privacy Act

The Right to Financial Privacy Act of 1978 (RFPA)[31] governs the release of customer financial information to federal government authorities. The act defines both the circumstances under which a financial institution can volunteer information about customers' financial records to federal government authorities, and the applicable procedures and requirements to follow when the federal government requests customers' financial information.

If a government authority requests the release of customer financial information, the RFPA, as a general rule, requires that financial institutions obtain customers' consent prior to granting access to or release of their financial information to the requesting government authority. Without a customer's authorization, the financial institution must first be presented with a valid subpoena or search warrant by the government authority before access may be granted to copies of the customer's financial records.

There are several important exceptions, however, three of which are discussed below.

1. Voluntary Disclosure by a Financial Institution

    Section 3403(c) of the RFPA addresses a very limited exception to the RFPA, wherein a financial institution may notify government authorities about information they believe to be relevant to a possible violation of any statute or regulation, including criminal activity. The information that may be disclosed under this exception is limited to the name or other identifying information of the individual, corporation or account involved, and the nature of the suspected illegal activity. No records may be released under this exception.

2. Disclosure Pursuant to a Request by a Government Authority Conducting Foreign Intelligence Activities

Section 3414(a) of the RFPA permits the production of customer financial records without customer consent if the request is from a government authority authorized to conduct foreign intelligence activities. Before providing the records, however, the financial institution must first receive a certificate of compliance from the government authority requesting the records verifying that the appropriate provisions of the RFPA have been complied with, thus protecting the institution from liability related to the release.

In addition, Section 3414(a)(5)(A) of the RFPA requires a financial institution to comply with a request for financial records made by the FBI when the FBI director certifies in writing that the records are sought for foreign counterintelligence purposes, and that there are specific and articulable facts giving reason to believe that the customer or entity whose records are sought is a foreign power or an agent of a foreign power.

In both of the above scenarios, the financial institution may not disclose to the customer that the federal agency has sought or obtained access to their financial records.

3. Disclosure Required due to Imminent Danger

Section 3414(b)(1) provides that a federal government authority may obtain financial records if the authority determines that a delay in obtaining access to the records would create imminent danger of any of the following:

 – Physical injury to any person
 – Serious property damage
 – Flight to avoid prosecution

As with the foreign intelligence exception, the government authority seeking the financial records must first provide the financial institution with a certificate of compliance, acknowledging that all requirements of the RFPA have been met.

2.6 The Electronic Communications Privacy Act

Title III of the Omnibus Crime Control and Safe Streets Act of 1968[32] (also known as "The U.S. Wiretap Statute") was designed primarily to prevent unauthorized government access to private electronic communications. The Electronic

Communications Privacy Act of 1986 (ECPA), an amendment to the Wiretap Statute, expanded the scope of existing federal wiretap laws to include protection for all newer forms of electronic transmissions, such as video, audio, text and data (e.g., telephones, computers, cell phones, faxes and text messaging).

In general, the ECPA protects the communications of U.S. citizens from government surveillance by requiring a court order for wiretaps and the interception of communications. The ECPA also prohibits private-sector providers of electronic communications services (e.g., Internet service providers) from divulging message content.

Title I of the ECPA protects and prohibits the interception and disclosure of wire, oral and electronic communications (e-mail, for example) while in transit and sets out stringent criteria needed for obtaining a search warrant. Title II, Stored Wire and Electronic Communications and Transactional Records Access, protects communication held in electronic storage—most notably, messages stored on computers. In addition, the use of a pen register[33] and/or trap and trace devices[34] to record dialing, routing, addressing and signaling information used in the process of transmitting wire or electronic communications is prohibited without a search warrant.

Employers and providers of wire and electronic communication services may provide information and assistance to persons authorized by law to intercept wire, oral or electronic communications or to conduct electronic surveillance, provided that there is either a:

- Valid court order directing such assistance; or
- Written certification from an authorized official that no warrant or court order is required for the desired information/assistance.

In accordance with the ECPA, employers are generally prohibited from both intercepting an employee's electronic communications and accessing stored communications without employee consent. However, such prohibitions are, for all intents and purposes, nullified because of the business use and employee consent exceptions articulated in the act. Most employers now escape ECPA liability by notifying the employee that their communications may be subject to monitoring and then requiring employee consent to the monitoring prior to the issuance and/or use of employer-owned equipment, such as computers and other portable electronic devices.

While several provisions of the ECPA were made arguably less stringent when amended by the USA Patriot Act, as a general rule, the government is still forbidden from listening in on the conversations of private citizens without first obtaining a warrant. The ECPA received attention when the Supreme Court ruled in 2007 that President Bush violated the act by ordering recordings of conversations without first obtaining a warrant. In addition, provisions of the act, which allowed the FBI to issue national security letters to internet service providers ordering them to disclose records about their customers, have since been ruled unconstitutional.[35]

2.7 The USA Patriot Act

The Uniting and Strengthening America by Providing Appropriate Tools Required to Intercept and Obstruct Terrorism Act of 2001 (USA Patriot Act), more commonly referred to simply as the Patriot Act, was signed into law on October 26, 2001, just 45 days after the September 11, 2001 terrorist attacks.[36] It substantially expanded the surveillance and investigative authority of U.S. law enforcement agencies, amending more than 15 important statutes, including the BSA, FISA, and the RFPA. The act expanded the definition of terrorism to include "domestic terrorism," thus enlarging the act's applicable sphere to both domestic and international arenas.

Among other provisions, the act increased the ability to track and intercept communications, both for law enforcement and foreign intelligence purposes, and to search, under specified circumstances, telephone and e-mail communications, as well as medical and financial records. It also eased restrictions on foreign intelligence gathering within the United States; expanded the secretary of the Treasury's authority to regulate financial transactions, particularly those involving foreign individuals and entities; and enhanced the discretion of law enforcement and immigration authorities in detaining and deporting immigrants suspected of terrorist acts.

Parts of the act have been criticized from its inception for weakening protections of civil liberties.[37] In particular, opponents of the law have criticized its authorization of indefinite detentions of immigrants; "sneak and peek" searches, through which law enforcement officers search a home or business without the owner or occupant's permission or knowledge;[38] the expanded use of national security letters, which allow the FBI to search telephone, e-mail and financial records without a court order; and the expanded authority of law enforcement agencies to access business records, including library and financial records. Since the act's passage, several legal challenges have been brought against it, and federal courts have ruled that a number of provisions are unconstitutional.

Both detractors and supporters have viewed other parts of the act, however, as welcome and necessary.[39] A case in point is Section 701, which authorizes the establishment and operation of information-sharing systems to enhance the investigation and prosecution abilities of participating law enforcement agencies.

The act was reauthorized, and amended and signed into Public Law 109-178 on March 9, 2006. The major changes that were enacted include a) a provision to allow judicial review of production orders by amending Section 501 of FISA; and b) a provision defining a library is not a wire or electronic communications service provider for the purposes of in Section 2510(15) of this title.

Most recently, the act was reauthorized and signed into Public Law 112-14 on May 26, 2011. It reauthorizes the act until June 1, 2015. The law extended two controversial provisions of the 2001 act: one allowing for roving wiretaps, and the other allowing searches of business records in the pursuit of terrorist threats. A third provision gives the government power to watch non-American "lone wolf" suspects with no certain ties to terrorist groups. These three provisions are considered valuable tools by law enforcement officials, but are opposed by privacy advocates due to concerns about privacy rights abuses.

2.8 The REAL ID Act

The REAL ID Act of 2005 is a nationwide effort intended to prevent terrorism, reduce fraud and improve the reliability and accuracy of identification documents issued by U.S. state governments.[40] The act has many varying provisions, including enhanced security at U.S. borders, more stringent requirements for asylum and new criteria pertaining to the deportation of aliens involved in terrorist activity. But the provision generating the most interest and controversy concerns the establishment and implementation of national standards for state-issued driver's licenses and non-driver identification cards. As currently written, the national standards for these cards address what data must be included on the card, the documentation required for issuance of the card and how the states must share their databases.

The goal of the REAL ID Act was to establish national standards for the state-issued licenses and identification cards. This was due, in large part, to the lack of uniformity among states in the documentation required prior to issuing the card. More lax documentation requirements in some states arguably eased acquisition of state-issued cards by several of the terrorists involved in the attacks on September 11, 2001.

There has been significant opposition and controversy surrounding this act. While the new law sets forth national standards, some argue that the REAL ID Act fails to institute a national identification card system in that the issuance of the cards and the maintenance of the databases remain in state hands. Many others are equally opposed, but on the grounds that a national identification card should not be developed because of privacy and civil liberty concerns relating to the sharing of personal data between government agencies. Although there was opposition from the states after it was enacted in 2005, 41 states, the District of Columbia and three territories have since embraced the implementation rule.

On March 2, 2007, the previously mandated state compliance deadline of May 11, 2008, was extended until December 31, 2009. On January 11, 2008, the U.S. Department of Homeland Security issued a final rule establishing the minimum-security standards for state-issued identification cards.[41] The new standards purportedly enhance the card's integrity and reliability, strengthen issuance capabilities, increase security at card-production facilities and reduce state implementation costs.[42] If the act is implemented as currently written, a federal agency will only accept a valid driver's license or identification card issued by a state that is in compliance with all requirements of the REAL ID Act. States will be permitted to issue noncomplying licenses and identification cards, providing that the card clearly indicates that it cannot be used for federal identification purposes. Subsequently, the Secretary of the U.S. Department of Homeland Security extended the mandated state compliance deadlines twice, from December 31, 2009 to May 2011, and from May 2011 to January 2013.

2.9 The Cable Communications Policy Act of 1984

The Cable Communications Policy Act of 1984 (CCPA) codified provisions in federal statutes to require cable TV operators to obtain consent from the customer and provide notice, choice, access and redress to customers prior to releasing personal data about the consumer, except for instances where they are conducting legitimate business activity related to cable services or another service provided by the cable operator.[43] Personal information may also be released subject to a court order. Cable operators are required to properly destroy any personal information that is no longer needed. Finally, the act allows consumers to seek redress via a civil court for violations of these provisions.

The act provides for disclosure of cable subscriber data to a government entity with a court order that is justified by "clear and convincing evidence" that the subscriber is "reasonably suspected of engaging in criminal activity, and that the information sought would be material evidence in the case."[44] The subscriber must be given the opportunity to appear and contest the government entity's claims.

In 1992, CCPA was amended to include a customer privacy section stating that aggregated data that does not identify particular persons is not considered PII.

3. Conclusion

These laws cover various sectors of businesses within the United States and in cases where collection of data is required in order to operate sensitive programs such as health insurance or banking place additional protections for the consumer and provide transparency. Some of these statutes are aimed at combatting fraud and terrorism, which can be perceived as anti-private in that the collection and disclosure of the data is not made known to the subject.

The ongoing debate in the United States over anti-privacy laws likely will continue. Those opposed to such laws suggest that the government is infringing upon the privacy rights of citizens. They argue that such laws and regulations not only prevent these individuals from remaining anonymous, but potentially could harm them if personal information is misused or inadequately protected.

The government, on the other hand, cites the increased necessity to use personal information to detect, protect against, and deter increasing threats of crime and terrorism. Thus, any anti-privacy law or policy should delicately balance the threat to one's privacy against any benefit that might be derived from the collection and use of personal information.

Endnotes

1   Public Law 104–191.

2   U.S. Department of Health & Human Services, *Restrictions on Government Access to Health Information*, http://www.hhs.gov/ocr/privacy/hipaa/understanding/coveredentities/govtaccess.html.

3   PHI is defined as "Individually identifiable health information that is transmitted by electronic media, maintained in electronic media, or transmitted or maintained in any other form or medium. PHI excludes individually identifiable health information in: (i) education records covered by the

Family Education Rights and Privacy Act, as amended, 20 U.S.C. § 1232(g); (ii) records described at 20 U.S.C. § 1232g(a)(4)(B)(iv); and (iii) employment records held by a covered entity in its role as employer," www.hhs.gov/ocr/privacy/hipaa/administrative/securityrule/securityrulepdf.pdf, p. 42.

4   www.hhs.gov/ocr/privacy/hipaa/administrative/securityrule/securityrulepdf.pdf, p. 14.

5   20 U.S.C. § 1232g.

6   Department of Health and Human Services, *Breach Notification for Unsecured Protected Health Information,* www.gpo.gov/fdsys/pkg/FR-2009-08-24/pdf/E9-20169.pdf; *Interim Final Rule,* 45 CFR Parts 160 and 164, August 24, 2009.

7   OMB Memorandum M-07-16, "Safeguarding Against and Responding to the Breach of Personally Identifiable Information," May 22, 2007, www.whitehouse.gov/sites/default/files/omb/memoranda/fy2007/m07-16.pdf.

8   Department of Health and Human Services, *Guidance Specifying the Technologies and Methodologies That Render Protected Health Information Unusable, Unreadable, or Indecipherable to Unauthorized Individuals for Purposes of the Breach Notification Requirements under Section 13402 of Title XIII (Health Information Technology for Economic and Clinical Health Act) of the American Recovery and Reinvestment Act of 2009,* www.nacua.org/documents/HHSGuidance_SpecifyingTechnologiesMethodologiesRenderPHIUnusable.pdf; *Request for Information,* 45 CFR Parts 160 and 164, April 17, 2009.

9   15 U.S.C. §§ 6501-6508.

10 16 CFR 312.

11 Verifiable parental consent is defined in COPPA as "any reasonable effort (taking into consideration available technology), including a request for authorization for future collection, use, and disclosure described in the notice, to ensure that a parent of a child receives notice of the operator's personal information collection, use, and disclosure practices, and authorizes the collection, use, and disclosure, as applicable, of personal information and the subsequent use of that information before that information is collected from that child." 15 U.S.C. § 6501(9).

12 16 CFR 312.5(b)(2).

13 Federal Trade Commission, *FTC Seeks Comment on Proposed Revisions to Children's Online Privacy Protection Rule,* (September 15, 2011), www.ftc.gov/opa/2011/09/coppa.shtm.

14 15 U.S.C. §§ 6801-09.

15 12 U.S.C. § 1843(k).

16 Federal Trade Commission, *Federal Regulators Issue Final Model Privacy Notice Form,* (Nov. 17, 2009), http://www.ftc.gov/opa/2009/11/glb.shtm.

17 15 U.S.C. § 6821-27.

18 Consumer Financial Protection Bureau, *Learn About the Bureau,* http://www.consumerfinance.gov/the-bureau/.

19 20 U.S.C. § 1232g; 34 CFR Part 99.

20 U.S. Department of Education, Family Educational Rights and Privacy Act, http://www2.ed.gov/policy/gen/guid/fpco/ferpa/index.html.

21 *Id.*

22 *Id.*

23 Federal Trade Commission, *Fighting Fraud with the Red Flags Rule,* www.ftc.gov/bcp/edu/microsites/redflagsrule/index.shtml.

24 www.federalreserve.gov/newsevents/press/bcreg/bcreg20090611a1.pdf.

25 Federal Trade Commission, *Fighting Fraud with the Red Flags Rule,* www.ftc.gov/bcp/edu/microsites/redflagsrule/index.shtml.

26 See 50 U.S.C. §§ 1801-1811, 1821-29, 1841-46, and 1861-62.

27 A U.S. person includes citizens, lawfully admitted permanent resident aliens and corporations incorporated in the United States.

28 See 50 U.S.C. § 1801(f).

29 See *Amendments to the Foreign Intelligence Surveillance Act,* www.fas.org/sgp/crs/intel/m071906.pdf.

30 Protect America Act of 2007, Public Law 110-55.

31 Right to Financial Privacy Act, 12 U.S.C. § 3401 et seq.

32 The Electronic Communications Privacy Act of 1986, Public Law 99-508, Oct. 21, 1986, 100 Stat.1848, 18 U.S.C. § 2510.

33 See 18 U.S.C. § 3127(3): A "pen register" is a device or process that records or decodes dialing, routing, addressing or signaling information transmitted by an instrument or facility from which a wire or electronic communication is transmitted but does not include the contents of the communication itself.

34 See 18 U.S.C. §3127(4): A "trap and trace device" is a device or process that captures the incoming electronic or other impulses identifying the originating number or other dialing, routing, addressing and signaling information reasonably likely to identify the source of a wire or electronic communication, provided that the information does not include the contents of the communication itself.

35 See *Federal Court Strikes Down National Security Letter Provision of Patriot Act,* (Sept. 6, 2007), www.aclu.org/safefree/nationalsecurityletters/31580prs20070906.html.

36 *Uniting and Strengthening America by Providing Appropriate Tools Required to Intercept and Obstruct Terrorism Act of 2001,* Public Law 107-56 (2001).

37 *Patriot Act Draws Privacy Concerns,* CNET News.com (Oct. 26, 2001), "The Center for Constitutional Rights: The USA PATRIOT Act—What's So Patriotic About Trampling on the Bill of Rights?", (Nov. 2001) "FBI Bypasses the First Amendment to Nail a Hacker," *The Register* (Sept. 29, 2003); "Senate Republicans Warn That Patriot Act Will Not Be Renewed Unless Changes are Made," *San Francisco Chronicle* (Oct. 14, 2003); "Patriot Act Has Ashcroft Under Fire," *Atlanta Journal-Constitution* (Oct. 19, 2003).

38 www.abanet.org/natsecurity/patriotdebates/213-2#opening.

39 "'Trust me' just doesn't fly", News, *USA Today,* (April 12, 2005.) Anastasia Steranko, "PATRIOT Act inspires discussion of civil liberties", *The Pitt News,* (Sept. 19, 2003).

40 The Real ID Act of 2005, Public Law 109-13, is part of a larger act of the U.S. Congress titled Emergency Supplemental Appropriations Act for Defense, the Global War on Terror, and Tsunami Relief, 2005.

41 See www.uscis.gov/ilink/docView/FR/HTML/FR/0-0-0-1/0-0-0-145991/0-0-0-165820/0-0-0-176819.html.

42 See "DHS Releases REAL ID Regulation," (Jan. 11, 2008.), www.govtech.com/security/DHS-Releases-REAL-ID-Regulation.html.

43 47 U.S.C. 551.

44 47 U.S.C. 551(h)(1) and (2).

CHAPTER SIX

Privacy Program Development and Organization

Changes in information technology, as well as in the collection and use of growing amounts of data, have created a complex privacy landscape for both the private and public sectors. The government possession of data is often required in order to operate and manage programs such as Social Security, Medicare, veterans' benefits and tax collection. In many instances, individuals do not have a choice in providing data—they must do so if they want to receive certain types of government benefits or services.[1]

Amid growing use of technology and data for a multitude of missions and programs, and a rise in the number of data breaches in the past decade, federal agencies have been required to place more emphasis on privacy protection. This includes an intensified focus on adherence to various privacy-related statutes, such as the Privacy Act of 1974 and E-Government Act of 2002 (Section 208), as well as new and existing policies, such as presidential directives and Office of Management and Budget (OMB) guidance and memoranda.

This chapter provides an overview about the crucial elements required to develop an agency privacy program and privacy policy. It also highlights some of the mature federal agencies' privacy programs and best practices to assist new government privacy professionals.

1. Program Development

Revised by Roanne R. Shaddox, CIPP/US, CIPP/G

In the past decade, U.S. government agencies have faced an increasing number of legal and regulatory privacy requirements. Between 2003 and 2008, the OMB issued a record number of privacy-related memorandums due to the passage of the E-Government Act and a growing number of agency data breaches. (Among those breaches was the 2006 theft of a U.S. Department of Veterans Affairs laptop containing 26.5 million sensitive records.) These memorandums reinforced existing privacy and security protection requirements

The original text for this chapter was developed by Julie S. McEwen, CIPP/US, CIPP/G, CIPP/IT. New content for this revised edition was contributed by Roanne R. Shaddox, CIPP/US, CIPP/G, Deborah Kendall, CIPP/US, CIPP/G and Claire Barrett, CIPP/US, CIPP/G, CIPP/IT.

outlined in previous OMB memorandums and guidance, but also created new mandates. A key new mandate, included in OMB Memorandum M-05-08 required the head of each federal agency to appoint a senior agency official for privacy (SAOP). The SAOP reports to the head of the organization and is responsible for overseeing all privacy matters, including the development, implementation and enforcement of privacy policies. The SAOP requirement was a critical step in the evolution of agency privacy programs across the federal government during the 2000s, combined with new privacy program reporting requirements (discussed later in this chapter).

The decision about where to place the SAOP's responsibilities is often driven by the agency's mission and resources. Due to existing responsibilities for information resource management, the OMB permitted the appointment of the chief information officer (CIO) as the SAOP.[2] Many agencies have adopted this approach, while others have opted to place the SAOP responsibilities under the purview of the legal department (due to existing Freedom of Information Act [FOIA] and Privacy Act responsibilities) or under administration (due to existing records management responsibilities). For some agencies, there also may be a legislative requirement to appoint a chief privacy officer (CPO) to develop and manage department-wide privacy programs. This is the case with the Department of Homeland Security (DHS) and the Department of Justice, each of which has a distinct legislative mandate. In addition, the departments of Transportation and Treasury (and related agencies) are required to appoint a CPO to oversee agency-wide privacy programs under Section 522 of the 2005 Consolidated Appropriations Act.[3] For smaller agencies, one individual, such as the CIO, may serve both as the SAOP and the CPO. In larger agencies, the roles are usually separate, with the CPO either directly reporting to the SAOP or coordinating with the SAOP in the execution of the privacy protection responsibilities.

1.1 Federal CIO Council Privacy Committee "Best Practices" White Paper

To assist federal agencies in their efforts to develop and manage privacy programs, the federal CIO Council Privacy Committee issued a white paper in 2010 titled, "Best Practices: Elements of a Federal Agency Privacy Program,"[4] ("the Elements Paper"). The committee is an interagency coordinating body; its members are federal agency SAOPs and CPOs who issue white papers on a wide range of topics and provide expertise to the CIO Council and the OMB on numerous initiatives.

The Elements Paper identifies seven fundamental building blocks of a robust privacy program, summarized as follows:

Element 1: *Leadership:* Designation of a senior-level official as the SAOP/CPO who is accountable for overseeing the implementation of a robust privacy program

Element 2: *Privacy Risk Management and Compliance Documentation:* Identifying privacy risk in business processes and information technology

(IT) systems and documenting compliance with privacy protection laws, regulations and policies

Element 3: *Information Security:* Protecting PII that is collected, used, shared, retained, disclosed or destroyed through appropriative administrative, technical and physical safeguards

Element 4: *Incident Response:* Establishing a robust plan for managing potential or actual breaches of PII

Element 5: *Notice and Redress for Individuals:* Providing clear notice to the public and having mechanisms for individual participation to ensure access, correction and redress regarding PII use

Element 6: *Privacy Training and Awareness:* Providing comprehensive and job-specific training for employees and contractors about the appropriate handing of PII in accordance with policies and procedures

Element 7: *Accountability:* Ensuring compliance with all applicable privacy protection requirements and the successful execution of Elements 1–6, as well as performing internal and external assessments and audits of PII protection activities and conducting reporting to senior management and the OMB

Many agencies use the Elements Paper to benchmark the maturity of their privacy programs, create or update policies and procedures, and assess program and resource needs.

1.2 Draft Appendix J: Privacy Control Catalog

Also in 2010, the CIO Council Privacy Committee undertook a landmark initiative with the National Institute of Standards and Technology (NIST) to create a set of measurable and enforceable federal privacy standards to complement existing IT security standards. These standards are detailed in NIST Special Publication 800-53, Security Controls for Federal Information Systems and Organizations, Revision 3.[5] The effort was driven by the need for a unified approach to identifying and addressing privacy and security requirements among the wide range of internal and external agency activities involving PII, including cloud computing and social media. The appendix recognizes that in today's digital world, federal organizations "cannot have effective privacy without a foundation of information security" and adds that privacy "is a value distinct from, but highly interrelated with, information security."

After nearly two years of drafting, reviewing, and gathering input from the federal privacy community and NIST, the first draft of a new appendix of privacy controls for Special Publication 800-53 was released for public comment in July 2011.[6] This draft document, Appendix J: Privacy Controls Catalogue[7] (hereinafter Appendix J), includes eight privacy-control families based on the Fair Information Practice Principles (FIPPs) and embodied in the Privacy Act, the E-Government Act (Section 208) and related OMB guidance: Authority and Purpose; Accountability, Audit and Risk Management;

Data Quality and Integrity; Data Minimization and Retention; Individual Participation and Redress; Security; Transparency; and Use Limitation. Each control family includes best practices for protecting PII as well as a set of controls that reflects the wide range of SAOP/CPO responsibilities. The privacy control families complement the detailed security controls in NIST SP 800-53 Appendix F.

The new privacy controls are designed to be implemented at the organization, department, agency, component, office, program or information-system level under the leadership of the SAOP/CPO. Coordination with other key stakeholders, including an agency's CIO, chief information security officer (CISO), legal counsel, records managers, and program officials, is essential to the control framework described in Appendix J.

In February 2012, NIST issued a second draft of Appendix J for public comment, along with the first public draft of Special Publication 800-53, Security and Privacy Controls for Federal Information Systems and Organizations, Revision 4. At press time, the final versions of NIST 800-53, Revision 4 and Appendix J were pending. However, the OMB has stated in its most recent Federal Information Security Management Act of 2002 (FISMA) reporting guidance for the 2012 fiscal year that "upon final publication of NIST SP 800-53, agencies will be expected to implement the privacy controls in Appendix J to satisfy requirements in the Privacy Act of 1974 and any privacy-related policies published by OMB."[8] Although federal agencies are already responsible for implementing most of the standards embodied in the proposed privacy controls, ultimately they will need to analyze and apply the controls in a manner consistent with their distinct authorities, missions and operational needs. In the future, NIST, working with the Federal Privacy Committee, plans to develop metrics and procedures for assessing compliance with the Appendix J controls.

2. NIST Risk Management Framework

Roanne R. Shaddox, CIPP/US, CIPP/G

NIST is an agency within the Department of Commerce. NIST has the lead responsibility for the development and issuance of security standards and guidelines for the federal government, contractors, and the United States critical information infrastructure.

The NIST has published a series of publications in support of its risk management framework (RMF). The RMF is a multi-tiered and structured methodology for creating a unified information security framework for the federal government in order to meet the vast array of requirements set forth in FISMA.

Information security is a key privacy principal and the success of government privacy programs depends on strong information security programs. Due to the focus on implementing the requirements of FISMA, to date, the various NIST RMF publications have not addressed in any depth the other key principals of privacy (such as notice or choice). The exception is the current NIST SP 800-53 (Revision 3) (described below) that contains one control requiring a privacy impact assessment (PIA). However, this is changing with the addition of the proposed Appendix J privacy controls to the draft NIST 800-53 (Revision 4) that clearly recognizes the need for agencies to address both security and privacy in a more holistic and robust manner.

This section highlights certain NIST publications that government privacy professionals should be aware of during the course of managing a privacy program. While the IT security staff primarily is responsible for the implementation of the requirements or guidance outlined in the current NIST publications, the privacy program staff does have an important role in several aspects of the agency's IT security risk management efforts. For example, the privacy program has lead responsibility for addressing the PIA control in the current NIST SP 800-53 (Revision 3) and for identifying and communicating to the IT staff the agency's IT systems containing PII (particularly sensitive PII), so that the systems can be appropriately categorized and controlled in accord with the publications described below. To support this effort, the privacy program needs to maintain an up-to-date inventory of all agency IT systems that collect and use PII (based upon PIAs and other types of privacy reviews) and must be prepared to respond to questions about the nature (for example, public or employee) and sensitivity of the PII maintained in such systems. In addition, the privacy program typically has lead responsibility for responding to data breaches involving PII that is discussed in NIST SP 800-122 below.

Note: the privacy program will have lead responsibility for implementing the pending Appendix J privacy controls once the publication becomes final.

2.1 Federal Information Processing Standards (FIPS) Publication 199, "Standards for Security Categorization of Federal Information and Information Systems"

Deborah Kendall, CIPP/US, CIPP/G

FISMA required NIST to develop and publish standards and guidelines for information security for the federal government, including "standards to be used by all federal agencies to categorize all information and information systems collected or maintained by or on behalf of each federal agency based on the objectives of providing appropriate levels of information security according to a range of risk levels." These security categorization standards provide a common framework for the federal government to provide better management, oversight and coordination of information security across all sectors of government, as well as consistent reporting to Congress and the OMB on the effectiveness and adequacy of information security policies and practices. This publication requires agencies to categorize their IT systems as low impact, moderate impact or high impact for the security objectives of confidentiality, integrity and availability. The publication offers the following definitions for those terms: "A loss of confidentiality is the unauthorized disclosure of information . . . A loss of integrity is the unauthorized modification or destruction of information . . . A loss of availability is the disruption of access or use of information or an information system."

2.2 FIPS Publication 200, "Minimum Security Requirements for Federal Information and Information Systems"

Deborah Kendall, CIPP/US, CIPP/G

This publication is the second of the mandatory security requirements by FISMA that specifies the minimum standards agencies must implement to protect government information systems or information. It provides a risk-based process for selecting security controls needed for minimum-security requirements, covering 17 security-related areas that protect the confidentiality, integrity and availability of federal IT systems and information.[9] Those areas are:

- Access control
- Awareness and training
- Audit and accountability
- Certification, accreditation, and security assessments
- Configuration management
- Contingency planning
- Identification and authentication
- Incident response
- Maintenance
- Media protection
- Physical and environmental protection
- Planning
- Personnel security
- Risk assessment
- Systems and services acquisition
- System and communications protection
- System and information integrity

One additional Information Security Program Management family in Appendix G of NIST SP 800-53 provides baseline controls for an organization-wide information security program. Although this family is not referenced in FIPS 200, it provides baseline security controls at the organizational level independent of any particular system.

Federal agencies must select the appropriate level of security controls based on the impact levels for information systems. Thus, organizations with low-impact systems must implement and use security controls from the low baseline of security controls defined in NIST Special Publication 800-53. Moderate-impact systems must, at a minimum, use appropriate controls from the moderate baseline of security controls, and so on.

2.3 NIST SP 800-122, "Guide to the Protecting the Confidentiality of Personally Identifiable Information"

Deborah Kendall, CIPP/US, CIPP/G

This publication was issued in April 2010, after a number of large public and private data breaches resulted in the loss of millions of records involving PII. Data breaches involving PII are detrimental to organizations, leading to public distrust, possible legal liabilities, and high costs of remediation, such as the costs of notifying the affected individuals and offering and providing credit monitoring. Thus, NIST recommends that organizations take a risk-based approach to protecting the confidentiality of PII. Federal agencies should conduct PII inventories and minimize the collection and retention of PII to only what is strictly necessary to accomplish their mission and business purposes. Subsequently, an agency should conduct periodic reviews of its PII holdings to determine if the data is still necessary and relevant to its programs and mission.

Because agencies categorize PII by the confidentiality impact-level factors (i.e., low, moderate and high), this publication lists potential issues an agency should consider when determining the impact level of each system. Those factors include identifiability, quantity of PII, data file sensitivity, context of use, obligations to protect confidentiality and the access to and location of PII. To ward off the misuse of data, agencies should:

- Create policies, procedures and controls for protecting the confidentiality based on the factors they adopt
- Conduct training for personnel who have access to PII; de-identify PII whenever possible; implement access control for systems and mobile devices; and provide transmission confidentiality, such as the encryption of data while in transit and auditing events
- Develop an incident response plan for data breaches, especially those involving PII
- Encourage a coordinated working relationship among CPOs, CIOs, CISOs and legal counsel when addressing issues related to collection, use, storage and handling of PII

2.4 NIST SP 800-53, "Recommended Security Controls for Federal Information Systems and Organizations"

Deborah Kendall, CIPP/US, CIPP/G

This publication provides guidelines for selecting and specifying security controls for systems that are developed and used by federal agencies to meet the requirements of FIPS 200, "Minimum Security Requirements for Federal Information and Information Systems." The guidelines apply to all parts of an information system that process, store, or transmit federal government information. These guidelines were developed to assist in obtaining more secure information systems and effective risk-based management within the federal sector. The guidelines provide a more consistent and repeatable approach for identifying and specifying security controls for IT systems. They set up minimum security control standards in accordance with FIPS 199, "Standards for Security Categorization of Federal Information and Information Systems;" provide a stable and flexible list of security controls to meet organizational protection needs as well as future protection needs based on changing technologies and requirements; create a baseline for development of metrics for determining security control effectiveness; and improve communication among organizations by providing common terminology for the implementation of risk management.

Within the management controls section of SP 800-53, NIST sets forth procedures for security assessment and authorization (SA&A).[10] A security assessment evaluates security controls within an information system, reporting on their implementation, operation, and results.[11] In addition, security authorization requires that an authorizing official—a designated senior-level executive or manager—authorizes the information system before it is used, and updates this authorization at least every three years or whenever there is a significant change to the system.[12] An SA&A has several similar elements to a PIA. Both procedures are risk-based analyses that identify potential risks as well as mitigation measures, and are updated as the system environment changes. Notable differences between an SA&A and a PIA are noted in Table 6.1.

Table 6.1: Differences between SA&A and PIA

SA&A	PIA
Security focused	Privacy focused
Information system focused	Information focused
User access/privileges minimized	User receipt of information minimized
Authorizing official must authorize system	No authorization equivalent
Report provided to the authorizing official	Report provided to the public
Periodic reauthorization required if system changes, or at least every three years	No reassessment required, as long as no changes have occurred

As previously stated, NIST SP 800-53 is being revised to include, among other things, the new proposed Appendix J Privacy Controls.

2.5 NIST SP 800-64, "Security Considerations in the System Development Life Cycle"

This publication assists federal agencies in integrating essential IT security steps into their established system development life cycle (SDLC) in the early stages. It should be viewed as a reference document in conjunction with other pertinent NIST publications rather than as a tutorial. It provides descriptions of the key security roles and responsibilities for most information system developments as well as information for those unfamiliar with the SDLC to help them understand the relationship between security controls and the SDLC. This publication provides a five-step SDLC as an example of one method of development, but it is not mandatory. Finally, the document also addresses IT projects that do not fit the traditional SDLC, such as service organization architectures, cross-organizational projects and IT facility development. The privacy program can assist the agency's SDLC efforts by integrating key privacy requirements, such as the need to conduct PIAs and publish Privacy Act system of records notices, when warranted.

3. Program Management

Revised by Roanne R. Shaddox, CIPP/US, CIPP/G

3.1 OMB Circular No. A-130, Appendix I

Appendix I to OMB's Circular A-130, "Federal Agency Responsibilities for Maintaining Records About Individuals," describes requirements for all federal agencies under the Privacy Act. It also details specific requirements for the Department of Commerce, the Office of Personnel Management (OPM), the National Archives and Records Administration (NARA), and the OMB itself.[13]

3.1.1 All Agencies

Importantly, Circular A-130 contains, among other things, requirements for developing and publishing Privacy Act system of records notices (SORNs) and for conducting mandatory reviews. Agencies are required to report on the outcome of the following reviews to the OMB via the annual FISMA/SAOP Report:

- Section M Contracts: Every two years, review a random sample of agency contracts that provide for the maintenance of a system of records on behalf of the agency to accomplish an agency function, in order to ensure that the wording of each contract makes the provisions of the Privacy Act binding on the contractor and his or her employees.

- Recordkeeping Practices: Every two years, review agency recordkeeping and disposal policies and practices in order to assure compliance with the Privacy Act, paying particular attention to the maintenance of automated records.

- Routine Use Disclosures: Every four years, review the routine use disclosures associated with each system of records in order to ensure that the recipient's use of such records continues to be compatible with the purpose for which the disclosing agency collected the information.

- Exemption of Systems of Records: Every four years, review each system of records for which the agency has promulgated exemption rules pursuant to the Privacy Act in order to determine whether such exemption is still needed.

- Matching Programs: Every year, review each ongoing matching program in which the agency has participated during the year in order to ensure that the requirements of the Privacy Act and OMB guidance have been met, along with any agency regulations, operating instructions, or guidelines.

- Privacy Act Training: Every two years, review agency training practices in order to ensure that all agency personnel are familiar with the requirements of the Privacy Act, the agency's implementing regulation, and any special requirements of their specific jobs.

- Violations: Every two years, review the actions of agency personnel that have resulted either in the agency being found civilly liable under the Privacy Act, or an employee being found criminally liable under the Privacy Act, in order to determine the extent of the problem and find the most effective way to prevent recurrence.

- SORNs: Every two years, review each system of records notice to ensure it accurately describes the system of records. Where minor changes are needed, (such as the name of the system manager) ensure that an amended notice is published in the *Federal Register*.

3.1.2 Department of Commerce
- Develop and issue standards and guidelines for ensuring the security of information protected by the Privacy Act in automated information systems

3.1.3 OPM
- Develop and maintain government-wide standards and procedures for civilian personnel information processing and recordkeeping directives to assure conformance with the Privacy Act
- Develop and conduct Privacy Act training programs for agency personnel, including both the conduct of courses in various substantive areas and the development of materials that agencies can use in their own courses

3.1.4 NARA

- Issue instructions on the format of the agency notices and rules that are required to be published under the Privacy Act.

- Compile and publish the rules and agency notices published under the Privacy Act in a form available to the public at low cost, every two years.

- Issue procedures governing the transfer of records to federal records centers for storage, processing, and servicing. For purposes of the Privacy Act, such records are considered to be maintained by the agency that deposited them. The archivist may disclose deposited records only according to the access rules established by the agency that deposited them.

3.1.5 The OMB

- Issue guidelines and directives to the agencies to implement the Privacy Act

- Assist the agencies, at their request, in implementing their Privacy Act programs

- Review new and altered systems of records and matching program reports submitted pursuant to the Privacy Act

- Compile the biennial report of the president to Congress in accordance with the Privacy Act

- Compile and issue a biennial report on the agencies' implementation of the computer matching provisions of the Privacy Act[14]

3.2 The Federal Enterprise Security and Privacy Profile (FEA-SPP)

In 2009, the Federal CIO Council Privacy Committee began developing new privacy sections for the Federal Enterprise Security and Privacy Profile (Version 3.0), which was later published in 2010. The FEA-SPP presents a methodology and roadmap for addressing the essential privacy and information security requirements of a federal organization's enterprise architecture. "The FEA-SPP is voluntary guidance applicable to any federal government agency. Instead of setting specific technical requirements, it provides best practices and recommendations to promote the successful incorporation of security and privacy into a government organization's enterprise architecture and to ensure appropriate consideration of security and privacy requirements in agencies' strategic planning and investment decision processes."[15]

As the FEA-SPP is intended for audiences that may not be familiar with federal agency privacy requirements, the document contains a description of "privacy fundamentals" to help foster an understanding of the key laws, regulations and policies that govern an agency's collection, maintenance, use and dissemination of PII (such as the Privacy Act, E-Government Act and related OMB guidance). Importantly, the document also contains a set of privacy control families based on FIPPs. Appendix F of the document provides a detailed description and explanation about how agencies can apply the privacy control families to assist their privacy compliance efforts. By integrating the privacy profile into the FEA-SPP, the goal is that an even broader range of federal agency officials and staff will be able to incorporate privacy considerations during the critical early stages of developing or updating federal information technology systems. Information from the FEA-SPP (Version 3.0) subsequently was used by the Privacy Committee to inform its work on the development of the draft NIST Appendix J: Privacy Control Catalogue.

3.3 Annual FISMA SAOP Report

In order to ensure that agencies are properly managing their privacy programs in accordance with the broad range of existing privacy requirements, the OMB requires the agency SAOP to submit an annual report as part of its annual FISMA reporting. Previously, the OMB issued annual reporting instructions (for example, M-11-33: "Fiscal Year (FY) 2011 Reporting Instructions for the Federal Information Security Management Act and Agency Privacy Management").[16] In 2012, the DHS undertook this responsibility as part of its overall leadership role on cyber security. In January 2012, the DHS released a set of reporting metrics, "FY 2012 Senior Agency Official for Privacy Federal Information Security Management Act Reporting Metrics."

In past years, reporting was completed by answering questions in a template that was sent to the OMB; however, today agencies are required to submit their FISMA report (including the SAOP Report) via an electronic system of reporting called CyberScope. Examples of the 10 privacy program metrics agencies must report on include:[17]

- Number of federal systems that contain personal information in an identifiable form
- Links to PIAs and SORNs on agency websites
- Documentation of the SAOP's fulfillment of responsibilities
- Privacy training programs and policies
- Categorization of written privacy complaints
- Documentation of privacy policy compliance reviews
- Agency use of persistent tracking technology

4. Federal Agency Privacy Policies and Procedures

Revised by Roanne R. Shaddox, CIPP/US, CIPP/G

U.S. government agencies and departments issue privacy policies and guidelines of their own to ensure the wide range of privacy protection obligations are met. These policies and guidelines vary widely in content and format (such as manuals and memoranda) and reflect the distinct missions and operations of the government organizations to which they apply. Some differences among privacy policies and procedures also reflect privacy provisions within legislation that apply to their specific agency.[18]

The SAOP or CPO often issues privacy policy at the departmental level in consultation with other officials in the organization, such as the CIO, CISO and legal counsel.[19] Privacy policy can apply broadly to a government agency, or it can be issued for specific programs or organizations within a government agency. General mission statements for government organizations sometimes refer to privacy, emphasizing the importance of privacy protection for the entire organization or a particular program within the agency. Guidance documents can be general or combined with templates to standardize reporting across a particular department or program.

The following are examples of privacy policies and guidance from federal departments and subordinate organizations, including foundational privacy principles and privacy mission statements, privacy policy and guidance for completing PIAs.

4.1 Foundational Privacy Principles and Privacy Mission Statements

An organization's privacy principles and privacy mission statement are aligned with that organization's particular mission. A number of government organizations have documented privacy principles. Examples of privacy principles from the Internal Revenue Service (IRS), the Census Bureau and the Department of Homeland Security (DHS).

4.1.1 IRS

The IRS's mission is to "provide America's taxpayers top quality service by helping them understand and meet their tax responsibilities and by applying the tax law with integrity and fairness to all."[20]

Given the IRS's function, it is critical to have the public's trust, and it is no surprise that the IRS was one of the first U.S. government organizations to publish its list of privacy principles. These principles establish how the IRS will conduct its business to ensure that taxpayers' privacy is protected.[21] The wording used in many of the principles flows directly from the requirements in the Privacy Act. The IRS privacy principles are:[22]

A. *Protecting taxpayer privacy and safeguarding confidential taxpayer information is a public trust.*

B. *No information will be collected or used with respect to taxpayers that is not necessary and relevant for tax administration and other legally mandated or authorized purposes.*

C. *Information will be collected, to the greatest extent practicable, directly from the taxpayer to whom it relates.*

D. *Information about taxpayers collected from third parties will be verified to the extent practicable, with the taxpayers themselves, before a determination is made, using the information.*

E. *Personally identifiable taxpayer information will be used only for the purpose for which it was collected, unless other uses are specifically authorized or mandated by law.*

F. *Personally identifiable taxpayer information will be disposed of at the end of the retention period required by law or regulation.*

G. *Taxpayer information will be kept confidential and will not be discussed with, nor disclosed to, any person within or outside the IRS, other than as authorized by law in the performance of official duty.*

H. *Browsing, or any unauthorized access of taxpayer information by any IRS employee, constitutes a serious breach of the confidentiality of that information and will not be tolerated.*

I. *Requirements governing the accuracy, reliability, completeness, and timeliness of taxpayer information will be such as to ensure fair treatment of all taxpayers.*

J. *The privacy rights of taxpayers will be respected at all times and every taxpayer will be treated honestly, fairly and respectfully.*

4.1.2 Census Bureau

The Census Bureau collects data to meet the nation's statistical needs. Because the data that the Census Bureau collects is often highly personal in nature and the Census Bureau depends on the trust of the individuals and businesses that supply the data, privacy protection is a high priority for the Census Bureau. Privacy is even mentioned in the Census Bureau's mission statement:[23]

> *The Census Bureau serves as the leading source of quality data about the nation's people and economy. We honor privacy, protect confidentiality, share our expertise globally, and conduct our work openly. We are guided on this mission by our strong and capable workforce, our readiness to innovate, and our abiding commitment to our customers.*

The Census Bureau emphasizes that the privacy principles serve as a reminder of its promise to protect the confidentiality of the information collected. The Census Bureau used a combination of the Organisation for Economic Co-operation and Development (OECD) privacy principles and the Fair Information Practices (FIPs) in the Privacy Act (both addressed in Chapter 1) as a starting point for creating the Census Bureau privacy principles, and has adapted them to align the privacy principles with the its mission. An introduction to the Census Bureau privacy principles and the principles themselves are:[24]

> *We depend on your cooperation and trust, and we promise to protect the confidentiality of your information. The Census Bureau's Privacy Principles remind us of this promise and help ensure the protection of your information throughout all of our activities.*
>
> *The Privacy Principles are our guidelines. They help us as we design surveys to consider respondents' rights and concerns. Every principle embodies a promise to you, the respondent.*
>
> - **Necessity:** *Do we need to ask this question? Do we need to collect this information? Every time we prepare to ask a question, we determine whether the information is truly necessary. All of the information we collect is used for federal programs.*
>   - *We promise to collect only information necessary for each survey and census.*
>   - *We promise that we will use the information only to produce timely, relevant statistics about the population and the economy of the United States.*
> - **Openness:** *Do you know why we are collecting your information?*
>   - *We collect information only for statistical purposes, and it is never used to identify individuals. Before participating, you have the right to know why we are conducting the survey or census, why we are asking specific questions, and the purposes for which the information will be used.*
>   - *We promise to inform you about the purpose and uses for every survey or census we conduct before you provide your answers to us.*
> - **Respectful Treatment of Respondents:** *Are our efforts reasonable and did we treat you with respect?*
>   - *We promise to minimize the effort and time it takes for you to participate in the data collection by efficient designs.*
>   - *We promise to use only legal, ethical and professionally accepted practices in collecting data.*

     – *We promise to ensure that any collection of sensitive information from children and other sensitive populations does not violate federal protections for research participants and is done only when it benefits the public good.*

- **Confidentiality:** *How do we protect your information? In addition to removing personally identifiable information, such as names, telephone numbers, and addresses, from our data files, we use various approaches to protect your personal information; including computer technologies, statistical methodologies, and security procedures.*

Our security measures ensure that only a restricted number of authorized people have access to private information and that access is only granted to conduct our work and for no other purposes. Every person who works with census confidential information collected by the Census Bureau is sworn for life to uphold the law.

Violating the confidentiality of a respondent is a federal crime with serious penalties, including a federal prison sentence of up to five years, a fine of up to $250,000, or both.

     – *We promise that every person with access to your information is sworn for life to protect your confidentiality.*

     – *We promise that we will use every technology, statistical methodology, and physical security procedure at our disposal to protect your information.*

4.1.3 DHS FIPPs
Claire Barrett, CIPP/US, CIPP/G, CIPP/IT

The DHS bears the distinction of being the first federal agency with a statutorily mandated privacy office charged with the responsibility of assuring that "personal information contained in Privacy Act systems of records is handled in full compliance with *fair information practices* as set out in the Privacy Act" (emphasis added). Accordingly, the DHS Privacy Office has established and implemented a set of FIPPs to review privacy when assessing and documenting the privacy implications of DHS activities, including a) assuring that the use of technologies sustains and does not erode privacy protections relating to the use, collection and disclosure of personal information; and b) assuring that personal information contained in the DHS Privacy Act systems of records is handled in full compliance with fair information practices as set out in the Privacy Act in accordance with Sections 222 (a)(1) and (a)(2) of the Homeland Security Act of 2002.

In 2008 the DHS Privacy Office issued a policy titled "The Fair Information Practice Principles: Framework for Privacy Policy at the Department of Homeland Security,"[25] formalizing the department's methodology for implementing the guiding principles of the Privacy Act, the E-Government Act and various OMB guidance.

Transparency: *DHS should be transparent and provide notice to the individual regarding its collection, use, dissemination, and maintenance of personally identifiable information (PII).*

Individual Participation: *DHS should involve the individual in the process of using PII and, to the extent practicable, seek individual consent for the collection, use, dissemination, and maintenance of PII. DHS should also provide mechanisms for appropriate access, correction, and redress regarding DHS's use of PII.*

Purpose Specification: *DHS should specifically articulate the authority that permits the collection of PII and specifically articulate the purpose or purposes for which the PII is intended to be used.*

Data Minimization: *DHS should only collect PII that is directly relevant and necessary to accomplish the specified purpose(s) and only retain PII for as long as is necessary to fulfill the specified purpose(s).*

Use Limitation: *DHS should use PII solely for the purpose(s) specified in the notice. Sharing PII outside the department should be for a purpose compatible with the purpose for which the PII was collected.*

Data Quality and Integrity: *DHS should, to the extent practicable, ensure that PII is accurate, relevant, timely, and complete.*

Security: *DHS should protect PII (in all media) through appropriate security safeguards against risks such as loss, unauthorized access or use, destruction, modification, or unintended or inappropriate disclosure.*

Accountability and Auditing: *DHS should be accountable for complying with these principles, providing training to all employees and contractors who use PII, and auditing the actual use of PII to demonstrate compliance with these principles and all applicable privacy protection requirements.*

The DHS FIPPs include eight principles that align with but do no replicate exactly the FIPPs as articulated by the OECD.

4.2 Privacy Policies

Privacy policies implement privacy principles and thereby reflect an organization's commitment to privacy protection. Examples of privacy policies in force today in the United States Postal Service (USPS), Department of Defense (DoD), and DHS are discussed below.

4.2.1 United States Postal Service

The USPS, an independent establishment of the executive branch of the U.S. government, has issued Handbook AS-353, Guide to Privacy and the Freedom of Information Act,[26] which describes the USPS policies and procedures for protecting the privacy of customers, employees and other individuals. The handbook emphasizes that the privacy and security of mail are core values of the USPS. In particular, it states that information from the contents or covers of any customer's mail may not be recorded, photocopied, filed or otherwise collected or disclosed within or outside the USPS, except for USPS operations and law enforcement purposes, as specified in 39 Code of Federal Regulations (CFR) 233.3.

In addition to describing privacy procedures and FOIA procedures, the handbook also contains sections that address the release and protection of USPS records, including general records management policy, records creation and designation guidelines, and high-level guidance on records retention, storage, retrieval and disposal. An appendix to the handbook contains the complete text of the SORNs.

The USPS implemented PIAs before they were required by statute and over time has developed an automated process to conduct PIAs, which has become an integral part of the Agency's Certification and Accreditation process. USPS Privacy and Information Security staff obtained a patent in 2011 for its PIA process, which is known within the agency as a Business Impact Assessment. The patent was awarded to the USPS for its innovative collaboration from the beginning of the technology lifecycle between the Privacy Office, business unit owners, and Information Security Office to identify PII in each new system and mitigate the risks of collecting and maintaining that data.

4.2.2 The DoD

The DoD reissued its Directive 5400.11, DoD Privacy Program, on May 8, 2007.[27] The document describes the general policies and responsibilities for DoD's privacy program, and authorizes publication of DoD Regulation 5400.11-R, Department of Defense Privacy Program, which contains the procedures that must be followed to implement the DoD privacy program.[28]

At least one branch of the U.S. military, the Air Force, also has issued its own privacy program document, Air Force Instruction (AFI) 33-332.[29] AFI 33-332 provides general guidance for operating the privacy program within the Air Force as well as instructions and a template for completing a PIA. The directive does not violate policy issued at a higher level but instead interprets higher-level policy as it pertains to Air Force operations.

The DoD also has issued DoD Directive OSD 12282-05, "Notifying Individuals When Personal Information is Lost, Stolen, or Compromised", to address the increasing threat of identity theft.[30] The directive states that when a DoD component becomes aware that protected personal information pertaining to a service member, civilian employee, military retiree or family member is disclosed, the component shall inform affected individuals as soon as possible but no later than 10 days after the disclosure of the personal information is discovered. OSD 12282-05 was issued in July 2005, before the OMB issued guidance on handling privacy incidents, and it is a good example of how government organizations sometimes issue their own policy to address developing threats in anticipation of issuance of OMB guidance.

4.2.3 The DHS

Previously in this chapter, there was an extended discussion of the DHS FIPPs. In addition to these principles, the DHS Privacy Office has issued a number of privacy policy and guidance documents.[31] Some of the policies come as action memoranda, such as the memorandum "Review of Safeguarding Policies and Procedures for Personnel-Related Data," which requires each DHS component to conduct a self-assessment of the handling of personnel-related data and to certify that personnel who handle such data have completed privacy and information security training.[32]

Policies issued in the form of guidance memoranda include Memorandum 2007-01, which regards the collection, use, retention and dissemination of information on non-U.S. persons (e.g., individuals who are not U.S. citizens or legal permanent residents).[33] In order to perform their functions, components within DHS, such as the Transportation Security Administration and U.S. Citizenship and Immigration Services, collect and use a large amount of information on non-U.S. persons.

Memorandum 2007-01 establishes the policy that DHS will handle non-U.S.-person PII that is held in systems containing data on both U.S. persons and non-U.S. persons in accordance with the FIPS in the Privacy Act. Because the Privacy Act applies only to U.S. citizens and legal permanent residents, DHS established the policy in Memorandum 2007-01 to standardize practices within DHS. The policy will help with advancing information sharing across borders to facilitate both travel and trade. It also will help to protect the privacy of U.S. persons overseas by treating non-U.S. persons in the same way that the United States would like to see its citizens treated when overseas.

DHS has issued a privacy policy for particular DHS programs, such as the US-VISIT Privacy Policy,[34] which provides answers to the following questions about the program's basic approach to privacy protection:

- What is the purpose of the US-VISIT program?
- Who is affected by the program?
- What information is collected?
- How is the information used?
- Who will have access to the information?
- How will the information be protected?
- How long is information retained?
- Who should one contact for more information about the US-VISIT program?

The section in the US-VISIT privacy policy addressing how information will be protected includes a discussion of the roles and responsibilities of DHS employees, system owners and managers, and third parties who manage or access information in the US-VISIT program.

4.3 Privacy Policy Enforcement

U.S. government agencies and departments have issued a number of privacy policies and guidelines in order to ensure their privacy protection obligations are met. These policies and guidelines vary widely in content and format, reflecting the distinct missions and operations of the government organizations to which they apply. Depending on these organizational characteristics, a single privacy policy may apply broadly to an entire government agency, or multiple policies may be issued for specific programs or organizations within a government agency. Some differences among privacy policies and procedures also reflect privacy provisions within legislation that apply to specific agencies. Agency privacy policy is often issued by the SAOP or CPO.

General mission statements for government organizations sometimes refer to privacy, emphasizing the importance of privacy protection for a particular organization or program. In order to realize this commitment, an organization will need to utilize methods of privacy policy guidance and enforcement. Policy guidance may be communicated to personnel in various formats, including manuals, instructions, regulations, and memoranda. These guidance documents can be general or combined with templates to standardize reporting across a particular department or program

The enforcement of privacy policies is a fundamental responsibility of federal agencies and their SAOPs/CPOs. Agencies use a variety of mechanisms to ensure compliance by agency employees, contractors and vendors. The following are examples of such efforts:

- The need to protect PII and Social Security numbers (SSNs), as highlighted in OMB M-07-16, inspired many agencies to turn to the use of new technologies to enforce compliance with privacy protection policies and mitigate risks to individuals and the agency. For example, many agencies have implemented automated "data loss prevention" (DLP) tools that are capable of, among other things, locating and blocking unsecured e-mails containing PII from leaving the agency's network. The DLP program may be housed within the privacy program or managed by another official, such as the CIO or CISO. Due to the sensitive nature of the program, the SAOP/CPO may need to develop specific policies and procedures for the use of such tools, in coordination with legal counsel and, where applicable, labor relations and the union. Escalation policies also are required to address both unintended and intended policy violations.

- The U.S. Census Bureau promises in its data protection policy to protect the confidentiality of information and to never identify individuals.[35] In order to ensure this confidentiality, the Bureau states that its personnel are bound by the requirements of federal law, with penalties including a federal prison sentence of up to five years and/or a fine of up to $250,000.[36] Within its privacy principles, the Bureau promises to use every technology, statistical methodology, and physical security procedure at its disposal to protect information.[37] In addition, the Bureau requires its employees to sign a sworn affidavit of nondisclosure, obligating them to protect the confidentiality of data for life.[38]

- The IRS states in its privacy principles that taxpayer information will be kept confidential, and that unauthorized access of taxpayer information by any IRS employee will not be tolerated. Enforcement of the IRS' privacy principles is partially legislative, under the Taxpayer Browsing Protection Act.[39] The act contains civil and criminal penalties for unauthorized inspection or disclosure of tax return information, including fines of up to $1,000 per incident, imprisonment of up to one year, and termination of employment. In addition, the IRS' Internal Revenue Manual holds its personnel responsible for complying with its Privacy Principles.[40] The manual sets forth requirements applicable to all IRS employees, stating that all employees shall adhere to IRS policies, prevent unnecessary record access and disclosure, complete privacy training, and report any unauthorized access or disclosure. The manual then provides additional responsibilities for senior management and other specific positions within the organization, including the requirement to take a proactive role in preventing unauthorized access and disclosure of taxpayer information.

- The DHS Privacy Office uses a privacy threshold analysis (PTA), as stated on its website, to "assess all new or proposed department programs, systems, technologies, or rule-makings (programs or systems) for privacy risks, and recommends privacy protections and alternative methods for handling personally identifiable information (PII) to mitigate privacy risks." Many federal agencies have adopted the PTA or a similar approach as a way to preliminarily determine the risks posed by new or changed technology systems, the need for a PIA and to enforce existing privacy policies. In addition, the DHS Privacy Office has implemented a new oversight mechanism called the Privacy Compliance Review (PCR). Again, according to the DHS Privacy Office website, the PCR is "designed as a constructive mechanism to improve a program's ability to comply with assurances made in existing privacy compliance documentation" including PIAs, SORNs, and/or formal agreements such as Memoranda of Understanding or Memoranda of Agreements.[41]

- OMB Circular A-130 requires agencies to conduct several reviews to monitor for compliance with key aspects of the Privacy Act. For example, agencies must conduct biennial reviews of Privacy Act SORNs to ensure they accurately describe their system of records. This includes identifying the need for amending existing SORNs, creating new SORNs or retiring SORNs.

- The E-Government Act (Section 208) requires agencies to publish online privacy policies on their public websites to disclose their PII handling practices. More recent OMB guidance requires agencies to disclose their use of web customization and tracking technology as well as use of third-party websites (social media, for example). The SAOP/CPO must periodically review and update the policy to reflect current agency activities. This often involves working with the agency's public affairs and website officials, who are knowledgeable about new website activities. Agencies also may use technology to automate the monitoring of their online privacy policy for compliance with federal requirements.

• Agencies also may develop other methods to enforce privacy policy compliance; for example, they may conduct physical inspections or reviews of agency facilities to identify unsecured documents and media containing sensitive information or PII and to raise awareness among managers and employees of the need to secure the items or dispose of the items in accordance with agency record retention and disposal requirements. Another method for enforcing policy is conducting in-depth privacy reviews of agency business processes, including meeting with program officials to identify the people, processes and technologies "touching" the PII and identify gaps in compliance that require remediation. These reviews may result in data flow maps that increase awareness among program, privacy and security officials about where sensitive data or PII may reside. Also, agencies may develop risk assessment methodologies to determine contractor and vendor compliance with contract clauses, confidentiality agreements, and privacy and security policies and procedures.

4.4 Guidance on PIAs

Government organizations have responded to the PIA requirements of the E-Government Act and OMB M-03-22 by developing PIA programs, including issuing guidance on the format and content of PIAs. Content and format requirements for PIAs vary among government organizations. Examples of three basic approaches are provided in the discussion below of the PIA programs for the IRS, Census Bureau and DHS.

4.4.1 IRS

In 1996, the IRS became the first U.S. government agency to formally issue guidance on the conduct of a PIA.[42] In 2000, this PIA guidance was named a best practice by the federal CIO Council.[43] Since that time, a number of government agencies, including the Department of Interior[44] and Department of Agriculture,[45] have adopted in their PIA formats characteristics similar to those of the IRS PIA format.

The first section of the IRS PIA must provide a system description. The system description is followed by information in four categories:[46]

• Data in the system
• Access to the data
• Attributes of the data
• Maintenance of administrative controls

Although the content of the questions in each section has changed to some extent over the years, the section titles and basic topics have not changed. The IRS requires completion of the PIA early in the system development life cycle process, and the PIA is one of the documents submitted as part of the SA&A process at the IRS.[47] The IRS recently launched a Privacy Impact Assessment Management System (PIAMS) to streamline and improve their PIA review and approval. The PIAMS also is used to create a centralized PIA repository and support PIA reporting, as part of the agency's annual FISMA/SAOP Report to the OMB. The questions asked in each section of the IRS PIA cover the following general topics:[48]

Data in the System
- Description of data used in the system
- Sources of the information, including:
  - IRS files and databases used
  - Data provided by other federal agencies, state and local agencies, and other third party sources
- Information collected from taxpayers/employees
- Method for verifying the accuracy of data collected from sources other than IRS records and taxpayers
- Method for checking data for completeness
- Currency of data
- Detailed documentation of data elements

Access to the Data
- Who has access to data
- How access is determined and restricted
- Controls to prevent data misuse
- Sharing of data with other internal systems
- Responsibility for protecting privacy rights of data subjects
- Sharing of data with other agencies, their use of the data, and their responsibility for properly using the data
- Limiting data shared with other agencies

Attributes of the Data
- Is data relevant and necessary for system purposes
- Derivation of new data or creation of previously unavailable data about individuals through data aggregation
- Placement of new data in an individual's record
- Determinations of individuals through use of new data
- Verification of data for relevance and accuracy

- Controls in place to protect both data and processes that are being consolidated and prevent unauthorized access
- Data retrieval methods, including retrieval by personal identifier
- Potential effects on the due process rights of taxpayers and employees of the following factors and how those effects are mitigated:
  - Consolidation and linkage of files and systems
  - Derivation of data
  - Accelerated information processing and decision making
  - Use of new technologies

Maintenance of Administrative Controls

- Assurance of equitable treatment of taxpayers and employees
- Maintenance of consistent use of system at all sites
- Possibility of disparate treatment of individuals or groups
- Retention periods of the data and documented procedures for eliminating data at the end of the retention periods
- Requirements for determining if data is sufficiently accurate, relevant, timely, and complete to ensure fairness in making determinations
- Use of technologies in ways that they have not previously been used; and effect upon taxpayer/employee privacy
- Capability to identify, locate, and monitor individuals and groups
- Controls used to prevent unauthorized monitoring
- SORN under which system operates and requirement to amend the SORN

4.4.2 Census Bureau

The Census Bureau has a Data Stewardship Program in place to address issues related to data confidentiality, data access and privacy. The mission of the program is to assure that the Census Bureau can effectively collect and use data while meeting its legal and ethical obligations, especially to respondents. The PIA is one tool for implementing and creating awareness of data stewardship policies. As a result, Census Bureau PIAs are labeled as "Data Stewardship/Privacy Impact Assessments" or "DS/PIAs."[49] The Census Bureau requires that DS/PIAs be completed early in the system development life cycle.[50]

The Census Bureau uses a complete Microsoft Excel© workbook for its DS/PIA tool, with each section of the DS/PIA appearing on a separate worksheet.[51] The assessment section of the DS/PIA tool consists of a series of questions that must be answered about a program's procedures, activities and application of current policy. The four Census Bureau privacy principles are the basis for the questions to be addressed in the DS/PIA.

The topics covered in the DS/PIA[52] under each of the privacy principles, as described in the Guide to U.S. Census Bureau Data Stewardship/Privacy Impact Assessment are:[53]

Privacy Principle 1: Mission Necessity

Questions cover:

- Breadth and depth of a data collection
- Whether sensitive topics are addressed

(Sensitive topics are defined as: abortion; alcohol, drug, or other addictive products; illegal conduct; illegal immigration status; information damaging to financial standing, employability, or reputation; information leading to social stigmatization or discrimination; politics; psychological well-being or mental health; religion; same-sex partners; sexual behavior; sexual orientation; taxes; and other information due to specific cultural or other factors.)

Privacy Principle 2: Openness

Questions cover:

- Tracking of notification for mandatory data collections and of consent for voluntary data collections
- Consent related to the use of proxies or data from third parties, which are often, but not always administrative records from other federal agencies
- Applicable SORNs

Privacy Principle 3: Respectful Treatment of Respondents

Questions cover:

- Actual data collection activities
- Targeting of population groups
- Burden
- Frequency of the collection
- Associated Paperwork Reduction Act Information Clearance Request Numbers

Privacy Principle 4: Confidentiality

Questions cover internal controls related to:

- Need-to-know access
- Use of off-site facilities
- Data transfers among systems
- Dissemination of products that have been protected by disclosure avoidance techniques
- Archiving plans
- Sensitive data (including sensitive topics, but broader) or information

The next section, the system write-up, describes the IT system to which the program is linked and how the IT Security Office determined the risk level of the system.

The sensitivity levels of the program are computed in the final two sections: the data sensitivity worksheet and the activity sensitivity worksheet, based on the answers provided in the assessment section. Risk points are assigned based on responses that reveal potential privacy threats. Mitigation points are assigned based on responses that document the application of current policies and procedures designed to reduce privacy threats. An overall score indicates whether the program poses minimal, average or excessive risk after the mitigation activities are taken into account.[54]

4.4.3 The DHS

The DHS Privacy Office has developed a framework to make privacy an integral part of day-to-day operations.[55] PIAs are a part of that framework, and are required to a) be completed early in the development life cycle of systems and programs, and b) be used throughout the life cycle to identify and manage privacy risks.[56]

The DHS requires that a PTA be performed first for a system or program to determine whether a new or revised PIA is necessary.[57] Official guidance and a template issued by the DHS Privacy Office are used to complete the PIA.[58] A unique feature of the DHS PIA template is that a subsection, called the Privacy Impact Analysis, appears at the end of each of the sections. In these subsections, the person who is completing the PIA must document an analysis of the risks pertaining to the particular topics in the sections and how to mitigate those risks. This requirement forces the PIA author to actively engage in analysis of privacy impact rather than merely answering questions about the system without thinking about the impact of the system's characteristics and operations.[59] Department of Justice PIAs have a format and content similar to those of DHS PIAs.[60] The topics covered in each section of the DHS PIA template are:[61]

1. Characterization of the information
   - List of information collected, used, disseminated, and maintained
   - Sources of the information
   - Why the information is being collected, used, disseminated, or maintained
   - How information collection is performed
   - How information is checked for accuracy
   - Legal authorities, arrangements, and/or agreements for information collection
2. Uses of the information
   - Description of information uses
   - Types of tools used to analyze data and type of data produced
   - Use of commercial or publicly available data

3. Retention

- Retention period and its approval by records officer and NARA

4. Internal sharing and disclosure

- Internal organizations with whom information is shared, what information is shared, and the purpose for sharing

- Methods of transmitting or disclosing information

5. External sharing and disclosure

- External organizations with whom information is shared, what information is shared, and the purpose for sharing

- Whether sharing of information is compatible with the original reason for collection, documentation of routine use, and legal mechanisms that allow sharing

- Methods of transmitting or disclosing information and security measures used to protect it during transmission

6. Notice

- Providing notice to individuals prior to collection of information

- Providing individuals with the opportunity to decline to provide information and consent to particular uses of the information

7. Access, redress, and correction

- Procedures for individuals to gain access to their own information

- Procedures for correcting inaccurate or erroneous information and how individuals are notified of those procedures

- Alternatives to a formal redress process

8. Technical access and security

- Procedures used to determine which users may access the system

- System access by contractors

- Privacy training provided

- Completion of security certification & accreditation

- Auditing measures and technical safeguards used to prevent misuse of data

9. Technology

- Type of project

- Current stage of development and project development life cycle used

- Use of technology that may raise privacy concerns

5. Protecting PII

Revised by Roanne R. Shaddox, CIPP/US, CIPP/G

In addition to developing and issuing policies and procedures, agencies must undertake several initiatives to protect PII in both paper and electronic form. Agencies have been guided in their efforts during the last decade by the documents discussed below.

5.1 The President's Identity Theft Task Force Report

In 2006, the president's Task Force on Identity Theft ("Task Force") was established by Executive Order 13402 in response to the growing number of breaches of PII by federal agencies, most notably the 2006 Department of Veterans Affairs breach that affected up to 26.5 million veterans. The Task Force was chaired by the U.S. Attorney General and was cochaired by the chairman of the Federal Trade Commission. According to its website, the creation of the Task Force represented the launching of "a new era in the fight against identity theft" and would work to develop "a coordinated approach among government agencies to combat this crime" that will include areas such as "identity theft awareness, prevention, detection, and prosecution."[62] The Task Force issued a set of interim recommendations in 2006, presented a strategic plan to the president in 2007 that contained 31 recommendations and issued a final report in 2008. In each instance, it was recognized that the public and private sectors have a role to play and many of the recommendations for the public sector formed the basis for OMB Memorandum M-07-16, described below.

5.2 Common Risks White Paper

In 2007, DHS and the OMB issued a white paper titled "Common Risks Impeding Adequate Protection of Government Information." In addition to the 10 risks identified in the paper, several recommendations were provided to help federal agencies reduce privacy and security risks to sensitive agency information. The risk areas include:

- Poor security and privacy training
- Contracts and data-sharing agreements that inadequately address the appropriate handling and safeguarding of PII
- Inventories that inaccurately describe the types, uses and locations of government information
- Poor record retention and disposal practices
- Privacy incidents not being reported in a timely manner
- Lack of audit trails to record how PII is being collected, used, shared and disclosed
- Inadequate physical security controls
- Inadequate information security controls

- Inadequate protection of remotely accessed information
- Lack of incorporation of privacy and security standards when acquiring information technology and information security products

5.3 OMB Memorandum M-07-16, "Safeguarding Against and Responding to the Breach of Personally Identifiable Information"

In this memorandum, the OMB reminds agencies of their existing privacy protection responsibilities under the Privacy Act, including the need to establish "rules of conduct for persons involved in the design . . . or maintenance of any system of records"; "establish appropriate administrative, technical and physical safeguards . . . to protect against any anticipated threats . . . which could result in substantial harm, embarrassment, inconvenience or unfairness to an individual"; and "maintain accurate, relevant, timely and complete information." In addition, OMB M-07-16 reminds agencies of four key existing security requirements that agencies must implement to protect PII and establishes several new privacy requirements, which include but are not limited to:[63]

- **Review and Reduce the Volume of PII and SSNs.** In an effort to reduce risk to individuals and the agency, OMB M-07-16 requires agencies to identify and reduce any unnecessary holdings of PII and SSNs. Typically, agencies create and use a "PII inventory" to track IT systems that maintain PII and SSNs, track the existence of privacy compliance documents, such as PIAs and Privacy Act SORNs, and support annual reporting to the OMB (discussed below). The SAOP/CPO also may provide the PII inventory to information security officials to assist with IT system categorization and certification and accreditation process.

  The maintenance of PII inventories is one of the most challenging aspects of a privacy program, and the methods used vary widely. For example, the Department of Treasury has developed a sophisticated web-based solution. Many other agencies use a simple spreadsheet or database approach. To ensure their inventories are up-to-date, agencies may periodically issue data calls to IT system and program owners, as well as use a PTA or similar process to identify and determine if an IT system or project or other electronic collection activity involves the use of PII or SSNs. The inventory is a living document that must continually be updated and reviewed to ensure its accuracy.

- **Develop a Breach Notification Policy.** Using guidance from OMB M-07-16, agencies must have a documented breach response plan and procedure that includes the establishment of a high-level response team led by the SAOP/CPO and consists of other agency officials, such as the CIO, CISO, legal counsel, public affairs and component- or division-level officials. In the event of a potential or actual loss of PII, the response team is responsible for reviewing the pertinent facts of an incident, assessing the likelihood that the loss will result in a high risk for identity theft, and determining whether to notify individuals affected by the loss. As the goal is to notify the affected individual(s) as soon as possible, the SAOP/CPO typically will establish a specific timeframe for performing the initial investigation and reaching a determination about whether there has been a loss of PII that poses a risk for identity theft. Depending on the nature of the incident, the agency's office of inspector general may get involved, as well as local or federal law enforcement officials.

- **Publish a Routine Use.** OMB M-07-16 recognizes that an "effective response necessitates the disclosure of information regarding the breach to those individuals affected by it, as well as to persons and entities in a position to cooperate, either by assisting in notification to affected individuals or playing a role in preventing or minimizing harms from the breach." Therefore, the OMB asked agencies to publish a routine use for "appropriate systems of records" allowing for the disclosure of breach-related information that could include PII. Many agencies implemented the new routine use contained in OMB M-07-16 immediately or as part of the mandatory biennial review of their agency's SORNs.

- **Inform and Train Personnel on PII Safeguarding Responsibilities.** Agencies are required under the Privacy Act and E-Government Act (Section 208) to provide employee and contractor awareness training about their responsibilities under the laws and applicable regulations. Similarly, under OMB M-07-16, agencies must ensure that managers, supervisors and employees are informed and trained about their responsibilities to safeguard PII. But OMB M-07-16 also required each agency to develop a Rules and Consequences Policy and to train employees on the consequences of violating their responsibility to safeguard PII. To meet this requirement, agencies typically conduct "new hire" training and annual mandatory awareness training addressing the wide range of responsibilities. Agencies may conduct standalone privacy and security training courses or combine them into one course that is delivered online. The Department of the Interior, for example, has not only combined privacy and security training into one course, but also combined records management training. Agency employees and contractors also are required to annually certify their acceptance of security and privacy responsibilities. Some agencies use a paper form that is signed by the individual and maintained by the supervisor, while others use the digital signature captured at the end of the online awareness-training module to satisfy this requirement. Additional role-based training is required for individuals who frequently handling PII records and, therefore, have greater privacy and PII protection responsibilities.

In addition, agencies must report annually to the OMB on the progress of their privacy management efforts, including in the areas of PII/SSN reduction and protection and breach response. Known as the Senior Agency Official for Privacy Report, it is used to fulfill various privacy-reporting requirements required by the E-Government Act (Section 208) and various OMB memoranda (e.g., OMB Circular A-130, OMB M-07-16).

To ease the burden on agencies, the OMB consolidated the privacy reporting with the agency's annual report required by FISMA. As part of the annual SAOP report, agencies must complete a questionnaire and provide written updates on their progress for identifying unnecessary holdings of PII and SSNs, as well as a copy of their breach response procedures whenever there is a significant update. The report is submitted by authorized agency officials using OMB's CyberScope system and must be approved by the head of the agency.

6. U.S. Government Workforce Management

Revised by Roanne R. Shaddox, CIPP/US, CIPP/G

Federal agencies must manage their workforces in an increasingly complex privacy landscape. The challenges range from conducting background checks to issuing credentials to monitoring networks to limiting the use of SSNs whenever possible.

6.1 Workforce Hiring Considerations

In 2007, the OPM issued guidance that stemmed from recommendations of the President's Identity Theft Task Force, entitled "Guidance on Protecting Federal Employee Social Security Numbers and Combating Identity Theft." The guidance seeks to "minimize the risk of identity theft and fraud . . . (1) by eliminating the unnecessary use of SSN as an identifier; and (2) by strengthening the protection of personal information, including SSNs, from theft or loss." The central focus of the guidance is federal employee personal information. The guidance reminded agencies of existing regulatory requirements and provided a list of measures that should be taken to protect personal information, such as:

- Eliminating the "unnecessary printing and displaying of the SSN on forms, reports, and computer display screens"

- Restricting "access to the SSN . . . to only those individuals whose official duty requires such access"

- Requiring "supervisory approval . . . before an authorized individual can access, transport, or transmit information or equipment containing Social Security numbers outside agency facilities"

- Establishing and communicating to employees "written procedures describing the proper labeling, storage, and disposal of printed material containing Social Security numbers and other personally identifiable data"

The guidance also references the development of a "new government-wide employee identifier" to help reduce the risk of identity theft. However, the effort eventually was abandoned due to technical and legal complexities.

6.1.1 Background Screening and Investigations

The OPM conducts background investigations for most federal agencies and their contractors, using a combination of contractor investigators (6,000) and career personnel (2,000) who also oversee investigative work and develop and implement policy. The OPM also conducts national security investigations for individuals who work in positions that require access to classified information.

In order for the OPM to perform an appropriate level of screening for a position, the position must be ranked according to its risk and sensitivity. Under OPM's guidance, agencies are responsible for designating each covered position "at a high, moderate or low risk level as determined by the position's potential for adverse impact to the efficiency or integrity of the service."[64] In addition, depending on the degree to which a position could affect national security, it must receive a sensitivity designation. These designations, ranked from greatest to least potential for damage, are: Special-Sensitive, Critical-Sensitive, Noncritical-Sensitive, and Non-Sensitive.[65] Once a position has been rated according to one of the three levels of risk and one of the four levels of sensitivity, the OPM can determine the necessary degree of background investigation.

Depending on the risk and sensitivity level of a job position, the OPM requires a different screening questionnaire. The correlation between these levels and questionnaire is generally as follows:[66]

- **Non-Sensitive Position Questionnaire.** For low risk, non-sensitive sensitivity levels.

- **Public Trust Position Questionnaire.** For moderate to high risk, non-sensitive sensitivity levels.

- **National Security Position Questionnaire.** For any level of risk combined with any sensitivity level greater than non-sensitive.

- **Selected Position Supplemental Questionnaire.** For positions with unique requirements. This questionnaire must be completed along with the Public Trust Position Questionnaire.

These questionnaires request varying levels of information from applicants, with the personal nature and sensitivity of the questions increasing with the sensitivity and risk of the position. Questionnaires request basic identification information such as name, date of birth, and Social Security number, as well as information regarding citizenship, residences, education, and employment history. National Security position questionnaires request information regarding military service, personal references, marital status, family, foreign contacts and activities, psychological and emotional health, criminal records, drug and alcohol use, finances, and group associations. In addition to the investigations and questionnaires, fingerprints are required, and periodic reinvestigations may be necessary.

Background investigations for certain government positions may require access to the applicant's financial records. The Fair Credit Reporting Act restricts access to an individual's credit reports that may be obtained from a consumer-reporting agency. In order for an agency to obtain a credit report on an individual, written notice must be provided to, and written consent received from, the applicant.[67] The background investigation may also require access to medical records. The Health Insurance Portability and Accountability Act of 1996 (HIPAA) requires individuals' written authorization for their medical records to be released for purposes not related to treatment, payment, or operations. If psychotherapy notes are being requested, the individual's authorization must specifically grant approval for their release.[68]

6.2 Internal Monitoring of Use of Federal Networks

Federal agencies use a wide range of technical measures to monitor their computer networks and other IT resources for, among other things, improper use and other prohibited activity by users. When logging onto the computer network, users typically see a warning banner that states that their activity is being monitored and that they should have "no expectation of privacy" when using the system. The act of logging into the network constitutes an employee's or contractor's consent to this monitoring. Agencies are also required to have in place "acceptable use" policies that outline prohibited and permissible uses of the network and other IT resources. Typically, the CISO is responsible for network monitoring policies and measures within an agency. However, close coordination between the CISO and the CIO, SAOP, and legal departments is required, due to the potential collection of sensitive PII that may be contained in electronic communications, such as emails, and to ensure that the activity is consistent with appropriate laws, regulations, and internal policies.

In order to meet mandates from OMB M-06-15, M-06-16, and M-07-16 to protect sensitive information and sensitive PII from unauthorized use or disclosure, agencies increasingly have deployed data loss prevention tools to monitor for unsecured sensitive information or sensitive PII that employees or contractors may be sending outside the agency's network. The tools are used to examine e-mails and their attachments for unencrypted SSNs or other types of sensitive information. The tools enable agencies to monitor the activity and block the transmission of the data. The system then alerts the appropriate personnel about the activity, such as the CISO or SAOP, so that action can be taken in accordance with internal policies and procedures. Depending on the nature of the incident, an agency's data breach procedures may need to be invoked. Due to the potential collection of PII, agencies also may conduct and publish a PIA for the activity and need to review the collection for any Privacy Act implications.

Agencies typically remind employees of their responsibilities to protect agency data and about the appropriate use of computer systems and electronic communications through annual privacy and security awareness training courses, during "new hire" orientations, or through e-mail messages to all employees and contractors.

6.3 Federal Identity Management and Authentication

6.3.1 Homeland Security Presidential Directive-12 (HSPD-12)

Issued in 2004, HSPD-12 stemmed from concerns about the need to improve the protection of federal buildings and facilities from a potential terrorist attack. In addition to enhancing security, the new credentials help to "increase government efficiency, reduce identity theft, and protect personal privacy." HSPD-12 contains eight policy requirements, most notably the establishment of a "mandatory, government-wide standard for secure and reliable forms of identification issued by the federal government to its employees and contractors"; promulgation by the secretary of commerce "a federal standard for secure and reliable forms of identification"; and establishment of programs by federal agencies to "ensure that identification issued by their departments or agencies to federal employees and contractors meets the standard."

Meeting the requirements of HSPD-12 and the standard subsequently issued by the Department of Commerce's NIST in 2005 presented significant challenges for most federal agencies, due to the cost and complexity of transitioning from existing credentialing systems and processes to the new one mandated by the directive.[69]

6.3.2 Federal Identity, Credential and Access Management (FICAM)

In 2010, the Federal Chief Information Officers Council and Federal Enterprise Architecture issued FICAM Roadmap and Implementation Guidance to address rising concerns related to identity management, such as identity theft and "inconsistent" enforcement of "trust relationships" while conducting transactions in the online environment. The FICAM initiative supports other government-wide initiatives in the area of cybersecurity and open government.[70]

6.3.3 OMB M-04-04, "E-Authentication Guidance for Federal Agencies"

In 2004, the OMB issued M-04-04 to address the rise in citizen use of the Internet to access government information and services. As stated in the memorandum, "to make sure government services are secure and protect privacy, some type of identity verification or authentication is needed." As such, agencies are required "to review new and existing electronic transactions to ensure that authentication processes provide the appropriate level of assurance." The guidance "establishes . . . four levels of identity assurance for electronic transactions requiring authentication":

- Level 1: Little or no confidence in the asserted identity's validity
- Level 2: Some confidence in the asserted identity's validity

- Level 3: High confidence in the asserted identity's validity
- Level 4: Very high confidence in the asserted identity's validity

The guidance outlines a five-step process for agencies to use to determine assurance levels:

1. Conduct a risk assessment of the e-government system

2. Map identified risks to the applicable assurance level

3. Select technology based on e-authentication technical guidance

4. Validate that the implemented system has achieved the required assurance level

5. Periodically reassess the system to determine technology refresh requirements

Agencies then select the appropriate technology to meet the technical requirements for the required level of assurance.[71]

7. Conclusion

To effectively protect the privacy rights of individuals and their PII, federal government agencies must develop and manage comprehensive privacy programs. This starts with the appointment of an SAOP/CPO who will develop, lead and enforce a strong governance, compliance and risk-management program. This also includes developing and implementing privacy policies and guidance documents for their specific organizations and programs, based on their interpretation of higher-level government privacy policies and procedures and agency best practices, and applying them to their agencies' distinct missions and operations. Finally, it includes undertaking employee and contractor awareness and training initiatives and having a robust breach response procedure for managing incidents and actual losses of PII. These combined efforts increase the effectiveness of privacy programs across agencies and enhance privacy protection across the federal government as a whole.

Endnotes

1   While an agency's Privacy Act Statement, for example, that appears on a paper or online form may state that the provision of sensitive data is voluntary, it also may state that by not providing such data, there may be a delay in the provision of the requested benefit or that the agency may not be able to process the request at all. Therefore, the practical effect is that the individual may feel that they have no choice but to provide the sensitive data in order to receive a benefit or service.

2   See Clinger-Cohen Act of 1996 and the related OMB Circular A-130, http://dodcio.defense.gov/ Portals/0/Documents/ciodesrefvolone.pdf.

3   Transportation and Treasury fall under the same law: the 2005 Consolidated Appropriations Act (Section 522).

4   The Elements Paper is available on the Federal CIO Council Privacy Committee website at www.cio.gov.

5   http://csrc.nist.gov/publications/nistpubs/800-53-Rev3/sp800-53-rev3-final.pdf.

6   Content from the Elements Paper was leveraged for this effort.

7   For further information, see http://csrc.nist.gov/publications/drafts/800-53-rev4/sp800-53-rev4-ipd.pdf.

8   OMB Memorandum M-12-20, "FY 2012 Reporting Instructions for the Federal Information Security Management Act and Agency Privacy Management," October 2, 2012.

9   Federal Information Processing Standards Publication 200, "Minimum Security Requirements for Federal Information Systems," March 2006.

10 NIST SP 800-53 CA Controls, http://web.nvd.nist.gov/view/800-53/family?familyId=CA.

11 NIST SP 800-53 CA-2.

12 NIST SP 800-53 CA-6.

13 Appendix I to Office of Management and Budget Circular A-130, "Federal Agency Responsibilities for Maintaining Records About Individuals," www.whitehouse.gov/omb/circulars_a130_a130appendix_i.

14 *Id.*

15 www.ocio.usda.gov/e_arch/ea_seca.html. For further information, see http://csrc.nist.gov/groups/SMA/ispab/documents/minutes/2004-09/Sept2004-Fed-Enterprise-Architecture-Security.pdf.

16 Office of Management and Budget, "FY 2011 Reporting Instructions for the Federal Information Security Management Act and Agency Privacy Management," September, 2011, www.whitehouse.gov/sites/default/files/omb/memoranda/2011/m11-33.pdf.

17 Department of Homeland Security, "FY 2102 Senior Agency Official for Privacy Federal Information Security Management Act Reporting Metrics," January 2012, www.dhs.gov/xlibrary/assets/nppd/fy12saopfismametrics.pdf.

18 DHS and the Department of Justice (DOJ) have specific privacy protection legislation, as do several agencies falling under Section 522 of the Consolidated Appropriations Act for Transportation, Treasury and Related Agencies.

19 For a comprehensive listing of individuals that the SAOP/CPO may need to coordinate with, see the Leadership section of the "Best Practices: Elements of a Federal Privacy Program" white paper.

20 Internal Revenue Service Mission Statement, www.irs.gov/uac/The-Agency,-its-Mission-and-Statutory-Authority.

21 The IRS is subject to the Taxpayer Browsing Protection Act (see bulk.resource.org/gpo.gov/laws/105/publ35.105.pdf), which designates willful unauthorized access to or inspection of taxpayer records as a crime, punishable by loss of job, fines and possibly prison terms. The IRS must also abide by Section 6103 of the Internal Revenue Code (see www.access.gpo.gov/uscode/title26/subtitlef_chapter61_subchapterb_.html), which has provisions to ensure that tax returns and return information are kept confidential.

22 Internal Revenue Manual, Section 4.10.1.6.10: Confidentiality of Taxpayer Information/Taxpayer Privacy, May 1999, www.irs.gov/irm/part4/irm_04-010-001.html.

23 Census Bureau, Facts About the Census Bureau, www.census.gov/aboutus/.

24 www.census.gov/privacy/data_protection/our_privacy_principles.html.

25 DHS Privacy Policy Guidance Memorandum, "The Fair Information Practice Principles: Framework for Privacy Policy at the Department of Homeland Security," December 29, 2008.

26 United States Postal Service, Handbook AS-353, *Guide to Privacy and the Freedom of Information Act*, September 2005, Updated with Postal Service Bulletin Revisions Through June 7, 2007, http://about.usps.com/handbooks/as353/welcome.htm.

27 DoD 5400.11, DoD Privacy Program, May 8, 2007, www.dtic.mil/whs/directives/corres/pdf/540011p.pdf.

28 DoD 5400.11-R, Department of Defense Privacy Program, May 14, 2007, www.dtic.mil/whs/directives/corres/pdf/540011r.pdf.

29 Air Force Instruction 33-332, Privacy Act Program, May 16, 2011, www.e-publishing.af.mil/shared/media/epubs/afi33-332.pdf.

30 DoD Directive OSD 12282-05, "Notifying Individuals When Personal Information is Lost, Stolen, or Compromised," July 15, 2005.

31 Section 222 of the Homeland Security Act of 2002 authorizes creation of the DHS Privacy Office, and requires the secretary of DHS to appoint a senior official in the department as the DHS CPO) with primary responsibility for privacy policy (see www.dhs.gov/xabout/structure/editorial_0510.shtm).

32 DHS Action Memorandum, "Review of Safeguarding Policies and Procedures for Personnel-Related Data," June 13, 2007, www.dhs.gov/xlibrary/assets/privacy/privacy_PIIPrimaryActionMemo_20070615.pdf.

33 DHS Privacy Policy Guidance Memorandum 2007-01, "Regarding Collection, Use, Retention, and Dissemination of Information on Non-U.S. Persons," January 7, 2009, www.dhs.gov/xlibrary/assets/privacy/privacy_policyguide_2007-1.pdf.

34 Department of Homeland Security, US-VISIT Privacy Policy, www.dhs.gov/us-visit-privacy-policy.

35 Census Bureau, Data Protection, www.census.gov/privacy/data_protection/.

36 13 U.S.C. §9, 214; 18 U.S.C. §3559, 3571.

37 Census Bureau, Our Privacy Principles, www.census.gov/privacy/data_protection/our_privacy_principles.html.

38 Census Bureau, Oath of Non-Disclosure, www.census.gov/privacy/data_protection/oath_of_non-disclosure.html.

39 26 U.S.C. §7213A; 26 U.S.C. §7431.

40 IRS Internal Revenue Manual, Part 10, Chapter 5, www.irs.gov/irm/.

41 For further information about the PCR process, see www.dhs.gov/privacy-compliance.

42 Internal Revenue Service Technical Manual: Privacy Impact Assessment, Version 1.3, Document 9927, December 17, 1996.

43 Federal Chief Information Officer's Council, Best Practices: Privacy, Internal Revenue Service Model Information Technology Privacy Impact Assessment, February 25, 2000.

44 The Department of Interior PIA template is available at www.doi.gov/ocio/privacy/Interior%20Privacy_Assessment_Template_No%20Explanations.doc.

45 See APHIS ePermits Release 2 Privacy Impact Assessment, July 20, 2005, www.usda.gov/documents/APHIS_Electronic_Permits_System(ePermits)PIA.pdf.

46 Completed IRS PIAs are available at www.irs.gov/privacy/article/0,,id=122989,00.html.

47 IRS, Internal Revenue Manual 10.8.1.3.5.3, Authorization, www.irs.gov/irm/part10/irm_10-008-001r.html.

48 IRS Privacy Impact Assessments, www.irs.gov/privacy/article/0,,id=122989,00.html.

49 Census Bureau, Guide to U.S. Census Bureau Data Stewardship/Privacy Impact Assessments (DS/PIAs), www.census.gov/privacy/pia/guide_to_ds-pias.html.

50 Census Bureau, Data Stewardship/Privacy Assessment Introduction, www.census.gov/privacy/pia/pias/EDMS_PIA.pdf.

51 The Census Bureau's DS/PIA tool and completed PIAs are available at: www.census.gov/privacy/pia/list_of_available_pias.html.

52 Census Bureau, Guide to U.S. Census Bureau Data Stewardship/Privacy Impact Assessments (DS/PIAs), hwww.census.gov/privacy/pia/guide_to_ds-pias.html.

53 *Id.*

54 Census Bureau, *Data Stewardship/Privacy Assessment Introduction*, www.census.gov/privacy/pia/pias/ EDMS_PIA.pdf.

55 Department of Homeland Security Privacy Office, *Operationalizing Privacy: Compliance Frameworks and Tools*, Presentation at the 2007 International Association of Privacy Professionals Privacy Summit, March 8, 2007.

56 Department of Homeland Security Privacy Office, *Privacy Impact Assessments: Official Guidance*, May 2007, www.dhs.gov/xlibrary/assets/privacy/privacy_pia_guidance_may2007.pdf.

57 The Department of Homeland Security PIA Threshold Analysis form is available at www.dhs.gov/ privacy.

58 DHS's PIA guidance is *Privacy Impact Assessments: Official Guidance*, Department of Homeland Security Privacy Office, May 2007, www.dhs.gov/xlibrary/assets/privacy/privacy_pia_guidance_ may2007.pdf. The DHS PIA template can be found at www.dhs.gov/xlibrary/assets/privacy/ privacy_pia_template.pdf. Completed DHS PIAs are published at www.dhs.gov/privacy-office-privacy-impact-assessments-pia.

59 In addition to the PIA guide, the DHS Privacy Office issued the *Privacy Technology Implementation Guide* in August 2007. This guide is to be used by technology managers and developers to integrate privacy protections into operational information technology systems. It is available at www.dhs. gov/xlibrary/assets/privacy/privacy_guide_ptig.pdf.

60 Department of Justice, Privacy and Civil Liberties office, Office of the Deputy Attorney General, *Privacy Impact Assessments: Official Guidance*, August 7, 2006, www.usdoj.gov/pclo/pia_manual.pdf.

61 *Privacy Impact Assessments: Official Guidance*, Department of Homeland Security Privacy Office, May 2007, www.dhs.gov/xlibrary/assets/privacy/privacy_pia_guidance_may2007.pdf.

62 For further information about the Task Force, see www.idtheft.gov/about.html.

63 Per OMB M-07-16, the four requirements are: "(a) Assign an impact level to all information and information systems; (b) implement minimum security requirements and controls; (c) certify and accredit information systems; (d) train employees," www.whitehouse.gov/sites/default/files/omb/ memoranda/fy2007/m07-16.pdf.

64 5 CFR §731.106(a).

65 5 CFR §731.106(c)(2).

66 Office of Personnel Management, *Requesting OPM Personnel Investigations*, www.opm.gov/ investigate/resources/INV15Apr2012.pdf.

67 15 U.S.C. 1681 *et seq.*

68 Public Law 104-191.

69 For further information about the standard, see http://csrc.nist.gov/groups/SNS/piv/index.html.

70 For further information, see www.idmanagement.gov/documents/FICAM_Roadmap_ Implementation_Guidance.pdf.

71 See IT Law Wiki, http://itlaw.wikia.com/wiki/Assurance.

CHAPTER SEVEN

Records Management, Data Sharing and Disclosure

1. Records Management

Revised by Matthew J. Olsen, CIPP/US, CIPP/G

An effective federal privacy program relies on a rigorous records management program to classify, preserve, archive and protect records that include personally identifiable information (PII).

The Federal Records Act of 1950 requires the establishment of standards and procedures to ensure efficient and effective records management to:[1]

(1) *Provide accurate and complete documentation of the policies and transactions of the federal government*

(2) *Control the quantity and quality of records produced by the federal government*

(3) *Establish and maintain mechanisms of control with respect to records creation, in order to prevent the creation of unnecessary records, and with respect to the effective and economical operations of an agency*

(4) *Simplify the activities, systems, and processes of records creation, maintenance and use*

(5) *Ensure judicious preservation and disposal of records*

(6) *Direct continuing attention on records from their initial creation to their final disposition, with particular emphasis on the prevention of unnecessary federal paperwork*

The original text for this chapter was developed by Charissa L. Smith, CIPP/US, CIPP/G. New content for this revised edition was contributed by Matthew J. Olsen, CIPP/US, CIPP/G and Michael Hawes, CIPP/G whose contributions are noted throughout the sections of the chapter.

The objectives of the Federal Records Act interact with federal privacy to:

- Ensure appropriate maintenance of a record that allows access rights to the subject of the record, as established by subsection (d)(1) of the Privacy Act of 1974.
- Minimize the collection of PII.
- Ensure the destruction of PII when there is no longer a business, legal, or historical need for the record. Considering that only one to three percent of federal records are permanently maintained, it is vital to plan for the timely destruction of records.

The National Archives and Records Administration (NARA) is charged with providing guidance and assistance with respect to records management and maintaining those records that are of sufficient value to warrant permanent preservation.

1.1 Defining Records Management

The Federal Records Act defines records management as "the planning, controlling, directing, organizing, training, promoting, and other managerial activities involved with respect to records creation, records maintenance and use, and records disposition in order to achieve adequate and proper documentation of the policies and transactions of the federal government and effective and economical management of agency operations."

Federal records managers have paid particular attention to the management of records that include PII. In the past, records management has been considered a low-priority administrative task across federal agencies; however, increased sensitivity to PII collection, especially in alternative media and platforms, has highlighted the individual duty of all federal employees to understand and follow agency records management guidelines.

1.2 NARA Guidance on Records Management

The federal mandate that establishes NARA as the issuer of records management guidance is OMB Circular A-130, Management of Federal Information Resources.[2] This circular states that the archivist of the United States will administer the federal records management program in accordance with NARA, and assist the director of the Office of Management and Budget (OMB) in developing standards and guidelines relating to the records management program. Agencies must follow guidance from NARA as articulated in the NARA Code 36 CFR parts 1220–1238, as described in Table 7.1.

Table 7.1: NARA Code of Federal Regulations for Records Management

Code	Title	Description
36 CFR 1220	General Federal Records	Prescribes policies of federal agencies' records management programs
36 CFR 1222	Creation and Maintenance of Federal Records	Provides guidance to the heads of federal agencies in the creation of federal records
36 CFR 1228	Disposition of Federal Records	Provides guidance to the heads of federal agencies in the development of records schedules; provides overall guidance on record retention periods
36 CFR 1230	Micrographic Records Management	Promulgates standards and procedures to federal agencies for using micrographic technology
36 CFR 1232	Audiovisual Records Management	Prescribes policies and procedures for managing audiovisual records
36 CFR 1234	Electronic Records Management	Establishes basic requirements related to the creation, maintenance, use, and disposition of electronic records
36 CFR 1236	Management of Vital Records	Prescribes policies and procedures for establishing a program for the identification and protection of vital records

Source: National Archives and Records Administration, 36 CFR, Parts 1220–1238.

In particular, Code 36 CFR 1234 covers the disposition of records in electronic format, which has become increasingly important as the number of electronic records grows. (NARA's Electronic Records Management Initiative is one of 24 E-Government initiatives managed by the OMB.) Key issues include using tools that ease the electronic transmission of records by agencies to NARA; and implementing rules, policies and procedures to manage the storage, access and destruction of those records while protecting anything that includes PII.

The dynamic nature of electronic records poses numerous integrity, security and disclosure risks. The sheer volume of government records containing PII requires privacy professionals to view them not just from a privacy perspective, but also from a records management perspective.

NARA has also promulgated guidance regarding the consideration of format or medium in scheduling records, including:

- NARA Bulletin AC 02-2011, Guidance on Managing Mixed-Media Files: www.archives.gov/records-mgmt/bulletins/2011/2011-04.html

- NARA Bulletin NWM 08.2010, Frequently Asked Questions About Managing Federal Records in Cloud Computing Environments: www.archives.gov/records-mgmt/faqs/cloud.html

- NARA Bulletin NWM 25.2010, Report on Federal Web 2.0 Use and Record Value: www.archives.gov/records-mgmt/resources/web2.0-use.pdf

- NARA Bulletin 2010-05, Guidance on Managing Records in Cloud Computing Environments: www.archives.gov/records-mgmt/bulletins/2010/2010-05.html

However, NARA also promotes the concept of media neutrality in the proper retention of a record.[3] While the format of a record is one consideration in proper PII management, the purpose for which the record was created is also a key factor. For example, rather than focusing on a retention period for agency e-mail, the proper retention period is more likely to be based on *why* the record was created.

Further, NARA establishes general records schedules (GRS), which provide mandatory disposal authorization for temporary administrative records common to several or all agencies of the federal government. These include records relating to civilian personnel, fiscal accounting, procurement, communications, printing and other common functions and certain nontextual records.[4] Agencies may also be required to develop or update existing records schedules. In particular, agencies need to ensure that legal obligations are met, including applying all privacy rules to any new disposition schedule.[5] Agencies may choose to retain information longer than NARA guidance suggests, but this should be communicated by the agency in the system of records notice (SORN).

1.3 Interaction of Records Management and Privacy

Subsection (e)(4)(E) of the Privacy Act requires agencies to include within a SORN "the policies and practices of the agency regarding storage, retrievability, access controls, retention, and disposal of the records." Proper coordination with the agency records managers and NARA is the only way to ensure accurate information regarding the proper retention and disposal instructions for the information contained within a SORN. Records managers can identify whether an agency records schedule or GRS covers the information in a system.

If a new agency records schedule is required, the privacy office must take into consideration the timeline for NARA approval of that schedule for publishing the SORN and allowing the program office to begin maintaining PII in the system.

Proper management of records is also essential in documenting the controls used for systems security, which, in turn, helps ensure the proper protection of PII. National Institute of Standards and Technology (NIST) Special Publication 800-37 requires, agencies to maintain the records on controls including security plans, security assessment reports and plans of action and milestones.[6] It is considered a best practice to document privacy controls, plans, and results of privacy assessments.

1.4 Conclusion

It is important for government privacy professionals to understand records management, and it is certainly essential to engage agency records managers in SORN development and overall protection of PII. Document retention and disclosure policies must be flexible and practical enough to permit implementation, while still being firm and consistent enough to meet the stated laws, rules and regulations—all while protecting PII. This framework is critical to an agency's ability to operate in a modern information environment.

2. Interagency Sharing of Personal Data

Revised by Matthew J. Olsen, CIPP/US, CIPP/G

OMB Memorandum M-11-02, "Sharing Data While Protecting Privacy," discusses the current environment for interagency data sharing. The memorandum notes numerous benefits related to data sharing, including:

- Timely and improved access to reliable and high-quality data to inform decision-making by the administration as well as Congress
- Increased transparency, better service and reduced risk of waste, fraud and abuse with respect to public programs
- More informed research on public policy as a result of an increased number of theoretical and empirical studies which rigorously analyze and augment the understanding of federal programs within government for the public at large
- Improved government efficiency and reduced paperwork burdens as a result of more informed decision making and a reduction in burdensome, excessive and duplicative data collection activities

However, agencies must also ensure continued privacy protections under the Privacy Act. When the sharing involves benefits funded by the federal government, agencies must also ensure protections under the provisions of the Computer Matching and Privacy Protection Act of 1988, which amended the Privacy Act. A key concept of the Privacy Act is that the disclosure of information from a system of records must be for a purpose compatible with the purpose for which the information is originally collected.

OMB Memorandum 01-05, "Guidance on Inter-Agency Sharing of Personal Data—Protecting Personal Privacy," provides guidelines for the protection of personal privacy for data sharing between federal agencies. The OMB recognizes the need to encourage efficiency in federal programs through the use of data sharing to reduce errors, identify and prevent fraud, evaluate program performance, locate intended beneficiaries and reduce the information collection burden on the public. The memorandum also encourages agencies to use the guidelines for other data-sharing activities. Specifically, the OMB guidance requires:

- **Notice:** When an agency uses data sharing to verify program eligibility or recover delinquent debt, it must provide notice at the time (and periodically thereafter) to the program applicant that the information the applicant provides may be subject to matching.

- **Consent, as appropriate:** The consent of the individual must be obtained electronically or in writing prior to the agency sharing the personal data.

- **Redisclosure limitations:** Data-sharing programs may not redisclose received information, except as allowed by the Matching Act.

- **Accuracy:** Reasonable procedures must be in place to ensure the accuracy of shared data. Further, the Matching Act prohibits agencies from taking adverse action against individuals based on the results of the information produced by a matching program, unless an independent verification is performed. The Computer Matching and Privacy Protection Act also requires agencies to notify the individual and provide an opportunity for the individual to contest those findings; notification must take place at least 30 days before adverse action is taken against the individual.

- **Security controls:** Agencies must employ adequate and effective security controls. This requirement makes it incumbent on the originating agency to ensure that the recipient organization also has employed adequate and effective security controls. There must be advance agreement between the organizations about the level and nature of the security controls, based on the risks associated with the potential loss of the shared data. Data security remains the responsibility of the originating agency.

Agencies must employ managerial, operational and technical security controls that are appropriate for the prevailing level of risk and the harm that would result from a security breach. Specifically, agencies should evaluate physical security needs and consider network security controls (access, application and administrator controls), including the potential use of encryption of in-transit data, audit trails and antibrowsing features.

- **Minimization:** Agencies are encouraged to determine what specific information, is required for data matching and data-sharing activities so that they only share information necessary to verify an individual's eligibility for a program.

- **Accountability:** The Privacy Act provides for civil and criminal penalties against agencies that do not adhere to the principles described in OMB Memorandum 01-05. To mitigate risk to applicants and agencies, the agencies should institute specific training programs that stress accountability and explain penalties for breach of confidentiality. Additional oversight mechanisms, including self-audits, should be considered.

- **Privacy Impact Assessments (PIAs):** PIAs, as described in Chapter 2, are critical in building a plan to protect privacy during the development of a new system, including systems in which records are shared between agencies.

2.1 Transmission and Disclosure of PII

The proposed transmission of PII among federal agencies requires the identification and examination of all relevant technical, security and administrative issues. A memorandum of understanding between agencies governs the purpose, methods of transmission, use of the PII (including constraints on use), relevant authorities, specific responsibilities of the organizations transmitting and receiving the PII, and risks associated with its transmission.

NIST Special Publication 800-47, "Security Guide for Interconnecting Information Technology Systems," provides detailed guidance on areas of consideration when connecting systems and sharing information. Specifically, it provides guidance for establishing interconnection security agreements (ISAs) between organizations. When developing an ISA, agencies are encouraged to consider a variety of factors:[7]

- Level and method of interconnections
- Impact on existing infrastructure and operations
- Hardware and software requirements
- Data sensitivity
- User community
- Services and applications
- Security controls
- Segregation of duties
- Incident reporting and response
- Contingency planning
- Data elements and ownership

- Data backup
- Change management
- Rules of behavior
- Security training and awareness
- Roles and responsibilities
- Scheduling
- Cost and budgeting

OMB Memorandum M-04-26, "Personal Use Policies and 'File Sharing' Technology," details "specific actions agencies must take to ensure the appropriate use of certain technologies used for file sharing across networks." The memorandum provides guidance in two areas: downloading illegal or unauthorized copyright content and inappropriate use. With respect to the former, ethical and responsible practices are mandated when using the Internet. The memorandum prohibits downloading illegal or unauthorized copyright content on federal computer systems and networks as well as those operated by government contractors.

Regarding inappropriate use of PII, OMB M-04-26 cites the recommended guidance on limits of personal use[8] from the Chief Information Officers Council. Examples of personal use cited by the council include:

- The creation, downloading, viewing, storage, copying or transmission of materials related to illegal gambling, illegal weapons, terrorist activities and any other illegal activities or activities otherwise prohibited.

- The unauthorized acquisition, use, reproduction, transmission, or distribution of any controlled information, including computer software and data that includes privacy information; copyrighted, trademarked or material with other intellectual property rights (beyond fair use); proprietary data; or export controlled software or data.

OMB M-04-26 identifies specific agency compliance actions. In particular, it requires agencies to establish personal-use policies consistent with the CIO Council's recommendations. Further, it requires that agencies train all employees on personal-use policies and the proper use of file sharing. It also requires security controls that comply with the Federal Information Security Management Act and the use of NIST security standards and guidance, especially for security planning and risk assessment. OMB M-04-26 also stresses the need for detailed operational controls. Where file sharing occurs, the memorandum emphasizes the importance of technology management and well-defined rules of behavior and controls to counter improper file sharing.

As mentioned in Chapter 2, the OMB has issued and supplemented Privacy Act guidelines for agencies, including computer-matching guidance. In June 1989, the OMB published "Final Guidance Interpreting the Provisions of Public Law 100-503, the Computer Matching and Privacy Protection Act of 1988."[9] The underlying act itself amended the Privacy Act, and was designed to safeguard records when agencies match data among their systems. These agencies must publicly disclose the matching and explain its scope. The OMB's guidelines state that federal agencies that perform matching programs must "(a) publish matching agreements; (b) report matching programs to the OMB and Congress; and (c) establish internal boards to approve their matching activity." These matching agreements must contain notice, access, accuracy and security procedures, as well as an explanation of the program's purpose, justification, and expected results. In addition, the terms of matching agreements must be reviewed and approved by a data integrity board. Notice of matching agreements must be published in the *Federal Register*, and the matching agreement itself must be provided to Congress before the matching programs can become operational.

In addition to its guidance protecting PII during inter-agency sharing of data, the OMB has issued advice regarding the selection of computer software to contain this data. OMB Memorandum M-04-16, Software Acquisition, sets forth privacy guidance regarding information technology investment decisions.[10] The memorandum states that the OMB's information technology policies, including those presented in Circular A-130, have been set forth in a manner that is both technology and vendor neutral, and that agency implementation of these policies should be neutral as well. Furthermore, when making IT acquisition decisions, agencies must consider the total cost of ownership—including the cost of addressing data security and privacy risks. Agencies must also consider the impact of both proprietary and open source software license requirements on the security and total cost of ownership of the software.

Federal agencies are, in some instances, required to transmit data to other nations. Trans-border transfer of PII calls for a high level of security. Different countries have a variety of privacy laws, many of which contain provisions similar to U.S. privacy laws.

2.2 The Common Rule

A specific area that has received increased attention is the protection of human subjects in federally funded research. The Federal Policy for the Protection of Human Subjects (known as the Common Rule) is codified in a number of Codes of Federal Regulations (CFRs) as they apply to specific agencies. Some agencies, such as the Department of Labor, have not codified the Common Rule.

The Common Rule includes requirements for obtaining and documenting informed consent and for Institutional Review Board (IRB) membership, function, operations, research review and record keeping. Specific protections are mandated for pregnant women, in-vitro fertilization, fetuses, prisoners and children.

The U.S. Department of Health and Human Services (HHS) regulations are typically applied throughout federal agencies regardless of the funding source for the particular research. Cross-institutional research is typically governed by HHS regulations as well.

The Office for Human Research Protections carries out the mandates of 45 CFR part 46 for HHS.

Confidentiality and protection of PII must be explicitly addressed in informed consent documents when applicable. This issue is considered so important that the requirement to document informed consent may be waived if the consent document itself will be the only thing linking a subject to the research and exposure of their participation will result in a significant risk of harm.

The IRB is responsible for making such determinations. IRBs are required for all research receiving funding, directly or indirectly, from any agency operating under the Common Rule. IRBs review research protocols, informed consent documents, and other investigative materials to ensure protection of the welfare and rights of human subjects. IRBs are required to protect the privacy of subjects whenever possible. The primary duties of an IRB are:[11]

- Ensure compliance with all federal regulations
- Ensure protection of the rights and welfare of human subjects
- Suspend or terminate approval of ongoing research, if necessary
- Approve, require modifications, or disapprove research
- Conduct ongoing review of approved research
- Communicate with research investigators

As the research arm of HHS, the National Institutes of Health (NIH) provides leadership in protecting the privacy of research study participants. In March 2002, NIH announced the availability of "certificates of confidentiality," which allow investigators and others who have access to research records to refuse to disclose identifying information on research participants in any civil, criminal, administrative, legislative or other proceeding, whether at the federal, state or local level. Any IRB-approved research project that collects PII is eligible for a certificate of confidentiality.

An important oversight body for the protection of human subjects and their privacy is the HHS Secretary's Advisory Committee on Human Research Protections (SACHRP). The SACHRP influences protection, not only within HHS, but also among the federal agencies that have adopted the Common Rule. Multiple federal agencies are invited to serve as ex-officio members of SACHRP. The SACHRP considers a wide range of topics related to the protection of human research subjects. Most importantly, it recommends needed revisions of the Common Rule to Congress.

3. Privacy and Federal Statistical Data Collections

Michael Hawes, CIPP/G[12]

Statistical data collections serve an important function for the federal government, as well as for society at large. From the once-per-decade census of all U.S. residents to allocate representation in Congress to the monthly and quarterly economic indicators that track the performance of the U.S. economy, federal statistics provide invaluable information about the country. Federal agencies also use statistical data and analyses to make important policy and program decisions, and to evaluate the relative success and effectiveness of federal programs. In fact, the federal government has over 100 agencies that receive $500,000 or more per year in direct funding for statistical programs and activities.[13] Many of these programs acquire the data for their statistical analyses directly from individuals or businesses through surveys and censuses. Many others make use of data already collected and maintained by the federal government for other purposes (tax information, program participation, etc.). These statistical data collections, and the uses of the data once they have been collected, have certain privacy implications that differ from those of nonstatistical data collections and uses.

Numerous federal privacy laws impact the work of federal statistical agencies and programs. These laws can be roughly divided into three categories: 1) federal laws with privacy provisions relating to data sharing and burden reduction, 2) federal laws and regulations relating to the confidentiality of data collected or used for statistical purposes, and 3) federal legal requirements relating to notification and informed consent.

3.1 Data Sharing, Administrative Records and Respondent Burden

Advances in computing technology during the 1970s led to a profound shift in the operations of U.S. statistical agencies. As data processing became faster, simpler and easier to perform, governmental agencies increasingly turned toward data collection from individuals to inform their policy decisions and conduct their operations. Growing public dissatisfaction with the rising burden of federal information collection led the U.S. Congress to create the Commission on Federal Paperwork. The recommendations from that commission led to the passage of the Paperwork Reduction Act (PRA) of 1980 (for more information, see Chapter 3).

The primary goal of the PRA is to minimize the burden of federal information collection on individuals and businesses, while maximizing the availability and quality of information collected.[14] In pursuit of this goal, one major strategic objective of the PRA is to have statistical agencies reduce their direct collection needs in favor of acquiring data from other governmental sources that have already collected it in support of their own operations. Similarly, Section 6 of the Census Act exhorts the Census Bureau to use other government agencies' data "to the maximum extent possible."[15] Data collected from other entities, collectively referred to as "administrative records," has become a major source of information for U.S. statistical agencies.

Several federal laws facilitate the sharing of administrative records for statistical purposes. The Privacy Act contains two laws specifically authorizing the sharing of administrative record data. Exception (b)(4) permits disclosure of Privacy Act protected information to the U.S. Census Bureau "for purposes of planning or carrying out a census or survey or related activity pursuant to the provisions of Title 13," exception (b)(5) allows disclosure of records that are not individually identifiable to "a recipient who has provided the agency with advance adequate written assurance that the record will be used solely as a statistical research or reporting record...."[16] Unfortunately, in most cases, for administrative records to be useful as a substitute for the direct collection of certain information necessary for census and survey programs, this data must often be linked to other administrative record collections and/or to information collected as part of a census or survey. This makes the Privacy Act exception (b)(5) less useful, because the lack of personal identifiers would render the data impossible to link to other data sources. In these cases, agencies may be able to rely on the more common (b)(3) "routine uses" exception, provided the agency that originally collected the data has included general statistical uses as a "routine use" in their SORN (see Chapter 2).

It is also important to note that data sharing among federal agencies involving record linkage for statistical purposes is typically exempt from the requirements of the Computer Matching and Privacy Protection Act (see Chapter 2).[17]

3.2 Federal Confidentiality Protections for Statistical Data Collections

Statistical analysis is a scientific discipline and is highly dependent on the quality of the underlying data. Because statistical agencies collect information from individuals and businesses on topics for which there may be personal or financial incentives for the respondent not to answer, or to provide a false answer (such as matters relating to income, health or illicit behavior), it is important for the collecting agencies to be able to assure respondents that their responses will not be used in a manner that could hurt them. Consequently, there are a number of federal statutes that provide strong confidentiality protections for statistical data collections. Many of these confidentiality statutes are agency specific, reflecting the need for strong legal protections tailored to the sensitivities of that agency's data collections. For example, the U.S. Census Bureau conducts most of its data collections under the strong confidentiality guarantees of Section 9 of the Census Act, which establishes criminal penalties for unlawful disclosure of information protected by the act to anyone other than Census Bureau employees and those who have taken the Census Bureau's Oath of Non-Disclosure.[18] Other agencies have similar statutory confidentiality protections; for example, the Institute of Education Sciences (which includes the National Center for Education Statistics) uses the confidentiality provisions of the Education Sciences Reform Act;[19] the National Center for Health Statistics protects the confidentiality of its data under the Public Health Service Act;[20] and statistical data collected by the National Science Foundation is protected under the National Science Foundation Act of 1950.[21]

Federal agencies collecting data for statistical purposes may also make use of the confidentiality protections of the Confidential Information Protection and Statistical Efficiency Act (CIPSEA) (see Chapter 3). CIPSEA provides federal legal protections for any data collected by federal agencies under a pledge of confidentiality "for exclusively statistical purposes," and establishes criminal penalties for the unauthorized use or disclosure of that data.[22]

Frequently, statistical data collected or used by a statistical agency may enjoy federal confidentiality protections under multiple statutes. Administrative records data shared with statistical agencies is often protected by the privacy or confidentiality statutes of the program agency. For example, section 6103 of the Internal Revenue Code protects federal tax information collected by the Internal Revenue Service,[23] and protected health information collected by the HHS enjoys the privacy protections of the Health Insurance Portability and Accountability Act.[24] When administrative records data is shared with a statistical agency, it is typically protected under both the program agency's statutory protections and the statistical agency's confidentiality protections. Similarly, a statistical agency conducting a survey may provide its respondents with a legal pledge of confidentiality under both an agency-specific statute and under the broader protections of CIPSEA.

3.3 Public Release of Statistical Data

For the majority of statistical work performed by federal agencies to be valuable to policymakers, as well as to the public at large, federal statistical agencies need to be able to make public the results of the statistical collections and analyses they perform. Unfortunately, any release of statistical summaries, tables or analysis results derived from confidential data carries some risk of disclosing protected information.[25] To minimize these risks, statistical agencies frequently release tables and data files that have been subjected to a variety of disclosure limitation mechanisms. The objective is to provide the public with data in its rawest form possible, while reducing the likelihood that characteristics or information obtained from individual respondents can be reidentified within the publicly released data.

Under most circumstances, this publicly released data represents a low-risk mechanism of making valuable information available to decision makers and the public. When data is considered for release to the public, it may undergo any number of disclosure prevention mechanisms. These mechanisms often involve either the redaction (suppression) of some data, the introduction of statistical "noise" into the data, replacing the characteristics of some individuals in the data with the characteristics of others ("data swapping"), or the aggregation of individuals, groups or geographic areas to ensure large enough populations to sufficiently mask individual characteristics that may be unique in smaller populations.[26]

The application of these techniques requires, in many cases, the identification of variables that could either singly or in combination be sufficiently unique to allow the identification of a particular individual in the data set using otherwise publicly available information. The inclusion of administrative records into these data sets can significantly increase the number of variables that might allow for reidentification, particularly when those same administrative records have also been linked by other agencies to other data sources.[27] Similarly, the growing availability of large-scale commercial databases containing personal information, and the increasing sophistication of computerized matching techniques, increase the risk of reidentification of individuals in publicly released data, and require statistical agencies to continually reevaluate the effectiveness of their disclosure avoidance methodologies (see "Big Data" sidebar).

Big Data

"Big Data" is a term often used to describe the growing availability of large-scale commercial and private databases used for data mining. This data poses growing privacy concerns because of its potential use to predict individual behavior or to identify and extract sensitive information about individuals in other publicly released data files.[28]

3.4 Challenges of Notification and Consent

As with all federal data collections, the PRA requires statistical agencies to inform respondents of the purpose for which the information is being collected and the intended uses of that information.[29] Unlike with other federal data collections, however, where information is typically being collected to administer a program or provide a service or benefit where the outcome can be tangibly described in a manner that clearly conveys the benefit of providing the information (or the cost of not providing it), statistical uses of information are not as easily described in informed consent statements. In particular, respondents appear to have difficulty understanding the phrase "statistical purposes" (likely caused by the public's lack of general knowledge of statistics).[30] Providing more specific descriptions of the purpose and intended uses, however, may not be any better, because more specificity may constrain future statistical uses of the data and more lengthy descriptions tend to scare respondents into not participating in the information collection at all, or into providing false or inaccurate responses.[31]

Statistical agencies' increased reliance on administrative records as a supplement to or replacement for direct collections poses privacy challenges to program agencies as well, to the extent that program agencies need to incorporate future statistical uses of the administrative records data they collect into their own public notifications and consent statements.

4. Conclusion

As awareness of identity theft and other threats to privacy have increased, changing public attitudes regarding privacy issues have greatly impacted public participation rates in federal surveys.[32] Federal statistical agencies have a great interest in respecting the privacy of their respondents and protecting the confidentiality of their information, because much of these agencies' ability to collect quality information from the public relies on public perceptions and sensitivities related to privacy.

Endnotes

1   44 U.S.C. chapters 29, 31, and 33.

2   Office of Management and Budget Circular A-130, "Management of Federal Information Resources," November 28, 2000, www.whitehouse.gov/omb/circulars_a130_a130trans4/.

3   See NARA's Media Neutral Records Guidance, www.archives.gov/records-mgmt/initiatives/erm-guidance.html.

4   More detailed information can be found at The National Archives, Introduction to the General Records Schedules, www.archives.gov/records-mgmt/grs/intro.html.

5   The National Archives, Frequently Asked Questions about Records Scheduling and Disposition— How Do I Develop a Records Schedule? www.archives.gov/records-mgmt/faqs/scheduling.html#steps.

6   http://csrc.nist.gov/publications/nistpubs/800-37-rev1/sp800-37-rev1-final.pdf.

7   NIST Special Publication 800-47, "Security Guide for Interconnecting Information Technology Systems," 2002.

8   Federal CIO Council, "'Limited Personal Use' of Government Office Equipment Including Information Technology," May, 1999.

9   54 Fed. Reg. 25818 (1989).

10 Office of Management and Budget Memorandum M-04-16, "Software Acquisition," July 1, 2004, www.whitehouse.gov/omb/memoranda_fy04_m04-16.

11 Institutional Review Board, 45 CFR 42, 2008.

12 The cited section is an official U.S. government product and, as such, is in the public domain.

13 Committee on National Statistics, Principles and Practices for a Federal Statistical Agency, 4th ed., The National Academies Press, 2009, p. 66.

14 44 U.S.C. § 3501.

15 13 U.S.C. § 6(c).

16 5 U.S.C. § 552a(b)(4) and 5 U.S.C. § 552a(b)(5).

17 5 U.S.C. § 552a(a)(8)(B)(i-ii).

18 13 U.S.C. § 9.

19 20 U.S.C. § 9573.

20 42 U.S.C. § 242(m)(d).

21 42 U.S.C. § 1873(i).

22 Public Law 107-347.

23 26 U.S.C. § 6103.

24 Public Law 104-191.

25 Federal Committee on Statistical Methodology, Office of Management and Budget, Statistical Policy Working Paper 2: Report on Statistical Disclosure and Disclosure-Avoidance Techniques, 1978, p.1.

26 Federal Committee on Statistical Methodology, Office of Management and Budget, Statistical Policy Working Paper 22: Report on Statistical Disclosure Limitation Methodology, 2005.

27 General Accounting Office (currently the Government Accountability Office), Record Linkage and Privacy: Issues in Creating New Federal Research and Statistical Information, GAO-01-126SP, April 2001, pp. 68–72.

28 Omer Tene and Jules Polonetsky, "Privacy in the Age of Big Data: A Time for Big Decisions," 64 Stanford L. Rev. Online 63. (February 2, 2012,) www.stanfordlawreview.org/sites/default/files/online/topics/64-SLRO-63_1.pdf.

29 5 C.F.R. § 1320.8(b)(3).

30 Landreth, A. *SIPP Advance Letter Research: Cognitive Interview Results, Implications, & Letter Recommendations.* U.S. Census Bureau, Statistical Research Division Final Report (March 23, 2001).

31 A. Landreth, T. DeMaio, and E. Gerber, U.S. Census Bureau, Statistical Research Division Center for Survey Methods Research, Understanding Confidentiality-and Privacy-related statements in Respondent Materials for the 2010 Decennial: Results from Cognitive Interview Pretesting with Volunteer Respondents, (September 4, 2007).

32 Singer, E. and Presser, S. "Public Attitudes Toward Data Sharing by Federal Agencies," paper presented at the Census Bureau Annual Research Conference, Washington, DC (1996); Singer, E. and Van Hoewyk, J. "Trends in Attitudes Toward Privacy, Confidentiality, Data Sharing, 1995–2000," paper presented at the Proceedings of the Annual Meeting of the American Statistical Association, August 5–9, 2001.

CHAPTER EIGHT

Privacy Auditing and Compliance Monitoring

Throughout this book we have described the legal and practical frameworks to which U.S. government agencies and departments must adhere when maintaining personally identifiable information (PII). The frameworks include numerous laws and guidance dictating the requirements surrounding the collection, use and safeguarding of PII. Government privacy professionals need to understand and work within this legal framework to ensure their agency or department is implementing all of the applicable legal requirements.

In some cases, an agency may decide to embrace a privacy policy or privacy principles that go beyond what is legally mandated to ensure public trust and further reduce the risk of a privacy breach. When this happens, additional privacy requirements must be satisfied to support the more expansive privacy position.

Two of the most important functions in the life cycle of a comprehensive privacy program are compliance and monitoring.

- **Compliance** encompasses the processes aimed at ensuring that applicable privacy laws and organizational policies are being followed.

- **Monitoring** encompasses those processes that ensure implemented privacy requirements are operating as planned. Monitoring is critical to supporting compliance. The organization uses ongoing monitoring to verify that the privacy program is working. It is not enough to implement privacy requirements; government agencies are responsible for ensuring the implemented requirements are operating effectively.

The original text for this chapter was developed by Catherine M. Petrozzino, CIPP/US, CIPP/G, CIPP/IT. New content for this revised edition was contributed by Julie S. McEwen, CIPP/US, CIPP/G, CIPP/IT.

Compliance is not a stagnant function. Privacy laws and organizations evolve over time. Government privacy professionals must stay apprised of pending legislation, executive rule-making and the Office of Management and Budget (OMB) guidance to fully understand and plan for resulting impacts to their agencies. Likewise, as the agency's mission, operations, processes and policies change, government privacy professionals must ensure that compliance and monitoring functions are adjusted accordingly.

1. Independent Audits

Revised by Julie S. McEwen, CIPP/US, CIPP/G, CIPP/IT

As with any business, government agencies are subject to independent audits. An audit is a formal process for examining an organization's processes, records and controls to verify compliance with laws and policy. A number of government offices are legally tasked with conducting audits. These include the Office of the Inspector General (OIG) and the Government Accountability Office (GAO)

1.1 OIG

For large government organizations, independent audits are performed by the organizations' OIG. The office was created by the Inspector General Act of 1978, and, among other responsibilities, is tasked with:[1]

- Conducting and supervising audits and investigations relating to the programs and operations

- Providing a means for keeping the head of the establishment and Congress fully and currently informed about problems and deficiencies relating to the administration of such programs and operations, as well as the necessity for and progress of corrective action

Inspectors general are empowered to act independently and are required to submit biannual reports to Congress covering a wide array of possible topics, including privacy. They perform privacy audits on a discretionary basis or when legally required by Congress.

The specific privacy responsibilities of inspectors general include:

- Participating in the annual Federal Information Security Management Act (FISMA) report, which is submitted to the OMB and reports on how the privacy program meets federal laws, regulations and guidance (FISMA reporting is discussed below)

- Assessing a number of key privacy items, including the agency's privacy impact assessment (PIA) process

- Overseeing independent, biennial privacy audits of their organizations in accordance with the Consolidated Appropriations Act of 2005, Section 522 (d)[2]

1.2 The GAO

Another government organization tasked to perform audits is the GAO, an independent organization that supports Congress. According to the GAO website, its work includes the following responsibilities:[3]

- Auditing agency operations to determine whether federal funds are being spent efficiently and effectively
- Investigating allegations of illegal and improper activities
- Reporting on how well government programs and policies are meeting their objectives

The GAO is allowed to access records of computer-matching programs to verify compliance with the matching agreement.

The law requires some government programs to undergo periodic GAO audits. However, in many other cases, the GAO performs audits at the direction of congressional committees or subcommittees. Not surprisingly, very public programs, especially those with well-publicized privacy problems or that are perceived as controversial or privacy invasive, frequently get the attention of Congress and the GAO.

1.3 Preparing for an Audit

Government auditors require evidence that controls are in place to meet key privacy requirements. Physical evidence may be either electronic or in hard copy, but some form of documentation is needed. Auditors cannot verify that controls are effective if they are undocumented.

A robust privacy program must record its operational privacy activities as part of its baseline operations. Table 8.1 below identifies the minimum set of records that government privacy professionals should maintain to effectively prepare for an audit. These records are minimal in that they map to requirements in various laws and mandates. Some of these records are generated daily, some annually (or even less frequently), and others somewhere in between. Government organizations with more stringent privacy policies may need additional records. For example, if an organization's privacy principles or policies state that explicit opt-in will be used for the collection of PII, then opt-in records must be maintained.

Table 8.1 Privacy Compliance Record Maintenance

RECORD TYPE	COMPLIANCE	NOTES
PII Store(s) Inventory	FISMA	An inventory of applicable electronic systems and hard copy records (such as paper copies) must be recorded and maintained.
System of Records Notice (SORN) Status and SORNs	Privacy Act, FISMA	Each PII store should be evaluated to determine if a SORN is needed. Either a SORN or documented justification for a SORN's absence should exist. Such a justification must identify who authorized the decision and include specific exemptions.
PIA Status and PIAs	E-Government Act, FISMA	Each electronic PII store should be evaluated to determine if a PIA is needed. Either a PIA or documented justification for a PIA's absence should exist. Such a justification must identify who authorized the decision.
Explicit Consents	Privacy Act	The Privacy Act requires written consent for certain disclosures of PII; the written consents should be maintained. (§552a.(b))
Account of Certain Disclosures	Privacy Act	The disclosure of Privacy Act-protected PII outside of normal processing and allowed exceptions should be recorded and maintained for five years after the disclosure. (§552a.(c))
Access/Amendment Requests for PII	Privacy Act	Access and amendment requests for Privacy Act-protected PII, the disposition of those requests, and the time consumed to process them should be maintained to validate that requirements are being followed. (§552a.(d))
Computer Matching Program Records	Privacy Act, FISMA	PII records processed by a computer matching program must be maintained and be accessible to other organizations (for example, the GAO) for auditing or investigatory purposes.
Contested Findings of Computer Matching Program	Privacy Act	All records pertaining to an individual's complaints about a matching program's findings and subsequent processing should be maintained to validate the requirements are followed. (§552a.(p))
Privacy Act Mandated Review	OMB Circular A-130, Appendix I	A record should be kept of the annual and two-, three- and four-year reviews mandated by OMB Circular A-130. See Chapter 6 for more details.
Privacy Violations Including Privacy Breaches	Privacy Act, FISMA, OMB M-07-16	Instances of agency Privacy Act violations and the details surrounding the violations must be recorded and maintained.

Persistent Tracking Use	E-government Act, FISMA	Records need to be maintained about where tracking technology is used, why it is needed, controls used to protect the tracked information, how the public is notified of tracking and the agency official who approved tracking.
Machine-Readable Web Privacy Policy Status	E-Government Act, FISMA	A record should be maintained for each of the agency's public websites on its status relative to having a machine-readable policy.
Privacy Training	Privacy Act, E-Government Act	Each person involved in the "design, development, operation, and maintenance" should be instructed on the privacy rules of behavior; and training records should be kept. (Privacy Act, §552a.(e)(9))
Freedom of Information Act (FOIA) Requests and Results	Freedom of Information Act	A record of all FOIA requests, appeals, denials, and processing time and fees must be kept.
Signed Acknowledgment of Responsibilities for Protecting Privacy and Security of Information	OMB M-07-16	Agencies must ensure that individuals who are authorized access to PII and their supervisors sign a document at least annually that clearly describes their responsibilities for protecting the privacy and security of that information.

Arguably, the most important entry in the table above is PII inventory. The PII inventory's maintenance is a fundamental activity for any privacy program. An organization runs tremendous risk if it does not know what PII it stores and where it is located. Automated information discovery tools can be used to add assurance that PII has been fully identified on the network.

It also is important for organizations to comply with any requirements prohibiting record retention. For instance, the U.S. Privacy Act of 1974 does not permit records to be maintained "describing how any individual exercises rights guaranteed by the First Amendment" unless explicitly authorized by law, the individual or as part of a law enforcement activity.[4]

1.4 Self-Assessments

Audits are used to verify compliance with laws and policies. Negative audit findings highlight privacy program gaps where laws and policies are not being satisfied or where there is an unacceptable risk that they will not be satisfied. Once a government privacy professional has built an operational privacy program, the program should periodically initiate a self-assessment to validate it is working as planned. The results of a self-assessment provide essential input for future privacy program planning and prepare the organization for independent audits.

Figure 8.1 shows the different levels of self-assessment. Self-assessments can be as informal as an organization examining its own practices with little reliance on formal evidence, or as formal as an independent audit with external reviewers and formal evidence. Although an agency self-assessment is simpler and quicker to perform than a diagnostic independent assessment, it may be less reliable and fail to detect gaps.

Figure 8.1: Self-Assessment Types (from most formal to least formal)

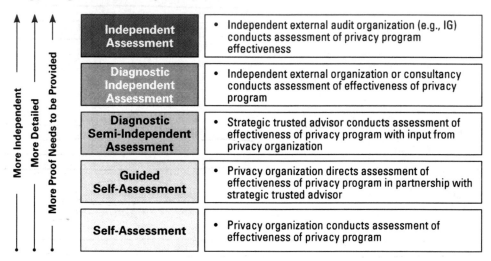

Levels of Privacy Assessment
Strategy: begin to move up the stack

Independent Assessment	• Independent external audit organization (e.g., IG) conducts assessment of privacy program effectiveness
Diagnostic Independent Assessment	• Independent external organization or consultancy conducts assessment of effectiveness of privacy program
Diagnostic Semi-Independent Assessment	• Strategic trusted advisor conducts assessment of effectiveness of privacy program with input from privacy organization
Guided Self-Assessment	• Privacy organization directs assessment of effectiveness of privacy program in partnership with strategic trusted advisor
Self-Assessment	• Privacy organization conducts assessment of effectiveness of privacy program

(vertical axis labels: More Independent / More Detailed / More Proof Needs to be Provided)

Source: Bruce J. Bakis and Julie S. McEwen, "How to Conduct a Privacy Audit," Presentation for the 2007 New York State Cyber Security Conference, June 6, 2007, www.mitre.org.

1.5 Post-Audit

Practitioner's Notebook—Defining and Managing the Scope of a Privacy Self-Assessment or Privacy Audit

One of the most daunting parts of completing a privacy self-assessment or a privacy audit is defining and managing the scope of the review. Federal agencies have a long list of privacy laws, regulations and guidance that they must follow, and it can be overwhelming to plan an assessment or audit addressing all of the appropriate privacy requirements. Agencies that have successfully conducted privacy self-assessments or audits have typically defined the scope of the reviews by using documentation of the high-level privacy objectives in their organizations. Documents to review include the privacy mission statement, which, flows from the organization's overall mission statement and identifies the focus of the organization's privacy operations. In addition, the organization's set of privacy principles provides the foundation for a privacy self-assessment or audit because the privacy principles reflect how the Fair Information Practice Principles are tailored within the organization's privacy program. Each organizational privacy principle serves as a focus area within the privacy self-assessment or audit. Then, key control elements are identified for each privacy principle. Lastly, control objectives are identified for each key control element. The result is a detailed list of control objectives to examine for the privacy self-assessment or audit that is comprehensive but still easy to track and manage because the control objectives flow directly from the organization's privacy principles. Using this method also decreases the likelihood that the scope of the privacy self-assessment or audit will be defined beyond the boundaries of the organization's mission. In addition, the following reference should be noted: National Institute of Standards and Technology (NIST) Special Publication (SP) 800-53, Security and Privacy Controls for Federal Information Systems and Organizations, Revision 4 (Initial Public Draft), Appendix J, Privacy Control Catalog. Appendix J contains a structured set of privacy controls based on international standards and best practices. Federal organizations are to select the appropriate controls for their environment and implement them, keeping in mind their organization's specific mission and business needs.[5] The controls in Appendix J can be used as input when developing the list of controls to examine for a privacy self-assessment or audit.

After the audit has been completed, the auditors generate a report that contains negative audit findings, which may include recommendations on how to address the findings. Government privacy professionals and other stakeholders in the management chain should carefully review each finding. When a consensus has been reached, the privacy professional should generate a comment that accepts a given finding, accepts the finding with conditions, or disagrees with the finding. The auditor then has an opportunity to respond to the comments.

Audit findings, comments and responses are usually publicly available, unless there are overriding considerations (such as national security concerns) that preclude their publication. Privacy-insensitive responses to audit findings can lead to a public outcry and the attention of nongovernmental organizations.

Government privacy professionals should then create a prioritized plan of action and milestones to address the agreed-upon findings. This will eliminate privacy program gaps and better prepare the agency for future audits and self-assessments, when the current findings will be reexamined.

2. Compliance Monitoring

Revised by Julie S. McEwen, CIPP/US, CIPP/G, CIPP/IT

2.1 Information Life Cycle

According to OMB M-03-22, "Guidance for Implementing the Privacy Provisions of the E-Government Act of 2002," agencies must consider the information "life cycle" (i.e., collection, use, retention, processing, disclosure and destruction) when assessing privacy risk. Accordingly, the privacy program should have controls to address and manage privacy risk, including compliance-based risk, at each phase of the life cycle.[6] Table 8.2 identifies the key privacy risk questions to address during different phases of the information life cycle.

Table 8.2: Information Life Cycle Privacy Risk Questions

Life Cycle Phase	Privacy Risk Questions
Collection	Is all collected PII relevant and necessary?
	Is PII collected directly from individuals as much as possible?
	Is PII received from other internal or external sources accurate, timely, relevant and complete?
Use	Is the use of PII consistent with all published notices and legal requirements?
	Is PII used for computer matching programs?
	Are individuals able to contest questionable findings?
Retention	Is PII retention consistent with the purpose of the system and National Records and Records Administration guidance?
	Are there multiple copies of PII that need to be monitored for expiration?
Processing	Does processing include adequate administrative, technical, procedural and physical controls to safeguard the PII?
	Is PII located on removable devices?
	Do individuals have access to their PII, and are they able to correct it?
Disclosure	Is personal medical information being disclosed?
	Is PII being disclosed in accordance with all published notices and legal requirements?
	Is written consent for disclosure obtained when legally required?
Destruction	Is PII securely destroyed in all locations where it is maintained?

2.2 Notice Requirements

The Privacy Act requires agencies to supply a SORN when they plan to maintain PII records. It also requires agencies to supply this notice to every individual asked to provide PII on the form used to collect the information, or on a separate form that can be retained by the individual. This notice should include why the information is being collected and the consequences to the individual of not supplying the PII.[7] This notice to the individual is often referred to as a Privacy Act Statement. Figure 8.4 contains a list of the information required by the SORN vs. the Privacy Act Statement.[8]

Table 8.3: Privacy Act Notice Requirements

Required Information	Systems of Records Notice	Privacy Act Statement
Name and location of system	X	
Authority to collect information (e.g., statute, executive order) and whether collection is voluntary or mandatory	X[9]	X
Effects of not supplying PII		X
Covered individuals	X	
Categories of records	X	
Principal purpose for collecting information	X[10]	X
Routine uses	X	X
PII policies and practices	X	
Privacy point-of-contact	X	
Information on how individual can access (and contest) PII	X	X
Sources of records in the system	X	X

Many agencies include fields that are unique to the Privacy Act Statement in their SORNs to provide more transparency to individuals. However, using the SORN as a Privacy Act Statement should be done with careful consideration. A Privacy Act Statement is intended to be succinct, so that it can be quickly read; SORNs, however, may span many pages.

2.3 Consent

Chapter 3 discusses the 12 exceptions under which agencies can disclose PII to another individual or agency. The Privacy Act requires an agency to seek explicit written consent of an affected individual before disclosing PII when none of these exceptions apply.[11] The government privacy professional should ensure that controls are in place to obtain an individual's consent when PII is being disclosed outside of a routine use or under allowable exceptions.

2.4 Reporting Obligations

The following section summarizes agencies' periodic compliance reporting requirements. Most of these reports are discussed in detail in earlier chapters.

2.4.1 Privacy Act: Computer-Matching Activities

A computer-matching report that summarizes the agency's matching activities should be submitted annually to the head of the agency and the OMB. According to the Privacy Act, the report should be generated by the agency's data integrity board (DIB) and include the following information:

- Matching programs in which the agency has participated
- Proposed matching agreements that were denied by the DIB
- DIB structural changes
- Reason for waiver of cost-benefit analysis
- Alleged or identified violations of matching agreements and corrective action (if any)
- Any other information required by the OMB

The computer-matching report must be made available to members of the public if requested.

2.4.2 FOIA

The FOIA requires that an annual report be submitted to the attorney general on or before February 1.[12] The report deals with FOIA requests from the past year, including the number of requests, appeals, denials, the time it took to process each request, and fees charged. This report must be made available to members of the public (if requested).[13]

2.4.3 The E-Government Act

OMB guidance for implementing the privacy provisions of the E-Government Act of 2002 requires an annual compliance report that includes:[14]

- PIA status
- Persistent tracking technology status
- Machine-readable privacy technology status

- Points of contact for information technology
- Web and website privacy policies

The OMB has consolidated the E-Government reporting into the FISMA report; this removes the need for a separate E-Government privacy report.

2.4.4 FISMA

Agencies complete the FISMA report annually and submit it to the OMB. The FISMA report is a collection of security and privacy-related information that includes reporting requirements for the Privacy Act and the E-Government Act as well as other significant privacy-related laws, regulations and guidance.

The FISMA reporting requirements change from year to year to reflect additional mandates and guidance from the previous year. Each year, the OMB publishes FISMA fiscal year reporting requirements. Agencies use an automated tool to submit their inputs. Chapter 3 contains detailed information on FISMA reporting. The following list summarizes the general privacy reporting categories that are typically included in the FISMA report:

- Inventory of systems that contain federal information in identifiable form, which require a PIA or SORN
- Links to PIAs and SORNs
- Senior agency official for privacy responsibilities
- Information privacy training and awareness
- PIA and web privacy policies and procedures
- Reviews mandated by the Privacy Act
- Written privacy complaints
- Policy compliance review
- Agency use of persistent tracking technology
- Contact information

As part of FISMA reporting, each agency must also report its progress on several initiatives:

- Breach notification policy if it has changed significantly since last year's report
- Progress update on eliminating unnecessary use of Social Security numbers
- Progress update on review and reduction of holdings of PII

2.4.5 Reporting Privacy Breaches

One other critical reporting obligation required by the OMB concerns privacy breaches. The OMB mandates that agencies report a suspected or confirmed breach involving PII to the United States Computer Emergency Readiness Team (known as US-CERT) within one hour of its discovery.[15]

2.4.6 Reporting Violations of The Health Insurance Portability and Accountability Act of 1996 (HIPAA)

Complaints about security and privacy violations regarding HIPAA should be reported to the Health and Human Services (HHS) Office for Civil Rights (OCR). HHS/OCR is responsible for enforcing the HIPAA Privacy and Security Rules. In addition to investigating complaints, HHS/OCR also conducts compliance reviews of covered entities and provides education and outreach activities so that covered entities are familiar with HIPAA requirements. OCR refers possible criminal violations of HIPAA to the Department of Justice. The HIPAA Privacy and Security Rules complaint process is illustrated in the Figure 8.2.[16]

Figure 8.2: HIPAA Privacy and Security Rule Complaint Process

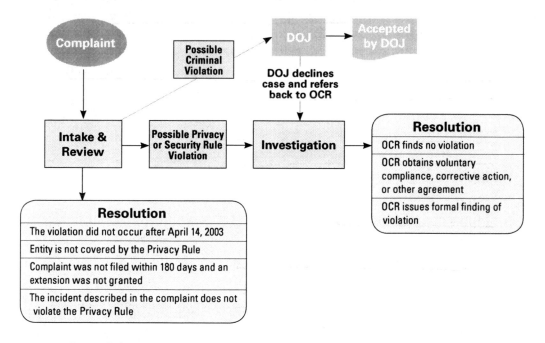

2.4.7 The Consolidated Appropriations Act

Section 522(a)(6) of the Consolidated Appropriations Act of 2005 requires the chief privacy officer to:[17]

> *prepare a report to Congress on an annual basis on activities of the Department that affect privacy, including complaints of privacy violations, implementation of Section 552a of title 5, 11 United States Code [i.e., Privacy Act], internal controls, and other relevant matters.*

As noted in Chapter 3, this act applies to a subset of agencies. However, other agencies (for example, the Department of Homeland Security) have legislatively mandated chief privacy officers who are similarly tasked with generating annual privacy reports to Congress. The contents of these reports mirror the contents stated in the Consolidated Appropriations Act, 2005.

In addition, Section 522(c)[18] of the act states that each covered agency "shall prepare a written report of its use of information in an identifiable form, along with its privacy and data protection policies and procedures and record it with the inspector general of the agency to serve as a benchmark for the agency."

Ideally, this report should be updated if the agency modifies either its use of information in identifiable form or its privacy and data protection policies and procedures.

3. Conclusion

Monitoring and compliance are mandatory components for any privacy program with legal and policy obligations. In addition, government privacy professionals must be diligent to ensure that the privacy program is in step with new legal and regulatory obligations as well as the agency's evolving privacy policy position. This not only makes audits much easier (and more pleasant) but also helps ensure the PII entrusted to the agency by the public is safeguarded appropriately and handled with respect.

While privacy programs aim to ensure that PII is handled appropriately, they ultimately exist to establish and preserve trust. Although this is also true for the private sector, the government context raises the stakes dramatically. The government's ability to compel disclosure of PII and use it in ways that can directly affect the freedom and welfare of individuals—and of society as a whole—carries with it enormous ethical and practical obligations. These obligations go beyond compliance with the letter of the law. They demand compliance with the *spirit* of the law.

A lack of public trust in the government's capacity to meet these obligations undermines both the legitimacy of government activities requiring PII and the willingness of the public to participate in or even permit those activities. At the end of the day, the role of government privacy professionals is to help build and sustain public trust in the government's treatment of PII. This book and the certification program that it supports are intended to further promote these efforts.

Endnotes

1   5 U.S.C. Appendix, Inspector General Act of 1978 § 2.

2   See Chapter 3 for more details on the required biennial privacy audits.

3   U.S. Government Accountability Office, *About GAO*, www.gao.gov/about/index.html.

4   Privacy Act of 1974, 5 U.S.C. § 552a.(e)(7).

5   National Institute of Standards and Technology (NIST) Special Publication (SP) 800-53, "Security and Privacy Controls for Federal Information Systems and Organizations," Revision 4 (Initial Public Draft), Appendix J, Privacy Control Catalog, pps. 352-354, (February 2012), http://csrc.nist.gov/publications/drafts/800-53-rev4/sp800-53-rev4-ipd.pdf.

6   Office of Management and Budget Memorandum M-03-22, "OMB Guidance for Implementing Privacy Provisions of the E-Government Act of 2002," September 26, 2003, www.whitehouse.gov/omb/memoranda/m03-22.html.

7   Privacy Act, 5 U.S.C. 552a(e)(3).

8   See Chapter 2 for more details surrounding the generation and update of SORNs.

9   Required by Office of Management and Budget Circular A-130, "Management of Federal Information Resources," November 28, 2000, Appendix I, 4.c.(3)(b)(2), www.whitehouse.gov/omb/circulars_a130_a130appendix_i.

10 Required by Office of Management and Budget Circular A-130, "Management of Federal Information Resources," November 28, 2000, Appendix I, 4.c.(3)(b)(1), www.whitehouse.gov/omb/circulars_a130_a130appendix_i.

11 Privacy Act, 5 U.S.C. § 552a(b).

12 Freedom of Information Act, 5 U.S.C. § 552.

13 More information on the FOIA report can be found in Chapter 3.

14 OMB Memorandum M-03-22, "OMB Guidance for Implementing Privacy Provisions of the E-Government Act of 2002," September 26, 2003, www.whitehouse.gov/omb/memoranda/m03-22.html.

15 See Chapter 6 for more information on responding to privacy breaches.

16 U.S. Department of Health and Human Services, Health Information Privacy, www.hhs.gov/ocr/privacy/hipaa/enforcement/process/index.html.

17 Consolidated Appropriations Act, 2005, Title V, § 522(a)(6), H.R. 4818-460, www.gpo.gov/fdsys/pkg/BILLS-108hr4818enr/pdf/BILLS-108hr4818enr.pdf.

18 Consolidated Appropriations Act, 2005, Title V, § 522(c), H.R. 4818-461, www.gpo.gov/fdsys/pkg/BILLS-108hr4818enr/pdf/BILLS-108hr4818enr.pdf.

Index

D

About the Authors

Executive Editor

Deborah Kendall, CIPP/US, CIPP/G

Deborah Kendall retired from the U.S. Postal Service's Privacy and Records Office in May, 2012, after 33 years of federal government service. She spent 14 years working in public policy at the USPS, the last 10 years of which she spent conducting privacy impact assessments, drafting system of records revisions and working on privacy policy for both customers and employees. Kendall assisted with the development of the first CIPP/G exam administered in 2005 and has been an active member of the IAPP since joining in 2002.

Prior to joining the USPS, Kendall worked at the Office of Personnel Management and the U.S. House of Representatives in various capacities including as a subcommittee staff director for seven years. She also served on a five-month detail at the Office of Management and Budget as the acting federal pay analyst during the George W. Bush administration. She graduated from George Mason University with a B.S. and resides in Arlington, Virginia with her husband and son.

Contributors

Claire Barrett, CIPP/US, CIPP/G, CIPP/IT

Claire Barrett joined the Department of Transportation (DOT) as the chief privacy and information asset management officer in February 2011 with the mission to preserve and enhance privacy protections for all individuals, to promote the transparency of DOT operations and to serve as a leader in the federal privacy community.

In her role as chief privacy officer, Barrett is responsible for evaluating department-wide programs, systems and technologies and rule-makings for potential privacy impacts and for providing mitigation strategies to reduce any privacy impact. She brings with her significant expertise in commercial and public-sector privacy law and operations, as well as in systems and security engineering. This diverse background informs the development and execution of privacy policy within the department and advice given senior leadership to ensure that privacy protections are implemented throughout the department.

Barrett also serves as the department's chief records management and information collections officers; together, these programs in conjunction with the privacy program seek to harmonize and leverage data and records management activities across the department. Her office provides policy and programmatic oversight and supports implementation of the same across the department.

Prior to joining the department, Barrett served as the deputy privacy officer for the Department of Transportation and the director of privacy programs and special projects for SRA International. She obtained her Master's degree in International Commerce and Politics from George Mason University and obtained her undergraduate degree in Political Science from James Madison University. Barrett is currently working on a Master's degree in Intelligence Analysis from Mercyhurst University and plans to begin pursuit of her Doctoral degree.

Jonathan R. Cantor, CIPP/US, CIPP/G

Jonathan R. Cantor joined the Department of Homeland Security as the deputy chief privacy officer in July 2012, and became acting chief privacy officer on August 1, 2012. He advises the department leadership and other senior leaders on domestic and international privacy laws, policies and programs. In his capacity as acting chief privacy officer, he also serves as acting chief Freedom of Information Act (FOIA) officer, responsible for coordinating the department's FOIA activities. He is a senior executive service official with nearly 15 years of experience in privacy, transparency, and access to information.

Cantor previously served as the senior privacy official at both the Department of Commerce and the Social Security Administration. He served as the Department of Commerce's first chief privacy officer charged with developing a departmental program, and served as its deputy chief FOIA officer, helping it greatly improve its FOIA program. He was also the executive director for privacy and disclosure at the Social Security Administration (SSA), responsible for revamping SSA's privacy regulations, leading Social Security's transition to a modern privacy program designed for the Internet age, and helping reinvent its FOIA process to virtually eliminate its FOIA backlog.

He also serves as a co-chair of the CIO Council's Privacy Committee, and previously as a co-chair of the Privacy Committee's Innovation and Emerging Technology subcommittee.

Mr. Cantor received his JD, with honors, from George Washington University, and his AB, cum laude, from Duke University.

Michael Hawes, CIPP/G

Michael Hawes is the statistical privacy advisor for the U.S. Department of Education. He advises the Department of Education's chief privacy officer and senior leadership on issues relating to data release, data management and disclosure avoidance, and oversees the Department's Privacy Technical Assistance Center (PTAC), which provides technical assistance on privacy and data security issues to state and local education agencies and to institutions of higher education. Prior to joining the Department of Education, Hawes served as a statistician and policy analyst for the U.S. Census Bureau, focusing on data stewardship and data management. Hawes is a statistician and a Project Management Institute–certified Project Management Professional (PMP).

Liz Lyons, CIPP/G

Liz Lyons, privacy analyst in the Privacy Office of the Department of Homeland Security (DHS), currently works in the compliance group on the development and review of privacy impact assessments and system of records notices. Prior to compliance, Lyons worked in the technology group as a subject matter expert on privacy issues involving cloud computing and cybersecurity. Before joining DHS, Lyons was an attorney in San Francisco, CA, and served in the Peace Corps in Lithuania. Lyons obtained her B.A. from Georgetown University and her J.D. from the University of San Francisco, School of Law. During law school, Lyons worked as a legal intern at the Electronic Frontier Foundation and spent a summer studying the UN-backed Cambodia war crimes tribunal. Lyons is a member of the Washington, DC, and California Bar.

Patricia Mantoan

Patricia Mantoan is a senior attorney with the General Law Division of the Office of the General Counsel, Department of Health and Human Services, with expertise in the Freedom of Information Act, Privacy Act, Federal Advisory Committee Act and other information laws. Mantoan advises all department components on information law issues. Mantoan has been with the Office of the General Counsel since 1997. She graduated from the George Washington University Law School. Before joining the Department of Health and Human Services, she was a judicial law clerk for the Honorable Wilkes C. Robinson at the U.S. Court of Federal Claims.

Julie S. McEwen, CIPP/US, CIPP/G, CIPP/IT

Julie S. McEwen is a principal information privacy and cybersecurity engineer and leads the privacy capability at the Cybersecurity and Privacy Technical Center at the MITRE Corporation. Prior to joining MITRE, McEwen managed privacy and cybersecurity programs and advised organizations on privacy and cybersecurity strategy and policy and technology issues while at the U.S. Department of Defense, Deloitte, IIT Research Institute, the Logistics Management Institute, and T. Rowe Price. With over 25 years of experience in privacy and cybersecurity, U.S. federal agencies and departments that she has supported include the Departments of Defense, Justice, Treasury, Homeland Security, Health and Human Services and Housing and Urban Development as well as the Census Bureau and U.S. House of Representatives. McEwen was co-editor of the first edition of *U.S. Government Privacy: Essential Policies and Practices for Privacy Professionals* (IAPP, 2009). She has served as one of the lead faculty for the IAPP's U.S. government privacy training program since 2006, is a member of the IAPP CIPP/G Certification Advisory Board, is a Project Management Professional (PMP) and a Certified Information Systems Security Professional (CISSP).

Kim Mott, CIPP/US, CIPP/G

Kim Mott is the privacy officer at the General Services Administration. Mott has been in this position since January 2007 and serves as the lead authority on privacy policies and regulations on how to protect, handle and secure personally identifiable information (PII). She chairs and co-chairs the breach notification and information assurance teams within the agency and is responsible for the Senior Agency Official for Privacy (SAOP) section of the Federal Information Security Management Act (FISMA) report. Mott is an active member of both the Privacy Committee of the Chief Information Officers (CIO) Council and the Innovative and Emerging Technology Subcommittee. She has fully participated with team efforts on various white papers involving privacy and was a panelist at various privacy events. Mott has a Master's Certificate in Project Management from the George Washington University School of Business. Previously, she was a management intern at the National Institutes of Health and an administrator at a trade association. Mott is married and has three kids.

Matthew J. Olsen, CIPP/US, CIPP/G

Matthew J. Olsen joined the Social Security Administration's Office of Privacy and Disclosure in August 2008 and recently completed a six-month detail with the Office of Management and Budget at the White House. He was previously the Freedom of Information Act (FOIA), Privacy Act and Records Management officer at the Peace Corps. Olsen also spent six years at the National Archives and Records Administration (NARA), including his final year and a half as the deputy FOIA officer within NARA's Office of General Counsel. Olsen has a B.A. and M.A. in history from Southern Illinois University, where he also served as a research assistant for the Ulysses S. Grant Association.

Rebecca J. Richards, CIPP/US, CIPP/G

Rebecca J. Richards joined the Department of Homeland Security as director of privacy compliance in 2004. In this capacity, Richards is responsible for the privacy compliance process at DHS. The Privacy Compliance process includes privacy threshold analysis, privacy impact assessment and Privacy Act system of records notice requirements. She educates employees and leaders on best practices for compliance with privacy policies. Richards was a 2008 Federal 100 award recipient from *Federal Computer Week* and a recipient of the Secretary of Homeland Security's Silver Medal Award in 2008. Richards was a contributor to the book, *Building a Privacy Program: A Practitioner's Guide* (IAPP, 2011).

Prior to her working at the Department of Homeland Security, Richards was director of policy and compliance at TRUSTe, the independent nonprofit privacy seal program. Prior to working at TRUSTe, Richards worked at the U.S. Department of Commerce as an international trade specialist working on the landmark U.S.-EU Safe Harbor accord.

Richards received her B.A. from University of Massachusetts, Amherst, a Masters in international trade and investment policy and an MBA from George Washington University.

Roanne R. Shaddox, CIPP/US, CIPP/G

Roanne R. Shaddox has over a decade of experience working with federal agencies on the development and implementation of privacy programs. In 2007, she joined the Federal Deposit Insurance Corporation's Privacy Program in the Division of Information Technology as a senior privacy specialist. In this capacity, Shaddox works on a wide range of strategic, policy, compliance and awareness initiatives aimed at maintaining a culture of privacy throughout the Corporation. Since 2010, Shaddox also has served as a co-chair of the interagency Best Practices Subcommittee of the Federal Privacy Committee under the Federal Chief Information Officers Council. Prior to joining FDIC, Shaddox served as a senior consultant to federal agencies on the management and enhancement of their internal privacy programs, including at the U.S. Department of Transportation, the Transportation Security Administration Office of National Risk Assessment and the Defense Security Service. During the 1990s, Shaddox served as chief of staff and special assistant to the assistant secretary at the National Telecommunications and Information Administration, U.S. Department of Commerce, where, in addition to assisting with the day-to-day management of the agency, she worked on a wide range of e-commerce and digital divide policy and outreach initiatives.

Alexander C. Tang, CIPP/US, CIPP/G

Alexander C. Tang is an attorney in the legal counsel division of the Federal Trade Commission (FTC), Office of General Counsel. He has served as vice-chair of the agency's internal Privacy Steering Committee, legal advisor to the FTC's chief privacy officer and co-chair of the innovation and emerging technology subcommittee of the Federal CIO Council Privacy Committee. His wide-ranging legal portfolio includes the Privacy Act of 1974, E-GOV, FISMA, FOIA, ECPA, RFPA, HIPAA, procurement, records management, personnel/EEO and ethics. He also provides legal support on FTC rulemakings and programs, including FACTA, GLBA, COPPA, identity theft and the National Do-Not-Call Registry. He has spoken on privacy issues in mobile and cloud computing, electronic discovery and social media. He has received the Janet Steiger and Paul Rand Dixon awards for his contributions to the FTC's law enforcement mission.